Lumen Programming Guide

Writing PHP Microservices, REST and Web Service APIs

Paul Redmond

Apress®

Lumen Programming Guide: Writing PHP Microservices, REST and Web Service APIs

Paul Redmond
Phoenix, Arizona
USA

ISBN-13 (pbk): 978-1-4842-2186-0   ISBN-13 (electronic): 978-1-4842-2187-7
DOI 10.1007/978-1-4842-2187-7

Library of Congress Control Number: 2016953766

Managing Director: Welmoed Spahr
Lead Editor: Steve Anglin
Technical Reviewer: Jacob Jensen
Editorial Board: Steve Anglin, Pramila Balan, Laura Berendson, Aaron Black, Louise Corrigan, Jonathan Gennick, Robert Hutchinson, Celestin Suresh John, Nikhil Karkal, James Markham, Susan McDermott, Matthew Moodie, Natalie Pao, Gwenan Spearing
Coordinating Editor: Mark Powers
Copy Editor: Mary Behr
Compositor: SPi Global
Indexer: SPi Global
Artist: SPi Global
Cover image designed by Freepik

Distributed to the book trade worldwide by Springer Science+Business Media New York, 233 Spring Street, 6th Floor, New York, NY 10013. Phone 1-800-SPRINGER, fax (201) 348-4505, e-mail orders-ny@springer-sbm.com, or visit www.springeronline.com. Apress Media, LLC is a California LLC and the sole member (owner) is Springer Science + Business Media Finance Inc (SSBM Finance Inc). SSBM Finance Inc is a **Delaware** corporation.

For information on translations, please e-mail rights@apress.com, or visit www.apress.com.

Apress and friends of ED books may be purchased in bulk for academic, corporate, or promotional use. eBook versions and licenses are also available for most titles. For more information, reference our Special Bulk Sales–eBook Licensing web page at www.apress.com/bulk-sales.

Any source code or other supplementary materials referenced by the author in this text are available to readers at www.apress.com/9781484221860. For detailed information about how to locate your book's source code, go to www.apress.com/source-code/. Readers can also access source code at SpringerLink in the Supplementary Material section for each chapter.

Printed on acid-free paper

To Bernadette

Contents at a Glance

About the Author xi

About the Technical Reviewer xiii

Acknowledgments xv

Introduction xvii

■Chapter 1: Installing Lumen 1

■Chapter 2: Hello Lumen 7

■Chapter 3: Creating the Book Application 17

■Chapter 4: Starting the Books API 23

■Chapter 5: Creating, Reading, Updating, and Deleting Books 33

■Chapter 6: Responding to Errors 65

■Chapter 7: Leveling Up Responses 89

■Chapter 8: Validation 125

■Chapter 9: Authors 137

■Chapter 10: The /authors API Resource 165

■Chapter 11: Book Bundles 201

■Chapter 12: Ratings 219

■Appendix: Where to Go From Here 243

Index 245

Contents

About the Author xi

About the Technical Reviewer xiii

Acknowledgments xv

Introduction xvii

■Chapter 1: Installing Lumen 1

Homestead 1

Mac OSX 2

Linux 3

    Red Hat/CentOS 4

    Debian/Ubuntu 5

Windows 6

Conclusion 6

■Chapter 2: Hello Lumen 7

Setting Up a New Project 7

Routes 9

    The Hello World Route 10

    Route Parameters 10

Middleware and Responses 11

    Global Middleware 11

    Route Middleware 13

The Request and Response Objects 14

    The Request 15

    The Response 15

Onward 16

■**Chapter 3: Creating the Book Application** **17**

Building Something Amazing 17

Environment Setup 19

Checking Unit Tests 21

Setup Complete 22

■**Chapter 4: Starting the Books API** **23**

Creating the First Endpoint 23

Setting Up Models and Seed Data 26

Eloquent Books 30

Success 32

■**Chapter 5: Creating, Reading, Updating, and Deleting Books** **33**

Requesting an Individual Book 33

Creating a New Book 41

Updating an Existing Book 49

Deleting Books 53

Conclusion 63

■**Chapter 6: Responding to Errors** **65**

Test Database 65

    Model Factories 66

    Factories in Tests 66

Better Error Responses 69

    Framework Exception Handling 70

    JSON Exceptions 72

Testing the Exception Handler 74

Conclusion 88

■ **Chapter 7: Leveling Up Responses** **89**

Introducing Fractal 89

First Version of API Response Formatting 90

The Fractal Response Class 97

    The Book Transformer 97

    The Fractal Response Class... 101

Fractal Response Service 111

Integrating the Fractal Response Service 114

Conclusion 124

■ **Chapter 8: Validation** **125**

First Attempt at Validation 125

More Validation Constraints 129

Custom Validation Messages 132

Other Approaches.. 134

Conclusion 135

■ **Chapter 9: Authors** **137**

The Authors Database Schema 137

Fixing Broken Tests 145

Conclusion 163

■ **Chapter 10: The /authors API Resource** **165**

The GET /authors Endpoint.. 166

    The AuthorsTransformer 166

    The Author Controller.. 168

The GET /authors/{id} Endpoint 170

    A Basic Response 170

    Including Other Models in the Response 171

The POST /authors Endpoint.. 181

The PUT /authors/{id} Endpoint 188

The DELETE /authors/{id} Endpoint 197

Conclusion 199

■**Chapter 11: Book Bundles** **201**

Defining the Relationship Between Books and Bundles 201

The GET /bundles/{id} Endpoint 206

Adding a Book to a Bundle 214

Remove a Book from a Bundle 215

Conclusion 217

■**Chapter 12: Ratings** **219**

Database Design 219

Rating an Author 223

Adding an Author Rating 223

Deleting an Author Rating 233

Ratings in the Author API 236

Eager Loading Ratings 240

Conclusion 242

■**Appendix: Where to Go From Here** **243**

Laravel 243

Laracasts 243

Mockery 244

Guzzle 244

Index **245**

About the Author

Paul Redmond has worked as a web developer, entrepreneur, and mentor in software development for over a decade. He has built web applications within startups, agencies, and enterprise customers with open-source technologies. Paul is passionate about writing highly available applications with PHP, JavaScript, and RESTful APIs.

Paul lives in Scottsdale, Arizona with his wife, Bernadette, three boys, and one cat. He is usually wrangling code, kittens, and children, but finds time to enjoy reading fantasy/fiction, writing, and watching sports.

About the Technical Reviewer

Jacob Jensen is a software engineer who loves testing, automating, and clean code; he has a passion for teaching and learning, and has deep experience in web development, design patterns, object-oriented design, and a multitude of programming languages and platforms.

Acknowledgments

Writing a book is challenging. Editing a book more so.

Writing a book takes patience, persistence, time, and an abundance of help from others. When I first envisioned this title, its humble beginnings were in the form of an eBook. I conceptualized, wrote, edited, technically edited, designed, and marketed the concepts herein.

The Laravel (`https://laravel.com/`) framework and the Lumen micro framework have been inspiring in my day-to-day work. They provide a pleasant and productive development experience that rekindled my love for PHP and inspired me to share what I've learned with others. Additionally, the positive feedback and word-of-mouth about this book within the PHP and Laravel communities—specifically Taylor Otwell (`https://twitter.com/taylorotwell`), Michael Dyrynda (`https://dyrynda.com.au/`), and Amanda Folson (`http://amandafolson.net/`)—was unexpected and huge motivation to keep pressing forward and making the book better.

My early readers provided constructive feedback, small amounts of errata and grammar issues, and insight into what they liked about the manuscript. Early reader feedback showed that people were actually interested in my work, and found tips and tricks that helped them.

I would like to thank Steve Anglin and Mark Powers at Apress for guiding me through the writing process. They have made a dream of mine come true: to author a technical book. I am thankful for their help, and the help of everyone else at Apress who assisted me throughout the process.

Within my professional circle, the direct and indirect mentoring I've received from my colleague Justin Rainbow has helped shape me as a developer and I am much, much better off for it. Thank you. My colleague Jacob Jensen, the technical editor of this book, has been invaluable for motivating me, letting me bounce ideas off of him, and providing great feedback on a technical and peer level.

Writing a book is a big commitment, involving many late nights, and I owe my wife, Bernadette, and my children, Hayden, Masen, and Lincoln, the biggest thanks of all. Life is short. I am so fortunate to have a wonderful family that supports me. I love you guys!

Introduction

Lumen is a framework that is designed to write APIs. With the rising popularity of microservices (http://microservices.io/patterns/microservices.html), existing patterns like service-oriented architecture (https://en.wikipedia.org/wiki/Service-oriented_architecture), and increased demand for public APIs, Lumen is a perfect fit for writing the service layer in the same language as the web applications you write.

In my experience, it's not uncommon for PHP shops to write web applications with PHP and API services with something like Node.js (https://nodejs.org/en/). I am not suggesting that this is a *bad* idea, but I see Lumen as a chance to improve development workflows for PHP developers and for companies to standardize around a powerful set of complimentary frameworks: Laravel and Lumen.

You can write APIs quickly with Lumen using the built-in packages provided, but Lumen can also get out of your way and be as minimalist as you want it to be. Set aside framework benchmarks and open your mind to increased developer productivity. Lumen is fast, but more importantly, it helps me be more productive.

The Same Tools to Write APIs and Web Applications

Lumen is a minimal framework that uses a subset of the same components from Laravel (https://laravel.com/). Together Laravel and Lumen give developers a powerful combination of tools: a lightweight framework for writing APIs and a full-fledged web framework for web applications. Lumen also has a subset of console tools available from Laravel. Other powerful features from Laravel are included like database migrations, Eloquent Models (ORM Package), job queues, scheduled jobs, and a test suite focused on testing APIs.

The development experience between Lumen and Laravel is relatively the same, which means developers will see a productivity boost by adopting both frameworks. Together they provide a consistent workflow and can simplify the software stack for developers, release engineers, and operations teams.

Who This Book Is For

This book is for programmers that want to write APIs in PHP. Familiarity with the HTTP spec, Composer, PHPUnit, and the command line will help, but this book walks you through each step of building an API. You don't need to be an expert on these subjects, and more experienced developers can skip things they understand to focus on the specific code needed to write APIs in Lumen. This book does not cover every detail of using Lumen, but focuses on the most important concepts needed to write testable APIs with Lumen.

Conventions Used in This Book

The book is a hands-on guide to building a working API, so you will see tons of code samples throughout the book. I will point out a few conventions used so that you can understand the console commands and code. The code is meant to provide a fully working API; you can follow along or copy and paste code samples.

Code Examples

A typical PHP code snippet looks like this:

Example PHP Code Snippet

```
/**
 * A Hello World Example
 */
$app->get('/', function () {
    return 'Hello World';
});
```

To guide readers, approximate line numbers are used when you will be adding a block of code to an existing class or test file:

Example PHP Code Snippet

```
10   /**
11    * A Foobar Example
12    */
13   $app->get('/foo', function () {
14       return 'bar';
15   });
```

Longer lines end in a backslash (\) and continue to the next line:

Example of Long Line in PHP

```
$thisIsALongLine = 'Lorem ipsum dolor sit amet, consectetur adipisicing elit. Qu\
os unde deserunt eos?'
```

When you need to run console commands to execute the test suite or create files, the snippet appears as plain text without line numbers. Lines start with $, which represents the terminal prompt.

Example Console Command

```
$ touch the/file.php
```

Console commands that should be executed in the recommended Homestead[1] environment will be indicated like the following example. The book removes extra output from PHPUnit tests to make examples less verbose.

Console Command in the Homestead Virtual Machine

```
# vagrant@homestead:~/Code/bookr$
$ phpunit

OK (1 test, 4 assertions)
```

---

[1]https://laravel.com/docs/homestead

Code Errata and Feedback

Submit errata to lumenapibook@gmail.com, or via the book's apress.com product page, located at www.apress.com/9781484221860. Feel free to send in typos, inaccurate descriptions, code issues, praise, feedback, and code suggestions on better ways of doing something. Please don't be shy; these things make my book better!

Tips, Notes, and Warnings

YOUR ASIDE TITLE

This is an aside

 Hey, Listen!   Tips give you pointers related to concepts in the book.

⚠ **Danger!**   Warnings point out potential issues and security concerns.

ⓘ **Need the Info**   This aside provides additional info related to code and concepts.

ⓘ **Git Commit: Amazing Refactor!**   rm3dwe2f

This is an example of a code commit if you are following along and using git to commit your work.

💬 **Discussions**   This tip includes deeper discussions around topics in the book. Advanced users can generally skip these.

Tools You Will Need

All tools are recommended, but if you know what you're doing, you can set up your own coding environment and skip the recommended tools. You might even have these tools already; just make sure they are relatively up-to-date. All tools listed are free unless otherwise noted.

VirtualBox

This book uses a virtual machine to run the API application. You will need to download VirtualBox if you plan on using the recommended Homestead environment. VirtualBox works on Windows, Mac, and Linux (www.virtualbox.org).

Vagrant

Homestead also requires Vagrant (`www.vagrantup.com/`) to manage and provision virtual machines. Vagrant works on Windows, Mac, and Linux (Debian and CentOS).

Version Control

If you want to work along in the book and commit your code as you go (recommended), you need to install a version control system. I recommend git, but anything you want will do.

Editor/IDE

Most readers will already have a go-to editor. I highly recommend PhpStorm (`www.jetbrains.com/phpstorm/`), which is not free, but it pays for itself. Other common IDE options are Eclipse PDT and NetBeans.

If you don't like IDEs, I recommend Sublime Text (`www.sublimetext.com/`) or Atom (`https://atom.io/`). If you are on Mac, TextMate (`https://macromates.com/`) is another great choice. TextMate 2 is marked as "beta" but is reliable.

CHAPTER 1

■ ■ ■

Installing Lumen

Before you start diving into Lumen, you need to make sure PHP is installed. You'll also need a few other tools to develop a real application. You can get PHP a number of ways, but here is my recommendation for all platforms: Laravel Homestead (`laravel.com/docs/homestead`). I also include a few different ways to install PHP locally if you are interested, but the book examples will use Homestead. **I highly encourage using Homestead to work through this book.**

To work through the applications in this book, you will need

- PHP >= 5.5.9, as well as a few PHP extensions

- Composer

- MySQL Database

Homestead comes with a modern version of PHP called Composer (`https://getcomposer.org/`), and a few database options, so you don't need to worry about the requirements if you are using Homestead; if you are not using Homestead, you will need >= PHP 5.5.9 as outlined by the Lumen installation instructions (`https://lumen.laravel.com/docs/5.2/installation#installation`).

The last thing on the list is a database. Lumen can be configured to use different databases including MySQL, SQLite, PostgreSQL, or SQL Server. We will use MySQL (any MySQL variant will do) for this book. MySQL is the default database connection in the Lumen Framework database configuration (`https://github.com/laravel/lumen-framework/blob/5.2/config/database.php`) so we will stick with the convention.

Homestead

Laravel Homestead is the best development environment choice because it provides a complete development environment for *all* your Laravel and Lumen projects. Homestead provides some solid benefits for your development environment as well, including the following:

- Isolated environment on a virtual machine

- Works on Windows, Mac, and Linux

- Easily configure all your projects in one place

As mentioned in the introduction, Homestead requires Vagrant (`www.vagrantup.com/`) and VirtualBox (`www.virtualbox.org/`) so you will need to install both. Follow the installation instructions (`https://lumen.laravel.com/docs/5.2/installation#installation`) to finish setting up Homestead.

Electronic supplementary material The online version of this chapter (doi:10.1007/978-1-4842-2187-7_1) contains supplementary material, which is available to authorized users.

Once you complete the installation instructions you should be able to run the `vagrant ssh` command within the Homestead project and successfully ssh into your Homestead virtual machine. You will revisit Homestead to set up your sample application in Chapter 2, and then you will set up another application in Chapter 3 that you will work on throughout the remainder of the book.

When the install instructions instruct you to clone the Homestead git repository, I encourage you to clone it to ~/Code/Homestead to follow along with the book, or you can adapt the examples to match whatever you pick (see Listing 1-1).

Listing 1-1. Cloning the Homestead Project to ~/Code/Homestead

```
$ mkdir -p ~/Code
$ git clone https://github.com/laravel/homestead.git Homestead
```

Once you finish the Homestead installation instructions you should be able to ssh into the virtual machine (Listing 1-2).

Listing 1-2. SSH Into Homestead

```
$ cd ~/Code/Homestead
$ vagrant ssh
Welcome to Ubuntu 14.04.3 LTS (GNU/Linux 3.19.0-25-generic x86_64)

 * Documentation: https://help.ubuntu.com/
Last login: Tue Feb 2 04:48:52 2016 from 10.0.2.2
vagrant@homestead:~$
```

You can type "exit" or press Control+D to exit the virtual machine. The homestead repository will be at ~/Code/Homestead and this is the path you will use in this book for your applications. I encourage you to review the Homestead.yaml file at ~/.homestead/Homestead.yaml after you finish installing Homestead. Once you get Homestead installed, you can skip ahead to Chapter 2. See you in the next section!

■ **Optional Local Instructions** The following sections offer information if you are interested in running PHP locally, so feel free to skip them. I cannot guarantee these instructions, but for the most part they should work for you.

Mac OSX

If you want to develop locally on OS X, I recommend using Homebrew (http://brew.sh/) to install PHP and MySQL. The PHP installation that ships with OS X will probably suffice, but I will show you how to install PHP with Homebrew instead of dealing with the different versions of PHP that ship with different versions of OS X.

To install packages with Homebrew, you will need Xcode developer tools and the Xcode command line tools. XCode is a rather large download—I'll be waiting for you right here.

Once you have Xcode, follow the installation instructions (http://brew.sh/#install) on Homebrew's site. Next, you need to tell brew about "homebrew-php" so you can install PHP 5.6 (Listing 1-3).

Listing 1-3. Tap homebrew-php

```
$ brew tap homebrew/dupes
$ brew tap homebrew/versions
$ brew tap homebrew/homebrew-php
$ brew install php56 php56-xdebug
```

Once the installation finishes, verify that you have the right version of PHP in your path (Listing 1-4).

Listing 1-4. Verifying PHP

```
$ php --version
PHP 5.6.16 (cli) (built: Dec 7 2015 10:06:24)
Copyright (c) 1997-2015 The PHP Group
Zend Engine v2.6.0, Copyright (c) 1998-2015 Zend Technologies
```

Next, you need to install the MySQL database server with Homebrew (Listing 1-5).

Listing 1-5. Installing MySQL with Homebrew

```
$ brew install mysql
```

Once the MySQL installation is finished, make sure you can connect to the database server (Listing 1-6).

Listing 1-6. Connecting to MySQL

```
$ mysql -u root
Welcome to the MySQL monitor. Commands end with ; or \g.
Your MySQL connection id is 3795
Server version: 5.6.26 Homebrew
...
mysql>
```

I highly recommend updating the root password (http://dev.mysql.com/doc/refman/5.6/en/resetting-permissions.html) and adding another user besides root, which you will use to connect to MySQL. Although the database is local, securing MySQL is a good habit.

You can configure Apache or Nginx locally if you want to use a web server (Mac ships with Apache).

I'll leave the rest up to you, but it should be pretty easy to get PHP and a web server going on a Mac by searching Google.

Linux

Here are simple instructions to install PHP on Unix-like systems; this section includes the most popular distributions like CentOS and Ubuntu. This is not an exhaustive set of setup instructions but it should be enough to work with Lumen.

Red Hat/CentOS

To install a modern version of PHP on Red Hat and CentOS, I recommend using the Webtatic (https://webtatic.com/) yum repository. First, add the repository with the Webtatic release RPM; you should use the repository that matches your specific version (Listing 1-7).

Listing 1-7. Adding the Webtatic Repository

```
# CentOS/REHL 7
$ yum -y update
$ rpm -Uvh https://dl.fedoraproject.org/pub/epel/epel-release-latest-7.noarch.rpm
$ rpm -Uvh https://mirror.webtatic.com/yum/el7/webtatic-release.rpm

# CentOS/REHL 6
$ yum -y update
$ rpm -Uvh https://mirror.webtatic.com/yum/el6/latest.rpm
```

Next, install the following PHP packages and verify that PHP was installed properly (Listing 1-8).

Listing 1-8. Installing PHP Packages from Webtatic

```
$ yum install \
    php56w.x86_64 \
    php56w-mysql.x86_64 \
    php56w-mbstring.x86_64 \
    php56w-xml.x86_64 \
    php56w-pecl-xdebug.x86_64

# Verify
$ php --version
PHP 5.6.16 (cli) (built: Nov 27 2015 21:46:01)
Copyright (c) 1997-2015 The PHP Group
Zend Engine v2.6.0, Copyright (c) 1998-2015 Zend Technologies
```

Next, install the MySQL client and server (Listing 1-9).

Listing 1-9. Installing MySQL on REHL

```
$ yum install mysql-server mysql
```

Once MySQL is installed, you should set a root password (Listing 1-10).

Listing 1-10. Securing the MySQL Installation

```
$ /usr/bin/mysql_secure_installation
```

Follow the prompts and you should be all set!

Debian/Ubuntu

On Debian systems I recommend using the php5-5.6 PPA (https://launchpad.net/~ondrej/+archive/ubuntu/php5-5.6) from Ondrej Surý (https://launchpad.net/~ondrej) or the PHP 7 version of the same PPA. Installation of the PPA varies slightly between different versions. Most of the steps will remain the same, but the following are the steps for Ubuntu 14.04 and Ubuntu 12.04.

First, install a couple dependencies needed to add the PPA. If you are using Ubuntu 14.04, see Listing 1-11.

Listing 1-11. Installing Dependencies Needed and the PPA on Ubuntu 14.04

```
$ apt-get install -y language-pack-en-base
$ apt-get install -y software-properties-common --no-install-recommends
$ LC_ALL=en_US.UTF-8 add-apt-repository ppa:ondrej/php5-5.6
```

If you are using Ubuntu 12.04, run the code in Listing 1-12 instead.

Listing 1-12. Installing Dependencies and the PPA on Ubuntu 12.04

```
$ apt-get install -y language-pack-en-base
$ apt-get install -y python-software-properties --no-install-recommends
$ LC_ALL=en_US.UTF-8 add-apt-repository ppa:ondrej/php5-5.6
```

Note that non-UTF-8 locales will not work (https://github.com/oerdnj/deb.sury.org/issues/56) at the time of writing. Next, update and install the required packages and verify; the commands are the same for Ubuntu 14.04 and 12.04 (Listing 1-13).

Listing 1-13. Updating and Installing Packages

```
$ apt-get update
$ apt-get install -y \
    php5 \
    php5-mysql \
    php5-xdebug

# Verify
$ php --version
PHP 5.6.16-2+deb.sury.org~precise+1 (cli)
Copyright (c) 1997-2015 The PHP Group
Zend Engine v2.6.0, Copyright (c) 1998-2015 Zend Technologies
    with Zend OPcache v7.0.6-dev, Copyright (c) 1999-2015, by Zend Technologies
```

Next, install MySQL server and client packages, make the MySQL service start on boot, and start the service manually (Listing 1-14).

Listing 1-14. Installing MySQL Packages on Ubuntu

```
$ apt-get install \
    mysql-server \
    mysql-client
$ sudo update-rc.d mysql defaults
$ sudo service mysql start
```

During the installation of the `mysql-server` package you should be prompted to update the root password, which will look similar to Figure 1-1.

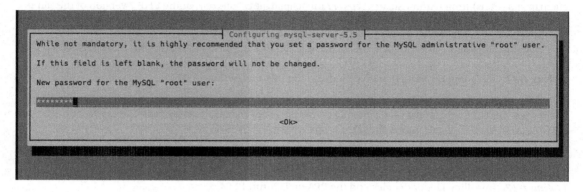

Figure 1-1. *Configuring MySQL Root Password*

Verify that you can connect to MySQL after you finish installing MySQL and setting a root password (Listing 1-15).

Listing 1-15. Connecting to MySQL

```
$ mysql -u root -p
Enter password:
...
mysql>
```

At this point, you should have everything required to get through this book using the built-in PHP server on a local Ubuntu machine.

Windows

I recommend using Homestead (`http://laravel.com/docs/5.1/homestead#installation-and-setup`) to work through this book on Windows.

Conclusion

You should now have a working environment that you can use to write Lumen applications! Let's summarize what we did in this chapter:

- Installed Vagrant and VirtualBox
- Installed the Homestead virtual machine
- Covered alternative ways of installing PHP and MySQL

I want to emphasize how easy Homestead makes getting a solid, portable development environment working with little effort. Now that you have PHP installed, it's time to learn Lumen!

CHAPTER 2

Hello Lumen

Let's dive right into Lumen. In this chapter, you'll learn how to set up a new Lumen project and you'll explore some of Lumen's basic features:

- Routing
- Middleware
- Requests
- Responses

To follow along, you should have the recommended Homestead environment from Chapter 1 installed.

Setting Up a New Project

Before you can get started, you need to create a new Lumen project in Homestead. To create a new project, ssh into Homestead virtual machine and use Composer to create a new Lumen project (Listing 2-1).

Listing 2-1. Creating a New Lumen Application in Homestead

```
# On your local machine
$ cd ~/Code/Homestead
$ vagrant ssh

# In the virtual machine
vagrant@homestead:~$ cd ~/Code
vagrant@homestead:~/Code$ composer create-project \
  laravel/lumen=~5.2.0 --prefer-dist hello-lumen
vagrant@homestead:~/Code$ cd hello-lumen
```

The book examples assume Homestead was cloned to the suggested path ~/Code/Homestead. Adjust the commands if you cloned Homestead elsewhere.

In the Homestead virtual machine, you change the directory to ~/Code, where your application files will live. Next, you use Composer's create-project command to create a new Lumen project. The last argument in the create-project command tells Composer to create the project in the path ~/Code/hello-lumen. Now that you've created a new project on the virtual machine, you should also see a shared local path at ~/Code/hello-lumen on your own machine.

© Paul Redmond 2016
P. Redmond, *Lumen Programming Guide*, DOI 10.1007/978-1-4842-2187-7_2

The next step is telling Homestead about the `hello-lumen` application. On your local machine, open `~/.homestead/Homestead.yaml` and find the default project under the `sites` key (Listing 2-2).

Listing 2-2. Default Sites Configuration in Homestead.yaml

```
sites:
    - map: homestead.app
      to: /home/vagrant/Code/Laravel/public
```

Replace it with the code in Listing 2-3 and save the file.

Listing 2-3. Default Sites Configuration in Homestead.yaml

```
sites:
    - map: hello-lumen.app
      to: /home/vagrant/Code/hello-lumen/public
```

Configure the project's hostname and the path to the `public` folder on the virtual machine. Save the file and run `vagrant provision` on your local machine to update Homestead with the new configuration changes (Listing 2-4).

Listing 2-4. Provision Vagrant Locally

```
> cd ~/Code/Homestead
> vagrant provision
```

Every time you update `Homestead.yaml` you will need to run the `vagrant provision` command.

Once Vagrant is finished provisioning the machine, the last step is adding an entry to the `hosts` file on your local machine. The `hosts` file will map the hostname `hello-lumen.app` to your virtual machine's IP address. You can find Homestead's IP address by finding the `ip` key in the `~/.homestead/Homestead.yaml` file—you should see something like `ip: "192.168.10.10"`.

Take note of the IP address so you can add it to the local `hosts` file. To update the `hosts` file on Mac or Linux, the file path is `/etc/hosts`; if you are on Windows, the file path is `C:\Windows\System32\drivers\etc\hosts`. Add the line from Listing 2-5 to your `hosts` file.

Listing 2-5. Adding Hostname to Hosts File

```
192.168.10.10 hello-lumen.app
```

Be sure to use the IP address found in your `~/.homestead/Homestead.yaml` file, not the IP shown in this book. It might be the same, but make sure.

After updating the `hosts` file, visit `http://hello-lumen.app/` in your browser and you should see something similar to Figure 2-1.

Figure 2-1. *Lumen default route*

You should now have a working hello-lumen project. Let's get to work!

Routes

Routing (https://lumen.laravel.com/docs/5.2/routing) is the first feature we will cover. Application routes in Lumen are defined in the app/Http/routes.php file. In the most basic form, routing configuration includes an HTTP verb (GET, POST, etc.) which accepts a URI and a Closure. We will use the Closure style routes in this chapter, but we will use controllers throughout the book.

The first routes will be two simple "Hello World" examples to introduce you to routing:

- /hello/world which responds with the text "Hello World"
- /hello/{name} which responds with a customized greeting

Before you define your own routes, if you open the file app/Http/routes.php, the default contents looks like Listing 2-6.

Listing 2-6. The Default Lumen Route in app/Http/routes.php

```php
<?php

$app->get('/', function () use ($app) {
    return $app->version();
});
```

The $app variable in the routes file is an instance of \Laravel\Lumen\Application which is defined in the bootstrap/app.php file. The application routes file is imported near the end of bootstrap/app.php (Listing 2-7).

Listing 2-7. The Bootstrap File Importing Routes

```php
$app->group(['namespace' => 'App\Http\Controllers'], function ($app) {
    require __DIR__.'/../app/Http/routes.php';
});
```

The Hello World Route

Your first route is a simple /hello/world route that responds with the text "Hello World". Open up the app/Http/routes.php file and add the route shown in Listing 2-8.

Listing 2-8. The /hello/world Route in app/Http/routes.php

```
18  $app->get('/hello/world', function () use ($app) {
19      return "Hello world!";
20  });
```

The $app->get() method accepts a URI and a \Closure that gets executed to create the response. The route returns a string response. If you visit http://hello-lumen.app/hello/world in your browser, you will see the response "Hello world!"

The $app instance has HTTP methods like get, put, post, and delete which are used to define routes. In this example, the defined route will respond to GET requests. If you try to send a POST request, you will get a 405 response (Listing 2-9).

Listing 2-9. Trying to POST to the Hello World Route

```
$ curl -I -XPOST http://hello-lumen.app/hello/world
HTTP/1.1 405 Method Not Allowed
Server: nginx/1.9.7
Content-Type: text/html; charset=UTF-8
Transfer-Encoding: chunked
Connection: keep-alive
allow: GET
Cache-Control: no-cache, private
date: Tue, 29 Dec 2015 06:28:46 GMT
```

Route Parameters

The second route you are going to add has a dynamic route parameter (Listing 2-10).

Listing 2-10. Your Second Route

```
22  $app->get('/hello/{name}', function ($name) use ($app) {
23      return "Hello {$name}";
24  });
```

The route URI has a required route parameter {name} which is then passed to the \Closure. You then return your concatenated $name variable, which creates the HTTP response shown in Listing 2-11.

Listing 2-11. Example Response from the Router

```
$ curl -i http://hello-lumen.app/hello/paul
HTTP/1.1 200 OK
Server: nginx/1.9.7
Content-Type: text/html; charset=UTF-8
Transfer-Encoding: chunked
Connection: keep-alive
```

```
Cache-Control: no-cache
Date: Sat, 26 Dec 2015 21:27:19 GMT

Hello paul
```

You can define multiple route parameters in one route and add constraints to them (only digits). I will go over plenty of route examples as you work through this book.

Middleware and Responses

Similar to express.js (http://expressjs.com/) and many other web frameworks, Lumen has HTTP middleware (https://lumen.laravel.com/docs/5.2/middleware). Middleware provides a way to filter incoming HTTP requests before a defined route handles the request. You can use middleware to do any number of things, like authentication, validating a signed request, and CORS support, to name a few. Middleware classes are typically created in the app/Http/Middleware path by convention; I suggest sticking to the convention unless you plan on writing a standalone package that includes middleware.

Lumen has two types of middleware configuration: global middleware and route middleware. What is the difference between the two types? Global middleware runs on every HTTP request and route middleware runs on specific routes (or groups of routes) configured to run the middleware. We will go over an example of each.

We will also cover an example of creating a response object in middleware. We will work with response objects throughout this book, but we will only touch on them lightly in this chapter.

Global Middleware

The first middleware example you will write is a simple request logger that logs every incoming request to the storage/logs/lumen.log application log file. Configuring the logging middleware to be a *global middleware* makes sense because we want to log all HTTP requests.

Start by creating the file app/Http/Middleware/RequestLogMiddleware.php with the contents shown in Listing 2-12.

Listing 2-12. Creating the RequestLogMiddleware

```php
1   <?php
2
3   namespace App\Http\Middleware;
4
5   use Log;
6   use Closure;
7   use Illuminate\Http\Request;
8
9   class RequestLogMiddleware
10  {
11      public function handle(Request $request, Closure $next)
12      {
13          Log::info("Request Logged\n" .
14              sprintf("~~~~\n%s~~~~", (string) $request));
15
16          return $next($request);
17      }
18  }
```

Middleware needs to define a handle method that accepts two parameters: the request object and a Closure instance. The request object is an instance of Illuminate\Http\Request and represents the current request.

Each middleware must call return $next($request) at some point in order to continue processing the request.

Now you need to register your new middleware in bootstrap/app.php (Listing 2-13).

Listing 2-13. Registering a Global Middleware

```
62  // $app->middleware([
63  //     App\Http\Middleware\ExampleMiddleware::class
64  // ]);
65
66  $app->middleware([
67      App\Http\Middleware\RequestLogMiddleware::class
68  ]);
```

The Application::middleware() method accepts an array of middleware class names. I have included the commented out middleware so you can see other types of middleware that ship with Lumen.

There is one more step to get the middleware working: you need to enable facades (https://laravel.com/docs/5.2/facades) so the Log class will work as expected.

In bootstrap/app.php, uncomment the code in Listing 2-14.

Listing 2-14. Enabling Facades in the Application

```
26  // $app->withFacades();
27  $app->withFacades();
```

With facades enabled, the new middleware will add a log entry to storage/logs/lumen.log for every request (Listing 2-15).

Listing 2-15. Partial Log Output from RequestLogMiddleware in lumen.log

```
[2015-12-26 21:47:53] lumen.INFO: Request Logged
GET /hello/paul HTTP/1.1
...
```

■ **Facades** The facade pattern provides a static interface to classes available in the service container (https://lumen.laravel.com/docs/5.2/container).

It offers a clean style that I personally like, but you are not required to use it.

Lumen offers various ways of resolving dependencies out of the container, which you will see in this book. Also be sure to read the "Resolving" section of the documentation (https://lumen.laravel.com/docs/5.2/container).

The middleware should be working. What happens if we forget to call $next($request)? To experiment, you would get the following response (Listing 2-16) by removing return $next($request) from the middleware (be sure to put it back).

Listing 2-16. What Happens When $next($request) Is Not Returned?

```
$ curl -i http://hello-lumen.app/hello/paul
HTTP/1.1 200 OK
Server: nginx/1.9.7
Date: Sat, 26 Dec 2015 21:54:00 GMT
Content-Type: text/html; charset=UTF-8
Transfer-Encoding: chunked
Connection: keep-alive
```

Middleware can also control **whether or not** the HTTP request should continue being processed. For example, an authentication middleware would deny access to guests trying to access secured parts of the application by sending a 403 Forbidden response instead of proceeding with the request. Middleware should either allow the request to continue or send a response back.

Route Middleware

Our next middleware will be *route middleware* for the /hello/{name} route. Create a new middleware class in app/Http/Middleware/HelloMiddleware.php with the code from Listing 2-17.

Listing 2-17. Creating the HelloMiddleware

```php
1   <?php
2
3   namespace App\Http\Middleware;
4
5   use Closure;
6   use Illuminate\Http\Request;
7
8   class HelloMiddleware
9   {
10      public function handle(Request $request, Closure $next)
11      {
12          if (preg_match('/balrog$/i', $request->getRequestUri())) {
13              return response('YOU SHALL NOT PASS!', 403);
14          }
15
16          return $next($request);
17      }
18  }
```

The HelloMiddleware checks the request URI against a case-insensitive regex pattern. If the URI matches the regex pattern, the middleware returns a 403 forbidden response error with the response() helper function. If the user is not asking to say hello to a balrog, the request will proceed as expected.

In order to use the HelloMiddleware you need to configure it in bootstrap/app.php (Listing 2-18).

Listing 2-18. Registering the HelloMiddleware

```
66  $app->middleware([
67      App\Http\Middleware\RequestLogMiddleware::class
68  ]);
69
70  $app->routeMiddleware([
71      'hello' => App\Http\Middleware\HelloMiddleware::class
72  ]);
```

The $app->routeMiddleware() method takes an associative array. The key hello is a shorthand reference to the middleware class; the shorthand key configures routes to use the middleware (Listing 2-19).

Listing 2-19. Configuring Your Route to Use the HelloMiddleware

```
22  $app->get('/hello/{name}', ['middleware' => 'hello', function ($name) {
23      return "Hello {$name}";
24  }]);
```

You have changed the second parameter in $app->get() to an array. The middleware key instructs your route to run the 'hello' middleware you defined in your bootstrap/app.php file. Note that the code example also drops use($app) in your Closure because you are not using $app inside the Closure.

Now if you try saying hello to a balrog the middleware will authoritatively stop the request (Listing 2-20).

Listing 2-20. Saying Hello to a Balrog

```
$ curl -i http://hello-lumen.app/hello/balrog
HTTP/1.1 403 Forbidden
Server: nginx/1.9.7
Content-Type: text/html; charset=UTF-8
Transfer-Encoding: chunked
Connection: keep-alive
Cache-Control: no-cache
Date: Sun, 27 Dec 2015 02:00:27 GMT

YOU SHALL NOT PASS!
```

We are done with your quick tour of middleware. To learn more about middleware, read the full documentation (https://lumen.laravel.com/docs/5.2/middleware). Another good resource is reading the source code of the middleware that ships with Lumen.

The Request and Response Objects

You will become quite familiar with getting data from requests and returning responses while building APIs with Lumen. We will quickly touch on each so you can get your feet wet. We will be using these objects extensively throughout the book, so using them should become second nature by the end of this book. Let's dive in to the request object first.

The Request

The request object (https://lumen.laravel.com/docs/5.2/requests) represents the HTTP request and is one of the essential objects that you need to familiarize yourself with. It provides methods to access basic information about the HTTP request and to access things like POST data and query string parameters, to name a few. To access the request in your routes, you type-hint the Illuminate\Http\Request class on your route. Type-hinting the request object (Listing 2-21) automatically injects the request from the service container (https://lumen.laravel.com/docs/5.2/container).

Listing 2-21. Using the Request Object

```
26  $app->get('/request', function (Illuminate\Http\Request $request) {
27      return "Hello " . $request->get('name', 'stranger');
28  });
```

In Listing 2-21, the route returns a string from the query string parameter name, and the second argument, 'stranger', is the default value returned when the name parameter is not present in the request. Making a request without the name parameter will return the responses shown in Listing 2-22.

Listing 2-22. Experimenting with Request::get()

```
$ curl http://hello-lumen.app/request
Hello stranger

$ curl http://hello-lumen.app/request\?name\=Paul
Hello Paul
```

The request object has many useful methods, and I highly encourage you to browse the source code and read all the documentation (https://lumen.laravel.com/docs/5.2/requests) on requests.

The Response

Lumen provides a response object to represent an HTTP response which provides convenient methods that make it easy to craft valid HTTP responses and return JSON, which is the response type you will return throughout this book—you are building APIs after all!

You can create a response in a number of ways, and I'll show you a few examples, including crafting a response from the Illuminate\Http\Response object and some convenience functions for easily responding with JSON. We will also build on the request object to show you some basic content negotiation.

The first way to create a response is returning an instance of the Illuminate\Http\Response object in a route (Listing 2-23).

Listing 2-23. Using the Illuminate Response Object

```
30  $app->get('/response', function (Illuminate\Http\Request $request) {
31      return (new Illuminate\Http\Response('Hello stranger', 200))
32          ->header('Content-Type', 'text/plain');
33  });
```

In Listing 2-23, we return the response object, set the status code to a 200 OK, and set the Content-Type header to text/plain. To expand on this example, let's do some inline content negotiation and return JSON when the client asks for it (Listing 2-24).

Listing 2-24. Responding with JSON

```
30  $app->get('/response', function (Illuminate\Http\Request $request) {
31      if ($request->wantsJson()) {
32          return response()->json(['greeting' => 'Hello stranger']);
33      }
34
35      return (new Illuminate\Http\Response('Hello stranger', 200))
36          ->header('Content-Type', 'text/plain');
37  });
```

In Listing 2-24, you use the Request object to check if the client is asking for JSON. If the client wants JSON, you use the response() helper function, which returns an instance of the Laravel\Lumen\Http\ResponseFactory. Now you can get a JSON greeting (Listing 2-25).

Listing 2-25. Returning a JSON Response

```
$ curl -H"Accept: application/json" \
    http://hello-lumen.app/response

{"greeting":"Hello stranger"}
```

The ResponseFactory has three convenient methods: make(), json(), and download(). You've seen json() already, but the above route could be written as shown in Listing 2-26 to use the make() method instead of initializing an instance of the response.

Listing 2-26. Using the ResponseFactory

```
30  $app->get('/response', function (Illuminate\Http\Request $request) {
31      if ($request->wantsJson()) {
32          return response()->json(['greeting' => 'Hello stranger']);
33      }
34
35      return response()
36          ->make('Hello stranger', 200, ['Content-Type' => 'text/plain']);
37  });
```

Some people might prefer to directly initialize the Response object, but I personally like using the response() helper function. I think the helper function cleans up code nicely and is convenient. Note that the third argument in make() accepts an optional array of HTTP response headers.

Onward

We are done with the tour of the basic parts of Lumen. In the next chapter, we will create another Lumen application and prepare to write test-driven features as we work through the remainder of the book.

CHAPTER 3

Creating the Book Application

Unfortunately, the world doesn't have much demand for "Hello World" APIs, and working on trivial applications is not going to help you for long. We are ready to start building something of more substance, driven by tests. For the remainder of this book, we will create a RESTful (hopefully) book API. The book API will represent two main RESTful resources (books and authors) and a few other resources. You will be writing a RESTful API, and while I try to follow good practices, it might not be perfectly "RESTful." I digress.

You will see some similarities between writing APIs and web applications in this book, such as routing, models, database associations, and the like. We will cover specific challenges and needs that differ from traditional web applications. As we work on the **book** and **author** resources, we will also include validation, ways to structure response data, and error handling, among other API-specific topics.

Before we can start writing the API, we need to define and set up the application to store your virtual library of books. In true web-naming fashion, our virtual library will be known to the world as **Bookr**.

Bookr will be developed in small, test-driven increments of code. You will get accustomed to running tests often, and I will show you a couple of my favorite workflows around testing. I think you will begin to realize how easily you can write fully-tested APIs with Lumen!

Source Code   If you get stuck or you want to see the source code, you can download it from `https://bitbucket.org/paulredmond/apress-bookr`.

Building Something Amazing

If you've used Laravel before, you are probably familiar with the love and attention to detail that make the Laravel ecosystem amazing! Without further ado, let's start by creating a new project on the Homestead virtual machine (Listing 3-1).

Listing 3-1. Creating a New Lumen Application in Homestead

```
# On your local machine
$ cd ~/Code/Homestead
$ vagrant ssh

# In the virtual machine
vagrant@homestead:~$ cd ~/Code
vagrant@homestead:~/Code$ composer create-project \
  laravel/lumen=~5.2.0 --prefer-dist bookr
vagrant@homestead:~/Code$ cd bookr
```

© Paul Redmond 2016
P. Redmond, *Lumen Programming Guide*, DOI 10.1007/978-1-4842-2187-7_3

Next, put your application under version control on the Homestead virtual machine (Listing 3-2).

Listing 3-2. Adding the Application to Version Control

```
# vagrant@homestead:~/Code/bookr$
$ git init
$ git add .
$ git commit -m"Initial commit of Bookr"
```

■ **Initial commit of Bookr** 67e024d (https://bitbucket.org/paulredmond/apress-bookr/ commits/67e024d)

Lumen ships with sensible .gitignore defaults so don't be concerned with running *git add* . for the initial commit.

■ **Keep Private Things Private** Avoid committing sensitive information (such as database passwords) to version control. Lumen uses the phpdotenv (https://github.com/vlucas/phpdotenv) library to load environment configuration, making it really easy to keep sensitive data out of your code.

Next, you need to configure your new application locally in ~/.homestead/Homestead.yaml. On your local machine, add the configuration shown in Listing 3-3.

Listing 3-3. Adding Bookr Site Configuration in Homestead.yaml

```
sites:
    - map: hello-lumen.app
      to: /home/vagrant/Code/hello-lumen/public
    - map: bookr.app
      to: /home/vagrant/Code/bookr/public

databases:
    - homestead
    - bookr
    - bookr_testing
```

You've added a site configuration and two databases that Homestead will create when you run *vagrant provision*. The *bookr* database is the development database, and the *bookr_testing* database will be your testing database in a later chapter. Save the configuration, and provision the virtual machine by running the code in Listing 3-4 locally.

Listing 3-4. Provisioning Vagrant Locally

```
$ cd ~/Code/Homestead
$ vagrant provision
```

Once provisioning is complete, you are ready to add *bookr.app* to your local system's hosts file. Update the hosts file entry you added in Chapter 2 by editing /etc/hosts (or C:\Windows\System32\drivers\etc\ hosts on Windows) and make it look like Listing 3-5.

Listing 3-5. Updating the Hosts File

```
192.168.10.10 hello-lumen.app bookr.app
```

Be sure you use the correct IP address from your _/.homestead/Homestead.yaml file!

You are done setting up the application on Homestead. If you visit http://bookr.app/ in your browser, you should now see the same "Lumen" text you saw in Chapter 2.

Now that you have a working application on Homestead, you should be able to connect to your MySQL databases. If you read the "Connecting to Databases" section (https://laravel.com/docs/5.2/ homestead#connecting-to-databases) in the Homestead documentation you should be able to connect with your favorite MySQL GUI app or the console. I personally like Sequel Pro (www.sequelpro.com/) on OS X. At the time of this writing, you can connect to Homestead's MySQL server with the code in Listing 3-6 from your local terminal if you have the MySQL client installed.

Listing 3-6. Connecting to Homestead Bookr Databases

```
> mysql \
-u homestead \
-h 127.0.0.1 \
-P 33060 \
-psecret

mysql> show databases;
+--------------------+
| Database           |
+--------------------+
| information_schema |
| bookr              |
| bookr_testing      |
| ...                |
+--------------------+
mysql> exit
Bye
```

Environment Setup

Now that the project is set up and under version control, you need to create a .env file. The .env file is used to set up an environment-specific configuration which is used by Lumen. I will show you how configuration files use environment variables later on. For now, copy the .env.example file that ships with Lumen for your development environment (Listing 3-7).

Listing 3-7. Copying the Example .env File

```
$ cd ~/Code/Homestead
$ vagrant ssh
# ...
vagrant@homestead:~$ cd Code/bookr/
vagrant@homestead:~$ cp .env.example .env
```

■ **Repeatable Environments** I recommend keeping .env.example under version control and up to date with any configuration used in your application. The .env file is ignored by git to keep sensitive data out of your repo. That means that another developer pulling your changes will not have any new environment variables you've added in his or her .env file.

Keeping track of environment variables can be frustrating when you pull changes and things stop working. Having an accurate starting point in .env.example makes it easy for a new developer to get an environment going and for developers to see what has been added or changed.

We will use as many conventions as possible in your environment. Since Lumen defaults to using MySQL, we will stick with that convention. Open .env (around Line 8 at the time of writing) and you will see the MySQL credentials shown in Listing 3-8.

Listing 3-8. The .env Database Connection Configuration

```
 8   DB_CONNECTION=mysql
 9   DB_HOST=localhost
10   DB_PORT=3306
11   DB_DATABASE=bookr
12   DB_USERNAME=homestead
13   DB_PASSWORD=secret
```

If you are using Homestead, the .env.example file already contains the correct MySQL credentials, and the only thing you need to change is DB_DATABASE=bookr; if you are using your own environment, adjust accordingly.

Quick feedback is fun. Its time to try out your new configuration! Run the code in Listing 3-9 on the Homestead server.

Listing 3-9. Running the artisan migrate Command

```
vagrant@homestead:~/Code/bookr$ php artisan migrate
Migration table created successfully.
Nothing to migrate.
```

Sweet! Your database and environment configurations are ready to go.

If we want to hit the ground running on the first endpoint in the next chapter, we need to do a little more setup. Lumen doesn't assume that we need or want to use object-relational mapping (ORM), but Eloquent (https://laravel.com/docs/5.2/eloquent) is a really nice ORM, and I personally think it's worth using in Lumen.

How do you enable Eloquent in Lumen? Back to your app bootstrap file, *bootstrap/app.php*, to uncomment a few lines. You should also enable Facades (https://laravel.com/docs/5.2/facades) at the same time, so uncomment the following two lines shown in Listing 3-10.

Listing 3-10. Enabling Facades and Eloquent

```
26   $app->withFacades();
27
28   $app->withEloquent();
```

Now commit your changes (Listing 3-11).

Listing 3-11. Commiting the Application Configuration

```
# vagrant@homestead:~/Code/bookr$
$ git commit -am"Enable Facades and Eloquent"
```

■ **Enable Facades and Eloquent**   00619f2 (https://bitbucket.org/paulredmond/apress-bookr/
commits/00619f2)

Before moving on to the final setup task, I'd like to show you quickly how these environment settings work. Lumen has all of the default PHP configuration files located in the vendor/laravel/lumen-framework/config folder. Feel free to take a peek now.

If you create a config/ folder in the root of the project, you can copy over config files and the application will read your copied file instead of the vendor config file.

The following code example is the default MySQL configuration that ships with Lumen, which may vary slightly from the time this was published. This example will give you an idea of how Lumen uses env() for configuration. By using env() you can use the .env file to get what you want without copying the vendor/laravel/lumen-framework/config/database.php configuration file to the project's config/ folder.

Default Database.php Config (Partial Source):

```
60  'mysql' => [
61      'driver'     => 'mysql',
62      'host'       => env('DB_HOST', 'localhost'),
63      'port'       => env('DB_PORT', 3306),
64      'database'   => env('DB_DATABASE', 'forge'),
65      'username'   => env('DB_USERNAME', 'forge'),
66      'password'   => env('DB_PASSWORD', ''),
67      'charset'    => 'utf8',
68      'collation'  => 'utf8_unicode_ci',
69      'prefix'     => env('DB_PREFIX', ''),
70      'timezone'   => env('DB_TIMEZONE', '+00:00'),
71      'strict'     => false,
72  ],
```

The env() function will get the value for the first argument; if the configuration doesn't exist, the second argument is the default. When you ran your failed migration command earlier, the application configuration was using the defaults.

Checking Unit Tests

Lumen uses PHPUnit for tests. When creating new projects, I recommend ensuring that PHPUnit is running properly. In my experience, if I don't test early and often, it becomes increasingly difficult to commit to testing in a project. Try running the PHPUnit suite that ships with Lumen:

Running phpunit Tests

```
vagrant@homestead:~/Code/bookr$ vendor/bin/phpunit
```

```
OK (1 test, 1 assertion)
```

PHPUnit is a composer dependency, and you execute tests by referencing *vendor/bin/phpunit*. If all went well, you should see green! Lumen ships with an example test class which is passing. The example tests let you know things are working as expected.

You will become very comfortable writing tests as you work through this book, but for now you just need to know you have everything working so you can focus on writing your application (Figure 3-1).

```
vagrant@homestead:~/Code/laravel-valet/bookr$ phpunit
PHPUnit 4.8.27 by Sebastian Bergmann and contributors.

.


Time: 364 ms, Memory: 6.00MB

OK (1 test, 1 assertion)
vagrant@homestead:~/Code/laravel-valet/bookr$ █
```

Figure 3-1. *PHPUnit success*

■ **PHPUnit Alias on Homestead**   On Homestead you can simply run `phpunit` without referencing the `vendor/bin` path.

Homestead creates an alias for you defined on your local machine in the `~/.homestead/aliases` file. You can also add your own aliases to that file.

I also have `./vendor/bin` to my path when I am not using Homestead: `export PATH=./vendor/bin:$PATH`

You can also install PHPUnit on your system. Refer to the official installation documentation (`https://phpunit.de/manual/current/en/installation.html`).

Setup Complete

With minimal setup, we are in good shape to start writing the first API endpoint: books. Setup was simple, but we covered many important steps that I like to perform at the beginning of an application. Getting a working database and unit tests will go a long way in helping us focus on writing the API. We are establishing conventions and good practices early.

CHAPTER 4

Starting the Books API

In this chapter, we will focus on writing our first API resource: /books. We will take this in small chunks and test it as we go. At the end of the next few chapters we will have a fully-tested /books resource doing basic CRUD operations. The /books resource will look like this:

Basic REST /books Resource

```
GET /books Get all the books
POST /books Create a new book
GET /books/{id} Get a book
PUT /books/{id} Update a book
DELETE /books/{id} Delete a book
```

Creating the First Endpoint

The first order of business to create a BooksControllerTest class and write your first failing test. You will then write the minimum amount of code required to get the test to pass. When you get back to green, you are free to refactor or add another feature.

I prefer my test's namespace to be organized under the same namespace as the application namespace. In our case, the controller namespace will be *App\Http\Controllers* and the tests for controllers will go under *Tests\App\Http\Controllers*. So let's write some code! See Listing 4-1.

Listing 4-1. Creating Your Test and Controller

```
# vagrant@homestead:~/Code/bookr$
$ mkdir -p tests/app/Http/Controllers
$ git mv tests/ExampleTest.php tests/app/Http/Controllers/BooksControllerTest.php
$ touch app/Http/Controllers/BooksController.php
```

In Listing 4-1, you rename the *ExampleTest.php* file as the *BooksControllerTest.php* with git since you don't want a fake example test. Feel free to create files however you want, but I will do it from the command line throughout the book for maximum portability.

Now you'll write and execute your first failing test for the *GET /books* route. Note the "use TestCase" import because you are namespacing your tests (Listing 4-2). You could also reference it with *extends \TestCase* and skip the use statement.

Listing 4-2. The BooksControllerTest.php File

```php
1   <?php
2
3   namespace Tests\App\Http\Controllers;
4
5   use TestCase;
6
7   class BooksControllerTest extends TestCase
8   {
9       /** @test **/
10      public function index_status_code_should_be_200()
11      {
12          $this->get('/books')->seeStatusCode(200);
13      }
14  }
```

Your test makes a request to the /books route and then expects to see a 200 status code. The visit and seeStatusCode methods are provided by the Laravel\Lumen\Testing\CrawlerTrait trait. You will become more familiar with the methods the CrawlerTrait provides as we work through the book.

Now run the test you just created and see what happens (Listing 4-3).

Listing 4-3. Failing the Test

```
vagrant@homestead:~/Code/bookr$ phpunit
F
...
FAILURES!
Tests: 1, Assertions: 1, Failures: 1.
```

I have omitted a stack trace, but basically your failing test received a 404 status code. Now, it's time to make our test pass, but you only write the least amount of code to get your test to passing and nothing more. You created the BooksController file earlier in the chapter, so now add the code in Listing 4-4.

Listing 4-4. The BooksController.php Class

```php
1   <?php
2
3   namespace App\Http\Controllers;
4
5   /**
6    * Class BooksController
7    * @package App\Http\Controllers
8    */
9   class BooksController
10  {
11      /**
12       * GET /books
13       * @return array
14       */
```

```
15    public function index()
16    {
17        return [];
18    }
19 }
```

You define an index method and return an empty array. You still haven't defined a route for your GET /
books endpoint, which you'll add below the default route in app/Http/routes.php, as shown in Listing 4-5.

Listing 4-5. Adding the BooksController@index Route

```
14 $app->get('/', function () use ($app) {
15     return $app->version();
16 });
17
18 $app->get('/books', 'BooksController@index');
```

This is the first time using a controller for the second argument of a route definition. Lumen assumes
the namespace of a controller to be App\Http\Controllers, and the second argument is in this format:
<controller_name>@<method>. The BooksController@index string passed to your route references the
public index method of the BooksController. With the controller and route in place, your test should pass
now (Listing 4-6).

Listing 4-6. Passing the Test

```
# vagrant@homestead:~/Code/bookr$
$ phpunit

OK (1 test, 1 assertion)
```

Now that your tests are back to green you are ready to add more features. We know this endpoint will
return a collection of books, so you will write a test for that (Listing 4-7).

Listing 4-7. Testing the JSON Response

```
15 /** @test **/
16 public function index_should_return_a_collection_of_records()
17 {
18     $this
19         ->get('/books')
20         ->seeJson([
21             'title' => 'War of the Worlds'
22         ])
23         ->seeJson([
24             'title' => 'A Wrinkle in Time'
25         ]);
26 }
```

The test introduces the seeJson() method, which converts the passed array into JSON and assures that
the JSON occurs somewhere within the response. I encourage you to read the official Lumen documentation
on testing (https://lumen.laravel.com/docs/5.2/testing). The "Testing JSON APIs" (https://lumen.
laravel.com/docs/5.2/testing#testing-json-apis) section has information on testing JSON responses.

As you would expect, if you run the tests, you will see failures. A failed test means you are ready to write implementation code. To reiterate, you will write the smallest amount of code to get tests passing again (Listing 4-8).

Listing 4-8. Returning a Collection of Books

```
11  /**
12   * GET /books
13   * @return array
14   */
15  public function index()
16  {
17      return [
18          ['title' => 'War of the Worlds'],
19          ['title' => 'A Wrinkle in Time']
20      ];
21  }
```

After adding the controller code, tests should be back to green (Listing 4-9)!

Listing 4-9. Passing Test for a Collection of Books

```
# vagrant@homestead:~/Code/bookr$
$ phpunit

OK (2 tests, 3 assertions)
```

ⓘ Git commit: Add /books Index Route

e21bf99 (https://bitbucket.org/paulredmond/apress-bookr/commits/e21bf99)

Now that you have passing tests, you are free to refactor the code and continue to ensure the tests still pass. With that in mind, it seems like a good time to introduce some real data from the database.

Setting Up Models and Seed Data

Our book API is not very useful right now without dynamic data, but we have a good testing foundation to make sure we can iterate and verify that our tests still pass. You can lean on your tests while you convert your controller to use a database. Lumen has some great features that make working with databases very pleasant!

Your first order of business is to define a Book model. What should that look like? What columns should you include? You could flesh out the entire data structure up front, but database migrations make it really easy to iterate on the database schema. For now, your schema will be very simple.

■ 💬 I encourage you to spend some time thinking about your database structure in the beginning. Aim for a mix of defining good structure up front without it paralyzing you from getting started on writing code.

Migrations allow you to iterate on the schema, but making good data decisions early can save you some headaches.

You will start by creating a database migration with the artisan console (https://laravel.com/docs/5.2/artisan) for the books resource (Listing 4-10).

Listing 4-10. The Books Database Migration

```
# vagrant@homestead:~/Code/bookr$
$ php artisan make:migration create_books_table --create=books
```

The *make:migration* command knows you intend to create a new database table from the *--create* flag. Your filename date will differ from my example, but will end with the same create_books_table.php file suffix.

ℹ Migrations   Database migrations (https://laravel.com/docs/5.2/migrations) are covered in great detail in the Laravel documentation. The Laravel migration documentation applies to Lumen.

In the generated migration you will see two methods: up() and down(). The up() method will be used to apply the migration and the down() method will roll back the migration. The artisan command takes care of down for you automatically because of the *--create* flag, so let's finish writing the up method (Listing 4-11).

Listing 4-11. The Books Table Migration

```
 8   /**
 9    * Run the migrations.
10    *
11    * @return void
12    */
13   public function up()
14   {
15       Schema::create('books', function (Blueprint $table) {
16           $table->increments('id');
17           $table->string('title');
18           $table->text('description');
19           $table->string('author');
20           $table->timestamps();
21       });
22   }
```

The migration is very readable and simple. Take note of $table->timestamps(), which will create two datetime columns: *created_at* and *updated_at*. Eloquent will also populate the timestamp columns for you automatically when you create and update records.

Now that you have the migration ready, let's run it (Listing 4-12).

Listing 4-12. Running Your First Database Migration

```
# vagrant@homestead:~/Code/bookr$
$ php artisan migrate
Migrated: 2016_07_28_232137_create_books_table
```

It seems to have worked! Check the database to be sure (Table 4-1).

```
mysql> use bookr;
mysql> show columns from books;
```

Table 4-1. *The Books Table Structure*

Field	Type	Key	Default
id	int(10) unsigned	PRI	NULL
title	varchar(255)		NULL
description	Text		NULL
author	varchar(255)		NULL
created_at	Timestamp		0000-00-00 00:00:00
updated_at	Timestamp		0000-00-00 00:00:00

Success! Now that you have a working database migration, you are going to need some data. How should we get data into the development database? We could version a SQL script that we execute when setting up an environment; we could connect to the database and add some rows by hand. At this point, either would be fine, but it will get clunky fast. Real fast. Fortunately (and not surprisingly) Lumen provides a better way with **database seeding**.

The database seeding files are located in the database/seeds folder—specifically the DatabaseSeeder. php file. Listing 4-13 shows what the stock DatabaseSeeder class looks like.

Listing 4-13. The Default Seeder Class

```
1   <?php
2
3   use Illuminate\Database\Seeder;
4
5   class DatabaseSeeder extends Seeder
6   {
7       /**
8        * Run the database seeds.
9        *
10       * @return void
11       */
12      public function run()
13      {
14          // $this->call('UserTableSeeder');
15      }
16  }
```

Line #14 is an example of how the DatabaseSeeder can call other seeder classes to keep things tidy. Based on the DatabaseSeeder example, it makes sense to make a seeder class for the books table. Create the file *database/ seeds/BooksTableSeeder.php* and call it from the DatabaseSeeder class. Once you create the seeder, you can use it to populate your development database with the artisan db:seed command (Listing 4-14).

Listing 4-14. The BooksTableSeeder

```php
1   <?php
2
3   use Carbon\Carbon;
4   use Illuminate\Database\Seeder;
5
6   class BooksTableSeeder extends Seeder
7   {
8       /**
9        * Run the database seeds.
10       *
11       * @return void
12       */
13      public function run()
14      {
15          DB::table('books')->insert([
16              'title' => 'War of the Worlds',
17              'description' => 'A science fiction masterpiece about Martians invading
                    London',
18              'author' => 'H. G. Wells',
19              'created_at' => Carbon::now(),
20              'updated_at' => Carbon::now(),
21          ]);
22
23          DB::table('books')->insert([
24              'title' => 'A Wrinkle in Time',
25              'description' => 'A young girl goes on a mission to save her father who has
                    gone missing after working on a mysterious project called a tesseract.',
26              'author' => 'Madeleine L\'Engle',
27              'created_at' => Carbon::now(),
28              'updated_at' => Carbon::now()
29          ]);
30      }
31  }
```

The DB::table() method returns an instance of the \Illuminate\Database\Query\Builder class, which has an insert method to insert a record to the database. The Builder::insert() method accepts an associative array of data. The code also introduces the Carbon (http://carbon.nesbot.com/) library, a standalone library for working with PHP's DateTime.

To use the book seeder, you need to call the BooksTableSeeder within the database/seeds/ DatabaseSeeder.php class (Listing 4-15).

Listing 4-15. Calling the BooksTableSeeder in the DatabaseSeeder Class

```
12  public function run()
13  {
14      // $this->call('UserTableSeeder');
15      $this->call(BooksTableSeeder::class);
16  }
```

You are now ready to seed the database with artisan. Since you created a new seeder class, you need to dump the composer autoloader. The database classes are autoloaded through composer's class map (https://getcomposer.org/doc/04-schema.md#classmap) setting, so each new seeder requires running the dump-autoload command (Listing 4-16).

Listing 4-16. Refreshing the Schema and Seeding the Database

```
# vagrant@homestead:~/Code/bookr$
$ composer dump-autoload
Generating autoload files

$ php artisan migrate:refresh
Rolled back: 2015_10_17_075310_create_books_table
Migrated: 2015_10_17_075310_create_books_table

$ php artisan db:seed
Seeded: BooksTableSeeder
```

I introduced a new artisan command called migrate:refresh, which will reset and rerun all migrations. The db:seed command populates the bookr database with the seed data you just defined.

■ **Artisan**   To get an overview of what each artisan command does, run *php artisan* to get a list of commands and a short description. You can even write your own commands.

Database migrations, database seeding, and Eloquent are the great features that set Lumen apart from other PHP micro-frameworks, in my opinion. Lumen is lightweight, but it offers features to help developer productivity that are not out of reach or difficult to enable.

Eloquent Books

Now that the books table has data, let's define a model representing the books table that you can use to query the database. Lumen (like Laravel) has access to Eloquent ORM, which is a fantastic ActiveRecord implementation for querying data and inserting/updating data.

Lumen does not ship with an artisan command for creating models, but creating one is not hard:

```
# vagrant@homestead:~/Code/bookr$
$ touch app/Book.php
```

The model is really simple at the moment (Listing 4-17).

Listing 4-17. The Book Eloquent Model

```
1   <?php
2
3   namespace App;
4
5   use Illuminate\Database\Eloquent\Model;
6
7   class Book extends Model
8   {
9
10  }
```

With the seeded data and Book model in hand, you are ready to wrap up the refactored *BooksController@index* route (Listing 4-18).

Listing 4-18. Putting the Book Model to Work

```
1   <?php
2
3   namespace App\Http\Controllers;
4
5   use App\Book;
6
7   /**
8    * Class BooksController
9    * @package App\Http\Controllers
10   */
11  class BooksController
12  {
13      /**
14       * GET /books
15       * @return array
16       */
17      public function index()
18      {
19          return Book::all();
20      }
21  }
```

Now it's time to run the test suite to see if your refactor broke anything:

```
# vagrant@homestead:~/Code/bookr$
$ phpunit

OK (2 tests, 3 assertions)
```

The refactor was simple and passed the first time. Sometimes refactors will lead to broken tests, which we will see later in this book. The goal of refactoring is that we start refactoring while tests are green, and then when we are done refactoring we should still be at green.

If you make a request to `http://bookr.app/books`, you should something resembling the response in Listing 4-19.

Listing 4-19. Example Response from /books

```
[
    {
        "id":1,
        "title":"War of the Worlds",
        "description":"A science fiction masterpiece about Martians invading London",
        "author":"H. G. Wells",
        "created_at":"2015-12-30 03:11:40",
        "updated_at":"2015-12-30 03:11:40"
    },
    {
        "id":2,
        "title":"A Wrinkle in Time",
        "description":"A young girl goes on a mission to save her father who has gone
        missing after working on a mysterious project called a tesseract.",
        "author":"Madeleine L'Engle",
        "created_at":"2015-12-30 03:11:40",
        "updated_at":"2015-12-30 03:11:40"
    }
]
```

Success

Boom! We've successfully refactored the BooksController to use a database and an Eloquent model. We will see plenty more examples of models throughout the book. Now we can move on to the rest of the /books endpoints. See you in the next chapter.

ⓘ **Git commit: Create books Table and BooksController**

729dff4 (`https://bitbucket.org/paulredmond/apress-bookr/commits/729dff4`)

CHAPTER 5

Creating, Reading, Updating, and Deleting Books

Now that you have a **Books** model, you are well-equipped to handle the management of books. You will continue to follow your test-driven development workflow as you complete the remaining CRUD operations of the /books API.

Listing 5-1 shows a quick refresher of your /books RESTful endpoints.

Listing 5-1. Basic REST /books Resource

```
GET     /books          Get all the books
POST    /books          Create a new book
GET     /books/{id}     Get a book
PUT     /books/{id}     Update a book
DELETE  /books/{id}     Delete a book
```

Requesting an Individual Book

You are going to start off with the GET /books/{id} route. Before you start coding, let's quickly define your high-level acceptance criteria for this route. You can do this within the tests/app/Http/Controllers/BooksControllerTest.php file by defining the skeleton test methods, as shown in Listing 5-2.

Listing 5-2. The GET books/:id Acceptance Criteria

```
28  /** @test **/
29  public function show_should_return_a_valid_book()
30  {
31      $this->markTestIncomplete('Pending test');
32  }
33
34  /** @test **/
35  public function show_should_fail_when_the_book_id_does_not_exist()
36  {
37      $this->markTestIncomplete('Pending test');
38  }
39
```

```
40  /** @test **/
41  public function show_route_should_not_match_an_invalid_route()
42  {
43      $this->markTestIncomplete('Pending test');
44  }
```

You mark these tests as incomplete while you work through each criterion. Running your test suite will provide the output shown in Listing 5-3.

Listing 5-3. Running phpunit with New Pending Tests

```
# vagrant@homestead:~/Code/bookr$
$ phpunit

OK, but incomplete, skipped, or risky tests!
Tests: 5, Assertions: 3, Incomplete: 3.
```

I want to point out that your tests rely on seed data. Using seed data for tests is not ideal, and you will address it in Chapter 6. In the meantime, you need to make sure that the database has seed data before running tests that rely on specific data in the database. You can always ensure that the database is fresh by running the code in Listing 5-4.

Listing 5-4. How to Refresh the Migrations and Seed the Database

```
# vagrant@homestead:~/Code/bookr$
$ php artisan migrate:refresh
$ php artisan db:seed
```

Let's get to work on the first acceptance criterion: *show_should_return_a_valid_book* (Listing 5-5). To meet this acceptance criterion, you need to

- Find the book in the database.

- Respond with the book's data.

- Make sure it responds with a correct status code.

- Assert that the JSON data returned is accurate.

Listing 5-5. Testing for a Valid Book

```
28  /** @test **/
29  public function show_should_return_a_valid_book()
30  {
31      $this
32          ->get('/books/1')
33          ->seeStatusCode(200)
34          ->seeJson([
35              'id' => 1,
36              'title' => 'War of the Worlds',
37              'description' => 'A science fiction masterpiece about Martians invading
                  London',
38              'author' => 'H. G. Wells'
39          ]);
40
```

```
41    $data = json_decode($this->response->getContent(), true);
42    $this->assertArrayHasKey('created_at', $data);
43    $this->assertArrayHasKey('updated_at', $data);
44  }
```

You've already seen *seeStatusCode* and *seeJson*. The only thing new in Listing 5-5 is the last three lines that get the response body (JSON) and decode it. The test simply checks the existence of *created_at* and *updated_at*, but does not test these values. Your seed data cannot guarantee consistent dates so it's impossible to test the values. In a later chapter, I will show you how to test date values once you start using proper test data.

Next, run the test (Listing 5-6), which will definitely fail. Can you come up with the reasons why the test fails?

Listing 5-6. Running the Failing Test Suite

```
# vagrant@homestead:~/Code/bookr$
$ phpunit
There was 1 failure:

1) Tests\App\Http\Controllers\BooksControllerTest::show_should_return_a_valid_bo\
ok
Failed asserting that 404 matches expected 200.

bookr/vendor/laravel/lumen-framework/src/Testing/CrawlerTrait.php:412
bookr/tests/app/Http/Controllers/BooksControllerTest.php:33
```

If you inspect the test failure closely, you will see that on **line 33** your test asserts a **200** HTTP status code, but a **404** response is given because no route exists yet. You will need to create a new route and controller method to get your tests back to green. Make the following changes in *app/Http/routes.php* (Listing 5-7) and *app/Http/Controllers/BooksController.php* (Listing 5-8).

Listing 5-7. Adding Show Route to routes.php

```
18  $app->get('/books', 'BooksController@index');
19  $app->get('/books/{id}', 'BooksController@show');
```

Listing 5-8. Adding Show Method to BooksController.php

```
22  /**
23   * GET /books/{id}
24   * @param integer $id
25   * @return mixed
26   */
27  public function show($id)
28  {
29      return Book::findOrFail($id);
30  }
```

The code for *BooksController@show* introduces the findOrFail method; the findOrFail method either returns a record or throws an exception of type *Illuminate\Database\Eloquent\ModelNotFoundException*.

The new route and the BooksController::show() method should be enough to get your test passing again (Listing 5-9).

Listing 5-9. Running PHPUnit Test for Returning a Valid Book

```
# vagrant@homestead:~/Code/bookr$
$ phpunit --filter=show_should_return_a_valid_book

OK (1 test, 7 assertions)
```

You will use PHPUnit's `--filter` flag to only run your latest test. The `--filter` flag, which accepts a regular expression, is a convenient way to limit which tests run; you will use it extensively in this book.

You are again back to green and you can move on to your next acceptance criterion, shown in Listing 5-10.

Listing 5-10. Testing Failure When a Book Does Not Exist

```
46  /** @test **/
47  public function show_should_fail_when_the_book_id_does_not_exist()
48  {
49      $this
50          ->get('/books/99999')
51          ->seeStatusCode(404)
52          ->seeJson([
53              'error' => [
54                  'message' => 'Book not found'
55              ]
56          ]);
57  }
```

Next, let's run the test to make sure it fails (Listing 5-11).

Listing 5-11. Running PHPUnit After Writing the Test

```
# vagrant@homestead:~/Code/bookr$
$ phpunit --filter=show_should_fail_when_the_book_id_does_not_exist

There was 1 failure:

1) Tests\App\Http\Controllers\BooksControllerTest::show_should_fail_when_the_book_id_does_
not_exist
Invalid JSON was returned from the route. Perhaps an exception was thrown?

FAILURES!
Tests: 1, Assertions: 1, Failures: 1.
```

Your latest test brings you back to failure. The *findOrFail* method will throw an exception if the id does not match a record in the database, resulting in a **404** error response with a Content-Type header of text/html. What you really wanted based on your test criteria is a **404** response with a friendly JSON error message. Time to update your *BooksController::store()* method to catch the *ModelNotFoundException* (Listing 5-12) and get tests back to green!

Listing 5-12. Responding to ModelNotFoundException BooksController::show()

```php
1   <?php
2
3   namespace App\Http\Controllers;
4
5   use App\Book;
6   use Illuminate\Database\Eloquent\ModelNotFoundException;
7
8   /**
9    * Class BooksController
10   * @package App\Http\Controllers
11   */
12  class BooksController
13  {
14      /**
15       * GET /books
16       * @return array
17       */
18      public function index()
19      {
20          return Book::all();
21      }
22
23      /**
24       * GET /books/{id}
25       * @param integer $id
26       * @return mixed
27       */
28      public function show($id)
29      {
30          try {
31              return Book::findOrFail($id);
32          } catch (ModelNotFoundException $e) {
33              return response()->json([
34                  'error' => [
35                      'message' => 'Book not found'
36                  ]
37              ], 404);
38          }
39      }
40  }
```

The entire controller is included to avoid confusion. Let's break down the changes:

- You wrap the Book::findOrFail() method in a try/catch block so you can catch the exception and respond with a **404**.

- If the id is found, a valid record is returned.

- The ModelNotFoundException is imported on line #6.

- You introduce the response() helper to create a response object.

- You then call json() on the response object to send a JSON response.

- The json() method accepts your array of data, and a HTTP status code.

Running your test suite will get you back to green (Listing 5-13). Getting back to green is a good feeling.

Listing 5-13. Running the Test for an Invalid Book id

```
# vagrant@homestead:~/Code/bookr$
$ phpunit --filter=show_should_fail_when_the_book_id_does_not_exist

OK (1 test, 2 assertions)
```

You have one final task to satisfy the acceptance criteria, and then you can move on to the next endpoint. The final test is to ensure that your BooksController::show route only matches integer ids. As of right now, your show route will happily match any parameter. Let's write a test for the route matching (Listing 5-14).

Listing 5-14. A Test for Route Matching

```
59  /** @test **/
60  public function show_route_should_not_match_an_invalid_route()
61  {
62      $this->get('/books/this-is-invalid');
63
64      $this->assertNotRegExp(
65          '/Book not found/',
66          $this->response->getContent(),
67          'BooksController@show route matching when it should not.'
68      );
69  }
```

Your test ensures that the response does not contain Book not found because that would mean the BooksController@show route was executed and the 404 response for the ModelNotFoundException was sent. You added a helpful message of "BooksController@show route matching when it should not" to explain that you do not want to match the BooksController@show route.

Let's run the test and see if it fails (Listing 5-15).

Listing 5-15. Running a Test for Invalid Show Route

```
# vagrant@homestead:~/Code/bookr$
$ phpunit --filter=show_route_should_not_match_an_invalid_route

There was 1 failure:

1) Tests\App\Http\Controllers\BooksControllerTest::show_route_should_not_match_an_invalid_
   route
BooksController@show route matching when it should not.
Failed asserting that '{"error":{"message":"Book not found"}}' does not match PCRE pattern
"/Book not found/".

/home/vagrant/Code/bookr/tests/app/Http/Controllers/BooksControllerTest.php:68
```

```
FAILURES!
Tests: 1, Assertions: 1, Failures: 1.
```

Since you have not changed the BooksController@show code yet, you get an expected failure. You need to change the route parameter to be constrained with a regular expression and then the test will pass (Listing 5-16).

Listing 5-16. Constrain the Show Route with a Regular Expression (app/Http/routes.php).

```
19   $app->get('/books/{id:[\d]+}', 'BooksController@show');
```

Now only requests where the id is an integer will match. Let's see if you can now pass the test (Listing 5-17).

Listing 5-17. Passing the Invalid Route Test

```
# vagrant@homestead:~/Code/bookr$
$ phpunit --filter=show_route_should_not_match_an_invalid_route

OK (1 test, 1 assertion)
```

Your acceptance criteria have been met for the GET /book/{id} route! You are ready to move on to creating new books. Commit your changes.

---

❶ Git commit Add /books/{id} Route

a39f235 (https://bitbucket.org/paulredmond/apress-bookr/commits/a39f235)

Listing 5-18 shows what your BooksControllerTest class looks like so far.

Listing 5-18. BooksControllerTest

```
1    <?php
2
3    namespace Tests\App\Http\Controllers;
4
5    use TestCase;
6
7    class BooksControllerTest extends TestCase
8    {
9        /** @test **/
10       public function index_status_code_should_be_200()
11       {
12           $this->visit('/books')->seeStatusCode(200);
13       }
14
15       /** @test **/
16       public function index_should_return_a_collection_of_records()
17       {
18           $this
19               ->get('/books')
20               ->seeJson([
21                   'title' => 'War of the Worlds'
22               ])
```

```php
23                    ->seeJson([
24                        'title' => 'A Wrinkle in Time'
25                    ]);
26        }
27
28        /** @test **/
29        public function show_should_return_a_valid_book()
30        {
31            $this
32                ->get('/books/1')
33                ->seeStatusCode(200)
34                ->seeJson([
35                    'id' => 1,
36                    'title' => 'War of the Worlds',
37                    'description' => 'A science fiction masterpiece about Martians invading
                     London',
38                    'author' => 'H. G. Wells'
39                ]);
40
41            $data = json_decode($this->response->getContent(), true);
42            $this->assertArrayHasKey('created_at', $data);
43            $this->assertArrayHasKey('updated_at', $data);
44        }
45
46
47        /** @test **/
48        public function show_should_fail_when_the_book_id_does_not_exist()
49        {
50            $this
51                ->get('/books/99999')
52                ->seeStatusCode(404)
53                ->seeJson([
54                    'error' => [
55                    'message' => 'Book not found'
56                    ]
57                ]);
58        }
59
60        /** @test **/
61        public function show_route_should_not_match_an_invalid_route()
62        {
63            $this->get('/books/this-is-invalid');
64
65            $this->assertNotRegExp(
66                '/Book not found/',
67                 $this->response->getContent(),
68                'BooksController@show route matching when it should not.'
69            );
70        }
71  }
```

You have been running specific tests. You need to make sure the whole suite passes before moving to the next feature, so see Listing 5-19.

Listing 5-19. Running the Full Test Suite

```
# vagrant@homestead:~/Code/bookr$
$ phpunit

OK (5 tests, 13 assertions)
```

Running the **whole suite** is important before moving on to make sure the entire test harness is sound before writing new features. You will build a dependable, albeit imperfect set of tests you can depend upon when refactoring and making major changes.

HOW IS THE MISSING ROUTE HANDLED?

Now that your `BooksController::show()` route only matches integer ids, how is an invalid route like `/books/this-is-invalid` handled? If Lumen can't find a route, the application will throw a `NotFoundHttpException`. If you investigate the response headers, you can see that Lumen responds with a `text/html` content type by default:

```
curl -I -H"Content-Type: application/json" \
-H"Accept: application/json" \
http://localhost:8000/books/this-is-invalid

HTTP/1.0 404 Not Found
Host: localhost:8000
Connection: close
Cache-Control: no-cache, private
date: Sun, 18 Oct 2015 07:25:30 GMT
Content-type: text/html; charset=UTF-8
```

The HTML response is not something an API consumer expects and you intend on making error responses JSON. For now, be aware of how things are working. You will revisit handling missing routes exceptions with JSON in the next chapter.

Creating a New Book

The next feature is creating a new book with the POST /books route. You will dive more into Eloquent and see how to handle POST data in the controller. Listing 5-20 shows the acceptance criteria for creating a new book in the tests/app/Http/Controllers/BooksControllerTest.php file.

Listing 5-20. The POST /books Acceptance Criteria

```
72  /** @test **/
73  public function store_should_save_new_book_in_the_database()
74  {
75      $this->markTestIncomplete('pending');
76  }
77
78  /** @test */
79  public function store_should_respond_with_a_201_and_location_header_when_successful()
80  {
81      $this->markTestIncomplete('pending');
82  }
```

Let's start with the store_should_save_new_book_in_the_database test (Listing 5-21). When things go as expected, this test will make sure that

- The response contains a "created": true JSON fragment.

- The book exists in the database.

Listing 5-21. Testing the Creation of a New Book

```
72  /** @test **/
73  public function store_should_save_new_book_in_the_database()
74  {
75      $this->post('/books', [
76          'title' => 'The Invisible Man',
77          'description' => 'An invisible man is trapped in the terror of his own
                creation',
78          'author' => 'H. G. Wells'
79      ]);
80
81      $this
82          ->seeJson(['created' => true])
83          ->seeInDatabase('books', ['title' => 'The Invisible Man']);
84  }
```

Your test inherits a $this->post() method, which accepts a URI and an array of post data. The test contains the seeInDatabase() method, which accepts a table name and an associative array in the format of column => value, and ensures the record is in the database. You can pass multiple columns to further constrain $this->seeInDatabase() assertions.

Running the test suite will result in a failure because you haven't defined the route or the controller method yet (Listing 5-22).

Listing 5-22. Running the Full Test Suite

```
# vagrant@homestead:~/Code/bookr$
$ phpunit

There was 1 failure:
```

```
1) Tests\App\Http\Controllers\BooksControllerTest::store_should_save_new_book_in_the_database
Invalid JSON was returned from the route. Perhaps an exception was thrown?
...
```

```
FAILURES!
Tests: 7, Assertions: 13, Failures: 1, Incomplete: 1.
```

You will start coding by adding a route to app/Http/routes.php (Listing 5-23).

Listing 5-23. Adding the POST Route

```
18  $app->get('/books', 'BooksController@index');
19  $app->get('/books/{id}', 'BooksController@show');
20  $app->post('/books', 'BooksController@store');
```

Your first version of the BooksController@store method is shown in Listing 5-24.

Listing 5-24. First Version of the BooksController::store() Method

```
41  /**
42   * POST /books
43   * @param Request $request
44   * @return \Symfony\Component\HttpFoundation\Response
45   */
46  public function store(Request $request)
47  {
48      $book = Book::create($request->all());
49
50      return response()->json(['created' => true], 201);
51  }
```

The store method is your first example using the service container (https://lumen.laravel.com/docs/5.2/container) to do method injection in a controller. The store method accepts an *Illuminate\Http\Request* instance that represents the current HTTP request.

Inside the method, the first line tries to create a new book in the database by passing post data from the request ($request->all()) to the Book::create() method. If the Book::create() method succeeds, it will return an instance of the new book. After creating the book, the method returns a JsonResponse object by calling response()->json(), which accepts an array of data and a status code. The JsonResponse object will convert the array into JSON before being sent to the browser.

⚠️ Your senses might be warning you that you are allowing mass assignment in the controller. While it is good to always keep mass assignment in mind, Eloquent does guard against mass assignment (https://laravel.com/docs/5.2/eloquent#mass-assignment), as you will see shortly.

Before you run your test, you need to also import Illuminate\Http\Request at the top of the BooksController (Listing 5-25).

Listing 5-25. Importing the Illuminate Request Class in the BooksController

```
1  <?php
2
3  namespace App\Http\Controllers;
4
5  use App\Book;
6  use Illuminate\Http\Request;
7  use Illuminate\Database\Eloquent\ModelNotFoundException;
```

You might think you've covered everything, so your test should pass, but it still fails (Listing 5-26).

Listing 5-26. The Failing Test Output

```
# vagrant@homestead:~/Code/bookr$
$ phpunit --filter=store_should_save_new_book_in_the_database

There was 1 failure:

1) Tests\App\Http\Controllers\BooksControllerTest::store_should_save_new_book_in_the_
database
Invalid JSON was returned from the route. Perhaps an exception was thrown?
...

FAILURES!
Tests: 1, Assertions: 0, Failures: 1.
```

The error message is identical to the last time you ran this test! You need to dig a little deeper to figure this out. Options include looking at the *storage/logs/lumen.log* file or adding some temporary debugging code to the request. Let's pursue the second option and add some debugging code to the BooksController (Listing 5-27).

Listing 5-27. Temporary Debugging Code

```
42  /**
43   * POST /books
44   * @param Request $request
45   * @return \Symfony\Component\HttpFoundation\Response
46   */
47  public function store(Request $request)
48  {
49      try {
50          $book = Book::create($request->all());
51      } catch (\Exception $e) {
52          dd(get_class($e));
53      }
54
55      return response()->json(['created' => true], 201);
56  }
```

You are attempting to debug the store method by catching any exception that happens when calling Book::create(). The code introduces the dd() function, which dumps the passed variable(s) and exits the script.

With the debug code in place, run the test again (Listing 5-28).

Listing 5-28. Running the Test with Debug Code in Place

```
# vagrant@homestead:~/Code/bookr$
$ phpunit --filter=store_should_save_new_book_in_the_database

"Illuminate\Database\Eloquent\MassAssignmentException"
```

The exception being caught is a mass assignment exception. I mentioned earlier that Eloquent guards against mass assignment out of the box, so you need to configure which fields are mass-assignable using the *protected $fillable = []* array in the Book model (Listing 5-29).

Listing 5-29. Defining Mass Assignable Fields (app/Http/Book.php)

```
1   <?php
2
3   namespace App;
4
5   use Illuminate\Database\Eloquent\Model;
6
7   class Book extends Model
8   {
9       /**
10       * The attributes that are mass assignable
11       *
12       * @var array
13       */
14      protected $fillable = ['title', 'description', 'author'];
15  }
```

ℹ You can also provide a `protected $guarded` property with values that should not be mass-assignable. You are taking the route that all columns should be protected, minus the exceptions you add to the `$fillable` array. See the "Mass Assignment" (`https://laravel.com/docs/5.2/eloquent#mass-assignment`) section in the Eloquent documentation for more information.

Before you remove the debugging code, try running the test again (Listing 5-30).

Listing 5-30. Running the Test After Defining Fillable Columns

```
# vagrant@homestead:~/Code/bookr$
$ phpunit --filter=store_should_save_new_book_in_the_database

OK (1 test, 2 assertions)
```

After defining the fillable fields, your test worked as expected! Now you need to revert the debugging code you added (Listing 5-31).

Listing 5-31. Reverting the Debugging Code

```
42  /**
43   * POST /books
44   * @param Request $request
45   * @return \Symfony\Component\HttpFoundation\Response
```

```
46    */
47    public function store(Request $request)
48    {
49        $book = Book::create($request->all());
50
51        return response()->json(['created' => true], 201);
52    }
```

The next test criterion makes sure that successfully creating a new book will respond with a *201* status code and a Location header matching the URI of the created resource (Listing 5-32).

Listing 5-32. Writing a Test for 201 Status Code and Location Header

```
86    /** @test */
87    public function store_should_respond_with_a_201_and_location_header_when_successful()
88    {
89        $this->post('/books', [
90            'title' => 'The Invisible Man',
91            'description' => 'An invisible man is trapped in the terror of his own
                 creation',
92            'author' => 'H. G. Wells'
93        ]);
94
95        $this
96            ->seeStatusCode(201)
97            ->seeHeaderWithRegExp('Location', '#/books/[\d]+$#');
98
99    }
```

The test will look familiar, except for the seeHeaderWithRegExp method, because you haven't defined it yet. To provide some convenience around checking header values, you define this custom assertion in the base test class *tests/TestCase.php* that your tests inherit (Listing 5-33).

Listing 5-33. New Test Assertions (tests/TestCase.php)

```
15    /**
16     * See if the response has a header.
17     *
18     * @param $header
19     * @return $this
20     */
21    public function seeHasHeader($header)
22    {
23        $this->assertTrue(
24            $this->response->headers->has($header),
25            "Response should have the header '{$header}' but does not."
26        );
27
28        return $this;
29    }
30
31    /**
```

```
32    * Asserts that the response header matches a given regular expression
33    *
34    * @param $header
35    * @param $regexp
36    * @return $this
37    */
38   public function seeHeaderWithRegExp($header, $regexp)
39   {
40       $this
41          ->seeHasHeader($header)
42          ->assertRegExp(
43              $regexp,
44              $this->response->headers->get($header)
45          );
46
47       return $this;
48   }
```

You added two public methods that help assert headers. The *seeHasHeader()* method asserts the mere existence of a header. The *seeHeaderWithRegExp* method chains a call to seeHasHeader and then uses PHPUnit's *assertRegExp* to see if the response header matches the passed regular expression. These methods use *Illuminate\Http\Response*, which wraps the Symfony\Component\HttpFoundation\ Response. I encourage you to become familiar with the request and response classes because you will use them frequently to build APIs.

After defining the new test methods, run the test (Listing 5-34).

Listing 5-34. Running the Test for the 201 Status Code and Location Header

```
# vagrant@homestead:~/Code/bookr$
$ phpunit \
--filter=store_should_respond_with_a_201_and_location_header_when_successful

There was 1 failure:

1) Tests\App\Http\Controllers\BooksControllerTest::store_should_respond_with_a_2\
01_and_location_header_when_successful
Response should have the header 'Location' but does not.
Failed asserting that false is true.

/home/vagrant/Code/bookr/tests/TestCase.php:25
/home/vagrant/Code/bookr/tests/TestCase.php:41
/home/vagrant/Code/bookr/tests/app/Http/Controllers/BooksControllerTest.php:97

FAILURES!
Tests: 1, Assertions: 2, Failures: 1.
```

Implement the Location header to get your test to pass (Listing 5-35).

Listing 5-35. Adding Location Header to BooksController@store

```
42  /**
43   * POST /books
44   * @param Request $request
45   * @return \Symfony\Component\HttpFoundation\Response
46   */
47  public function store(Request $request)
48  {
49      $book = Book::create($request->all());
50
51      return response()->json(['created' => true], 201, [
52          'Location' => route('books.show', ['id' => $book->id])
53      ]);
54  }
```

The json() method accepts an associative array of headers as the third argument, and you use this argument to set the Location header. The route() helper method takes a named route (https://lumen.laravel.com/docs/5.2/routing#named-routes) to create a URI for the value of the Location header. You haven't created a named route called books.show yet, so you need to define one now in *app/Http/routes.php* (Listing 5-36).

Listing 5-36. Adding the BooksController@show Named Route

```
18  $app->get('/books', 'BooksController@index');
19  $app->get('/books/{id:[\d]+}', [
20      'as' => 'books.show',
21      'uses' => 'BooksController@show'
22  ]);
23  $app->post('/books', 'BooksController@store');
```

The show route accepts an associative array with the named route 'as' => 'books.show' and the 'uses' key defines the controller.

---

❶ The dot notation used in the name route has no special meaning, but the namespace helps with organization. You could have named the route something like "show_book" if you wanted, but I personally follow the dot notation because it feels more organized.

Let's see if you code now passes the test suite (Listing 5-37).

Listing 5-37. Running the Full Test Suite

```
# vagrant@homestead:~/Code/bookr$
$ phpunit

OK (7 tests, 18 assertions)
```

Passing the tests means you are done with your BooksController@store route.

---

❶ Git commit: Create a New Book

1403e67 (https://bitbucket.org/paulredmond/apress-bookr/commits/1403e67)

Updating an Existing Book

Now that you can create a new book, the next feature is the ability to update an existing book. You will begin to understand (if you don't already) in this section that using your development database for tests is not a good idea; you will cover using a separate test database in Chapter 6. I hope you are getting a feel for using test-driven development to drive good design. Good design does not happen all at once, but through small increments of test and code cycles.

Listing 5-38 shows the acceptance criteria for updating an existing book record the BooksControllerTest class (tests/app/Http/Controllers/BooksControllerTest.php).

Listing 5-38. Acceptance Criteria for Updating a Book

```
101   /** @test **/
102   public function update_should_only_change_fillable_fields()
103   {
104       $this->markTestIncomplete('pending');
105   }
106
107   /** @test **/
108   public function update_should_fail_with_an_invalid_id()
109   {
110       $this->markTestIncomplete('pending');
111   }
112
113   /** @test **/
114   public function update_should_not_match_an_invalid_route()
115   {
116       $this->markTestIncomplete('pending');
117   }
```

The first test will ensure that only fillable fields can be changed and that the changes are persisted in the database. The response should also return the updated record data and a 200 OK status code (Listing 5-39).

Listing 5-39. Testing for a Successful Book Update

```
101   /** @test **/
102   public function update_should_only_change_fillable_fields()
103   {
104       $this->notSeeInDatabase('books', [
105           'title' => 'The War of the Worlds'
106       ]);
107
108       $this->put('/books/1', [
109           'id' => 5,
110           'title' => 'The War of the Worlds',
111           'description' => 'The book is way better than the movie.',
112           'author' => 'Wells, H. G.'
113       ]);
114
115       $this
116           ->seeStatusCode(200)
117           ->seeJson([
```

```
118                    'id' => 1,
119                    'title' => 'The War of the Worlds',
120                    'description' => 'The book is way better than the movie.',
121                    'author' => 'Wells, H. G.'
122            ])
123            ->seeInDatabase('books', [
124                    'title' => 'The War of the Worlds'
125            ]);
126  }
```

Your test assumes that a post with an id of 1 exists in the database from your seed data. You make a PUT request with changes all the fillable fields so you can assert that they get updated. Notice that the test tries to update the id, which should not be allowed. Before making the PUT request, your test makes sure a record doesn't already exist in the database. After updating the record, the test verifies the response, the status code, and that a record exists with the new changes in the database.

Your test will fail with your assertion of a 200 response status code because you haven't defined a route; instead you get a *405 Method Not Allowed* response (Listing 5-40).

Listing 5-40. Testing the Updating of a Book

```
# vagrant@homestead:~/Code/bookr$
$ phpunit

There was 1 failure:

1) Tests\App\Http\Controllers\BooksControllerTest::update_should_only_change_fillable_fields
Expected status code 200, got 405.
Failed asserting that 405 matches expected 200.

FAILURES!
Tests: 10, Assertions: 20, Failures: 1, Incomplete: 2.
```

With the failing test written, define the route (Listing 5-41) and the controller implementation (Listing 5-42).

Listing 5-41. Books Update Route (app/Http/routes.php)

```
18  $app->get('/books', 'BooksController@index');
19  $app->get('/books/{id:[\d]+}', [
20      'as' => 'books.show',
21      'uses' => 'BooksController@show'
22  ]);
23  $app->post('/books', 'BooksController@store');
24  $app->put('/books/{id:[\d]+}', 'BooksController@update');
```

Listing 5-42. First Attempt at Updating a Book (BooksController.php)

```
56  /**
57   * PUT /books/{id}
58   *
59   * @param Request $request
```

```
60    * @param $id
61    * @return mixed
62    */
63   public function update(Request $request, $id)
64   {
65       $book = Book::findOrFail($id);
66
67       $book->fill($request->all());
68       $book->save();
69
70       return $book;
71   }
```

The controller uses the findOrFail method you've already seen, which returns the book if it exists. The *$book->fill()* method, provided by Eloquent, takes an array of data from the request, but only updates the model's $fillable fields. Next, the $book->save() method is called and the updated book returned.

Run the tests after writing the implementation to see if you can move on (Listing 5-43).

Listing 5-43. Running the Update Test

```
# vagrant@homestead:~/Code/bookr$
$ phpunit --filter=update_should_only_change_fillable_fields

OK (1 test, 7 assertions)
```

I will spoil it for you: if you run the test again, it will fail the second time. Why does it fail? Because you are using the development database to run tests. The second time you run your test, it will see the updated record in the database when it should not (Listing 5-44).

Listing 5-44. Your Failing Test, Which Should Pass

```
$this->notSeeInDatabase('books', [
    'title' => 'The War of the Worlds'
]);
```

Until you start using a separate test database you will have to purge and seed the data before each test run (Listing 5-45).

Listing 5-45. Refreshing the Database Before Running Tests

```
# vagrant@homestead:~/Code/bookr$
$ php artisan migrate:refresh && php artisan db:seed
$ phpunit --filter=update_should_only_change_fillable_fields

OK (1 test, 7 assertions)
```

You are ready to work on the second acceptance criteria: *update_should_fail_with_an_invalid_id*. The final two acceptance criteria don't need to insert a record; they just make sure that your route matches integer digits and that non-existent records return a 404 response. Let's break the rules a little and write tests for both features at the same time (Listing 5-46).

Listing 5-46. Writing Remaining Tests for the Update Action (BooksController.php)

```
127  /** @test **/
128  public function update_should_fail_with_an_invalid_id()
129  {
130      $this
131          ->put('/books/999999999999999')
132          ->seeStatusCode(404)
133          ->seeJsonEquals([
134              'error' => [
135                  'message' => 'Book not found'
136              ]
137          ]);
138  }
139
140  /** @test **/
141  public function update_should_not_match_an_invalid_route()
142  {
143      $this->put('/books/this-is-invalid')
144          ->seeStatusCode(404);
145  }
```

Let's run all the update_should tests (Listing 5-47).

Listing 5-47. Running the Update Tests

```
# vagrant@homestead:~/Code/bookr$
$ php artisan migrate:refresh && php artisan db:seed
$ phpunit --filter=update_should

There was 1 failure:

1) Tests\App\Http\Controllers\BooksControllerTest::update_should_fail_with_an_invalid_id
ErrorException: Invalid argument supplied for foreach()
...

FAILURES!
Tests: 3, Assertions: 9, Failures: 1.
```

It looks like the only failing test is *update_should_fail_with_an_invalid_id*. You already dealt with this issue in the GET/books/{id} route when testing for an error message, so see if you can fix this test on your own before you see the solution (Listing 5-48).

Listing 5-48. Responding to Missing Books with a 404 (BooksController.php)

```
56  /**
57   * PUT /books/{id}
58   * @param Request $request
59   * @param $id
60   * @return mixed
61   */
62  public function update(Request $request, $id)
```

```
63  {
64      try {
65          $book = Book::findOrFail($id);
66      } catch (ModelNotFoundException $e) {
67          return response()->json([
68              'error' => [
69                  'message' => 'Book not found'
70              ]
71          ], 404);
72      }
73
74      $book->fill($request->all());
75      $book->save();
76
77      return $book;
78  }
```

Like the BooksController@show method, the @update method catches the ModelNotFoundException and responds with an error message and a 404 status code. This should get your test suite passing again (Listing 5-49).

Listing 5-49. Running the Full Test Suite

```
# vagrant@homestead:~/Code/bookr$
$ php artisan migrate:refresh && php artisan db:seed
$ phpunit

OK (10 tests, 28 assertions)
```

---

❶ Git Commit: Update a Book

475127d (https://bitbucket.org/paulredmond/apress-bookr/commits/475127d)

Deleting Books

Deleting books is the last part of CRUD, and the end of this really long chapter. Luckily, deleting is easy. Listing 5-50 shows the DELETE /books/{id} route criteria.

Listing 5-50. Delete Books Acceptance Criteria (BooksControllerTest.php)

```
148  /** @test **/
149  public function destroy_should_remove_a_valid_book()
150  {
151      $this->markTestIncomplete('pending');
152  }
153
154  /** @test **/
155  public function destroy_should_return_a_404_with_an_invalid_id()
156  {
```

```
157        $this->markTestIncomplete('pending');
158    }
159
160    /** @test **/
161    public function destroy_should_not_match_an_invalid_route()
162    {
163        $this->markTestIncomplete('pending');
164    }
```

Your first test will make sure you can successfully delete a book. The test expects a *204 No Content* status code and an empty response when deletion succeeds (Listing 5-51).

Listing 5-51. Testing for Successful Deletion (BooksControllerTest.php)

```
142    /** @test **/
143    public function destroy_should_remove_a_valid_book()
144    {
145        $this
146            ->delete('/books/1')
147            ->seeStatusCode(204)
148            ->isEmpty();
149
150        $this->notSeeInDatabase('books', ['id' => 1]);
151    }
```

Let's run the test to make sure it fails (Listing 5-52).

Listing 5-52. Running the Test for Destroying a Book

```
# vagrant@homestead:~/Code/bookr$
$ phpunit --filter=destroy_should_remove_a_valid_book

There was 1 failure:

1) Tests\App\Http\Controllers\BooksControllerTest::destroy_should_remove_a_valid_book
Expected status code 204, got 405.
Failed asserting that 405 matches expected 204.

/home/vagrant/Code/bookr/vendor/laravel/lumen-framework/src/Testing/CrawlerTrait\
.php:412
/home/vagrant/Code/bookr/tests/app/Http/Controllers/BooksControllerTest.php:153

FAILURES!
Tests: 1, Assertions: 1, Failures: 1.
```

The failed test responds with a 405 Method Not Allowed response. Lumen responds with the 405 without any work on your part until you define the DELETE /books/{id} route. A failed test means you are ready to implement your first version of the BooksController@destroy method and route (Listing 5-53).

Listing 5-53. BooksController::destroy() Method (BooksController.php)

```
80  /**
81   * DELETE /books/{id}
82   * @param $id
83   * @return \Illuminate\Http\JsonResponse
84   */
85  public function destroy($id)
86  {
87      $book = Book::findOrFail($id);
88      $book->delete();
89
90      return response(null, 204);
91  }
```

Just like your test outlines, you find the book and call $book->delete() on the model and omit a response body. You don't call response()->json() because you are not sending back a response body with a 204 response, indicating that the server successfully fulfilled the request but there is no content to send back.

You need to define the accompanying route (Listing 5-54) and then run the test (Listing 5-55).

Listing 5-54. The BooksController@destroy Route

```
18  $app->get('/books', 'BooksController@index');
19  $app->get('/books/{id:[\d]+}', [
20      'as' => 'books.show',
21      'uses' => 'BooksController@show'
22  ]);
23  $app->put('/books/{id:[\d]+}', 'BooksController@update');
24  $app->post('/books', 'BooksController@store');
25  $app->delete('/books/{id:[\d]+}', 'BooksController@destroy');
```

Listing 5-55. Running the Test for Destroying a Book

```
# vagrant@homestead:~/Code/bookr$
$ phpunit --filter=destroy_should_remove_a_valid_book

OK (1 test, 2 assertions)
```

After you delete the record in the database, your test will fail if you run it a second time because the record has been removed. Keep refreshing the migration and seeding data to wrap up this chapter. The final two tests are the same as the PUT /books/{id} tests (Listing 5-56).

Listing 5-56. Final BooksController::destroy() Tests

```
158  /** @test **/
159  public function destroy_should_return_a_404_with_an_invalid_id()
160  {
161      $this
```

```
162            ->delete('/books/99999')
163            ->seeStatusCode(404)
164            ->seeJsonEquals([
165                'error' => [
166                    'message' => 'Book not found'
167                ]
168            ]);
169  }
170
171  /** @test **/
172  public function destroy_should_not_match_an_invalid_route()
173  {
174      $this->delete('/books/this-is-invalid')
175          ->seeStatusCode(404);
176  }
```

You expect that your tests should fail (Listing 5-57).

Listing 5-57. Running the Tests for Deleting a Book

```
# vagrant@homestead:~/Code/bookr$
$ php artisan migrate:refresh && php artisan db:seed
$ phpunit --filter=destroy_

There was 1 failure:

1) Tests\App\Http\Controllers\BooksControllerTest::destroy_should_return_a_404_with_an_
invalid_id
ErrorException: Invalid argument supplied for foreach()
...

FAILURES!
Tests: 3, Assertions: 4, Failures: 1.
```

There's one final test to fail and then you can consider your initial BooksController complete. To pass the final test, you must catch the ModelNotFoundException like your other controller methods (Listing 5-58).

Listing 5-58. Respond with 404 Error if Missing (BooksController.php)

```
80  /**
81   * DELETE /books/{id}
82   * @param $id
83   * @return \Illuminate\Http\JsonResponse
84   */
85  public function destroy($id)
86  {
87      try {
88          $book = Book::findOrFail($id);
89      } catch (ModelNotFoundException $e) {
90          return response()->json([
91              'error' => [
92                  'message' => 'Book not found'
```

```
 93              ]
 94          ], 404);
 95      }
 96
 97      $book->delete();
 98
 99      return response(null, 204);
100  }
```

This code change should get your tests to pass (Listing 5-59).

Listing 5-59. Run the Full Test Suite

```
# vagrant@homestead:~/Code/bookr$
$ php artisan migrate:refresh && php artisan db:seed
$ phpunit

OK (13 tests, 33 assertions)
```

Success! You are done with your first version of the BooksController. The following listings show the full source code of the main files you are working on, including BooksController.php (Listing 5-60), BooksControllerTest.php (Listing 5-61), and routes.php (Listing 5-62).

Listing 5-60. BooksController.php

```php
 1  <?php
 2
 3  namespace App\Http\Controllers;
 4
 5  use App\Book;
 6  use Illuminate\Http\Request;
 7  use Illuminate\Database\Eloquent\ModelNotFoundException;
 8
 9  /**
10   * Class BooksController
11   * @package App\Http\Controllers
12   */
13  class BooksController
14  {
15      /**
16       * GET /books
17       * @return array
18       */
19      public function index()
20      {
21          return Book::all();
22      }
23
24      /**
25       * GET /books/{id}
26       * @param integer $id
27       * @return mixed
```

```
28          */
29      public function show($id)
30      {
31          try {
32              return Book::findOrFail($id);
33          } catch (ModelNotFoundException $e) {
34              return response()->json([
35                  'error' => [
36                      'message' => 'Book not found'
37                  ]
38              ], 404);
39          }
40      }
41
42      /**
43       * POST /books
44       * @param Request $request
45       * @return \Symfony\Component\HttpFoundation\Response
46       */
47      public function store(Request $request)
48      {
49          $book = Book::create($request->all());
50
51          return response()->json(['created' => true], 201, [
52              'Location' => route('books.show', ['id' => $book->id])
53          ]);
54      }
55
56      /**
57       * PUT /books/{id}
58       * @param Request $request
59       * @param $id
60       * @return mixed
61       */
62      public function update(Request $request, $id)
63      {
64          try {
65              $book = Book::findOrFail($id);
66          } catch (ModelNotFoundException $e) {
67              return response()->json([
68                  'error' => [
69                      'message' => 'Book not found'
70                  ]
71              ], 404);
72          }
73
74          $book->fill($request->all());
75          $book->save();
76
77          return $book;
78      }
```

```
79
80      /**
81       * DELETE /books/{id}
82       * @param $id
83       * @return \Illuminate\Http\JsonResponse
84       */
85      public function destroy($id)
86      {
87          try {
88              $book = Book::findOrFail($id);
89          } catch (ModelNotFoundException $e) {
90              return response()->json([
91                  'error' => [
92                      'message' => 'Book not found'
93                  ]
94              ], 404);
95          }
96
97          $book->delete();
98
99          return response(null, 204);
100     }
101 }
```

Listing 5-61. BooksControllerTest.php

```
1   <?php
2
3   namespace Tests\App\Http\Controllers;
4
5   use TestCase;
6
7   class BooksControllerTest extends TestCase
8   {
9       /** @test **/
10      public function index_status_code_should_be_200()
11      {
12          $this->visit('/books')->seeStatusCode(200);
13      }
14
15      /** @test **/
16      public function index_should_return_a_collection_of_records()
17      {
18          $this
19              ->get('/books')
20              ->seeJson([
21                  'title' => 'War of the Worlds'
22              ])
23              ->seeJson([
24                  'title' => 'A Wrinkle in Time'
25              ]);
26      }
```

```
27
28      /** @test **/
29      public function show_should_return_a_valid_book()
30      {
31          $this
32              ->get('/books/1')
33              ->seeStatusCode(200)
34              ->seeJson([
35                  'id' => 1,
36                  'title' => 'War of the Worlds',
37                  'description' => 'A science fiction masterpiece about Martians invading
                    London',
38                  'author' => 'H. G. Wells'
39              ]);
40
41          $data = json_decode($this->response->getContent(), true);
42          $this->assertArrayHasKey('created_at', $data);
43          $this->assertArrayHasKey('updated_at', $data);
44      }
45
46      /** @test **/
47      public function show_should_fail_when_the_book_id_does_not_exist()
48      {
49          $this
50              ->get('/books/99999')
51              ->seeStatusCode(404)
52              ->seeJson([
53                  'error' => [
54                      'message' => 'Book not found'
55                  ]
56              ]);
57      }
58
59      /** @test **/
60      public function show_route_should_not_match_an_invalid_route()
61      {
62          $this->get('/books/this-is-invalid');
63
64          $this->assertNotRegExp(
65              '/Book not found/',
66              $this->response->getContent(),
67              'BooksController@show route matching when it should not.'
68          );
69      }
70
71      /** @test **/
72      public function store_should_save_new_book_in_the_database()
73      {
74          $this->post('/books', [
75              'title' => 'The Invisible Man',
76              'description' => 'An invisible man is trapped in the terror of his own
                creation',
```

```
77              'author' => 'H. G. Wells'
78          ]);
79
80          $this
81              ->seeJson(['created' => true])
82              ->seeInDatabase('books', ['title' => 'The Invisible Man']);
83      }
84
85      /** @test */
86      public function store_should_respond_with_a_201_and_location_header_when_
    successful()
87      {
88          $this->post('/books', [
89              'title' => 'The Invisible Man',
90              'description' => 'An invisible man is trapped in the terror of his own
                creation',
91              'author' => 'H. G. Wells'
92          ]);
93
94          $this
95              ->seeStatusCode(201)
96              ->seeHeaderWithRegExp('Location', '#/books/[\d]+$#');
97
98      }
99
100     /** @test **/
101     public function update_should_only_change_fillable_fields()
102     {
103         $this->notSeeInDatabase('books', [
104             'title' => 'The War of the Worlds'
105         ]);
106
107         $this->put('/books/1', [
108             'id' => 5,
109             'title' => 'The War of the Worlds',
110             'description' => 'The book is way better than the movie.',
111             'author' => 'Wells, H. G.'
112         ]);
113
114         $this
115             ->seeStatusCode(200)
116             ->seeJson([
117                 'id' => 1,
118                 'title' => 'The War of the Worlds',
119                 'description' => 'The book is way better than the movie.',
120                 'author' => 'Wells, H. G.'
121             ])
122             ->seeInDatabase('books', [
123                 'title' => 'The War of the Worlds'
124             ]);
125     }
```

```php
126
127        /** @test **/
128        public function update_should_fail_with_an_invalid_id()
129        {
130            $this
131                ->put('/books/999999999999999')
132                ->seeStatusCode(404)
133                ->seeJsonEquals([
134                    'error' => [
135                        'message' => 'Book not found'
136                    ]
137                ]);
138        }
139
140        /** @test **/
141        public function update_should_not_match_an_invalid_route()
142        {
143            $this->put('/books/this-is-invalid')
144                ->seeStatusCode(404);
145        }
146
147        /** @test **/
148        public function destroy_should_remove_a_valid_book()
149        {
150            $this
151                ->delete('/books/1')
152                ->seeStatusCode(204)
153                ->isEmpty();
154
155            $this->notSeeInDatabase('books', ['id' => 1]);
156        }
157
158        /** @test **/
159        public function destroy_should_return_a_404_with_an_invalid_id()
160        {
161            $this
162                ->delete('/books/99999')
163                ->seeStatusCode(404)
164                ->seeJsonEquals([
165                    'error' => [
166                        'message' => 'Book not found'
167                    ]
168                ]);
169        }
170
171        /** @test **/
172        public function destroy_should_not_match_an_invalid_route()
173        {
174            $this->delete('/books/this-is-invalid')
175                ->seeStatusCode(404);
176        }
177    }
```

Listing 5-62. routes.php

```php
1   <?php
2
3   /*
4   |--------------------------------------------------------------------------
5   | Application Routes
6   |--------------------------------------------------------------------------
7   |
8   | Here is where you can register all of the routes for an application.
9   | It is a breeze. Simply tell Lumen the URIs it should respond to
10  | and give it the Closure to call when that URI is requested.
11  |
12  */
13
14  $app->get('/', function () use ($app) {
15      return $app->version();
16  });
17
18  $app->get('/books', 'BooksController@index');
19  $app->get('/books/{id:[\d]+}', [
20      'as' => 'books.show',
21      'uses' => 'BooksController@show'
22  ]);
23  $app->put('/books/{id:[\d]+}', 'BooksController@update');
24  $app->post('/books', 'BooksController@store');
25  $app->delete('/books/{id:[\d]+}', 'BooksController@destroy');
```

If you are following along, commit your changes before moving on to the next chapter.

ⓘ Git commit: Delete a Book

60ab6ca (https://bitbucket.org/paulredmond/apress-bookr/commits/60ab6ca)

Conclusion

You covered a lot of ground in this chapter, including

- Testing first and then writing a passing implementation
- Creating new records in a database with Eloquent
- Updating existing records in the database
- Deleting existing records in the database
- Using correct response codes for creating, updating, and deleting resources
- Defining a named route

The BooksController is clean and simple, with Eloquent doing the heavy lifting for your data. Your methods are small and concise, which makes code easier to digest and maintain.

CHAPTER 6

Responding to Errors

During your work on the Book API in Chapter 5 it became evident that you need to start using a separate test database. You also don't have very good error responses for API consumers yet. Responding to a client with an HTML error that expects JSON is not going to cut it anymore. When an API consumer interacts with your API, you want to respond with the correct Content-Type header. For now, you will assume all of your consumers want JSON, and in my experience, JSON is typically what consumers want.

Test Database

The main focus of this chapter will be error responses, but before you work on error responses you will sidestep and fix your glaring database testing issue. Lumen provides convenient and clever tools out of the box to support creating test data, such as

- Model factories
- DatabaseMigrations trait
- Faker data generator (https://github.com/fzaninotto/Faker)

The basic steps needed to start using the test database include

- Configuring PHPUnit to use the test database
- Creating a model factory definition for the Book model
- Modifying existing tests to use factory test data

Back in Chapter 3 you set up the *bookr_testing* database during your project setup in the Homestead.yaml file. If you don't have that database yet, you need to configure it now and rerun the vagrant provision.

If you recall your project environment setup, the MySQL database is configured using *phpdotenv*. You take advantage of that to set the test database used within PHPUnit. Open the *phpunit.xml* file in the root of the project and you will see opening and closing *<php></php>* tags that contain environment variables; you need to add the *DB_DATABASE* variable (Listing 6-1).

Listing 6-1. Configuring PHPUnit to Use the Testing Database

```
22   <php>
23       <env name="APP_ENV" value="testing"/>
24       <!-- Test Database -->
25       <env name="DB_DATABASE" value="bookr_testing"/>
26       <env name="CACHE_DRIVER" value="array"/>
27   </php>
```

I won't show the output if you run `phpunit` at this point, but you will get exceptions and failures, lots of them. Switching the database to *bookr_testing* means that you don't have any tables or data yet. You already have migrations, but to get data in your test database you need to configure a model factory and tweak your tests to take advantage of the *DatabaseMigrations* trait that Lumen provides.

Model Factories

Model factories provide fake test data that can be used to populate the test data before running a test. Factories generate random fake data you can use in a test, making your test data isolated and repeatable. In fact, each test requiring test data starts with a fresh database.

You only have one model right now, so you will define a factory you can use in your *BooksControllerTest.php*. All the model factory definitions should be added in the *database/factories/ ModelFactory.php* file (Listing 6-2).

Listing 6-2. Adding the Book Model Factory

```
21  $factory->define(App\Book::class, function ($faker) {
22      $title = $faker->sentence(rand(3, 10));
23
24      return [
25          'title' => substr($title, 0, strlen($title) - 1),
26          'description' => $faker->text,
27          'author' => $faker->name
28      ];
29  });
```

You define a Book factory with the first argument, *App\Book::class*, which references the model. The second argument in the factory definition is a *Closure*, which does the following:

- Uses Faker (https://github.com/fzaninotto/Faker) to generate a random sentence between 3 and 10 words long

- Returns an array of fake data using Faker's various "formatters"

- Removes the period (.) from the sentence formatter with `substr`

Factories in Tests

Now that you've defined a book factory (pun intended), you are ready to use it in your test to provide random fake test data. You will update all your existing tests that currently depend on your seeded data to start using the new factory. The only test file you have at this point is *tests/app/Http/Controllers/ BooksControllerTest.php*, so open it up in your favorite editor.

The first test is *index_should_return_a_collection_of_records*, which ensures that the *BooksController@index* method returns a collection of books (Listing 6-3).

Listing 6-3. Refactoring the *index_should_return_a_collection_of_records* Test

```
15  /** @test **/
16  public function index_should_return_a_collection_of_records()
17  {
18      $books = factory('App\Book', 2)->create();
19
```

```
20        $this->get('/books');
21
22        foreach ($books as $book) {
23            $this->seeJson(['title' => $book->title]);
24        }
25    }
```

The last code snippet is the first example of using the factory() helper function. You indicate that you want to use the *App\Book* factory, and that you want it to generate two book models. The second argument is optional, and if you omit it you will get one record back.

The *factory()* helper returns an instance of *Illuminate\Database\Eloquent\FactoryBuilder*, which has the methods *make()* and *create()*. You want to persist data to the database so you use create(); the make() method will return a model without saving it to the database.

The *factory()->create()* call returns the model instances and you loop over them to make sure each model is represented in the /books response.

Now that you've see the first example of using a factory, you need a way to migrate and reset your database before each test requiring the database. Enter the *DatabaseMigrations* trait provided by the Lumen framework (Listing 6-4).

Listing 6-4. Adding the DatabaseMigrations Trait

```
1    <?php
2
3    namespace Tests\App\Http\Controllers;
4
5    use TestCase;
6    use Laravel\Lumen\Testing\DatabaseMigrations;
7
8    class BooksControllerTest extends TestCase
9    {
10        use DatabaseMigrations;
11        // ...
12    }
```

The DatabaseMigrations trait uses a @before PHPUnit annotation to migrate the database automatically.

---

❶ Learn More About Model Factories

See the "Model Factories" (https://lumen.laravel.com/docs/5.2/testing#model-factories) section of the official documentation for information on how to use model factories.

It is time to run phpunit against your first test refactor (Listing 6-5).

Listing 6-5. Testing the First Test Refactor

```
# vagrant@homestead:~/Code/bookr$
$ phpunit --filter=index_should_return_a_collection_of_records

OK (1 test, 2 assertions)
```

Now that you have a working test with the Book model factory, you can knock out the remaining test cases that need model data. You will cheat a little and fix the remaining tests before you run the whole test suite again.

Next up is the GET /book/{id} route test, shown in Listing 6-6.

Listing 6-6. Refactoring *show_should_return_a_valid_book* to Use Factories

```
31  /** @test **/
32  public function show_should_return_a_valid_book()
33  {
34      $book = factory('App\Book')->create();
35      $this
36          ->get("/books/{$book->id}")
37          ->seeStatusCode(200)
38          ->seeJson([
39              'id' => $book->id,
40              'title' => $book->title,
41              'description' => $book->description,
42              'author' => $book->author
43          ]);
44
45      $data = json_decode($this->response->getContent(), true);
46      $this->assertArrayHasKey('created_at', $data);
47      $this->assertArrayHasKey('updated_at', $data);
48  }
```

Note that you use the *$book->id* to build the request URI and then assert the response from the *$book* instance. The remainder of the test stays the same.

Next up is using a model factory to test that only fillable fields can be updated (Listing 6-7).

Listing 6-7. Refactoring *update_should_only_change_fillable_fields* to Use Model Factories

```
104  /** @test **/
105  public function update_should_only_change_fillable_fields()
106  {
107      $book = factory('App\Book')->create([
108          'title' => 'War of the Worlds',
109          'description' => 'A science fiction masterpiece about Martians invading
             London',
110          'author' => 'H. G. Wells',
111      ]);
112
113      $this->put("/books/{$book->id}", [
114          'id' => 5,
115          'title' => 'The War of the Worlds',
116          'description' => 'The book is way better than the movie.',
117          'author' => 'Wells, H. G.'
118      ]);
119
120      $this
121          ->seeStatusCode(200)
122          ->seeJson([
123              'id' => 1,
```

```
124                'title' => 'The War of the Worlds',
125                'description' => 'The book is way better than the movie.',
126                'author' => 'Wells, H. G.'
127            ])
128            ->seeInDatabase('books', [
129                'title' => 'The War of the Worlds'
130            ]);
131  }
```

The test is the first example of passing an array to the *factory()->create()* to override model values. You are not required to pass specific data to get this test passing, but I think it makes the test more readable. When you pass an array to factory()->create() (and make) the values override the generated values produced by the Faker library. Note that you removed the *notSeeInDatabase()* assertion at the beginning because each test has a clean database, making the test unnecessary.

The next test to be refactored with a model factory is the one that ensures that a book can be deleted (Listing 6-8).

Listing 6-8. Refactoring *destroy_should_remove_a_valid_book* to Use Factories

```
153  /** @test **/
154  public function destroy_should_remove_a_valid_book()
155  {
156      $book = factory('App\Book')->create();
157      $this
158          ->delete("/books/{$book->id}")
159          ->seeStatusCode(204)
160          ->isEmpty();
161
162      $this->notSeeInDatabase('books', ['id' => $book->id]);
163  }
```

Your refactor is done. See if the tests can be passed now (Listing 6-9).

Listing 6-9. Test Suite After Model Factory Refactoring

```
# vagrant@homestead:~/Code/bookr$
$ phpunit

OK (13 tests, 32 assertions)
```

You can run phpunit multiple times and the tests will pass every time. Yay!

---

❶ Git commit: Use Model Factories and a Test Database for Tests

1c50b61 (https://bitbucket.org/paulredmond/apress-bookr/commits/1c50b61)

Better Error Responses

You are ready to improve your APIs error responses. Thus far you get back HTML when you have an application exception like a ModelNotFoundException, but an API consumer should get JSON. You could support other content types too, but you will focus on JSON responses for now.

Framework Exception Handling

So how does Lumen deal with exceptions out of the box? The Lumen application bootstraps an application instance (Laravel\Lumen\Application) which contains a few key traits: *Laravel\Lumen\Concerns\RoutesRequests* and *Laravel\Lumen\Concerns\RegistersExceptionHandlers*. You will find the *Application::run()* method is contained in the RoutesRequests trait (Listing 6-10).

Listing 6-10. The RoutesRequests Trait's run() Method

```
/**
 * Run the application and send the response.
 *
 * @param  SymfonyRequest|null  $request
 * @return void
 */
public function run($request = null)
{
    $response = $this->dispatch($request);

    if ($response instanceof SymfonyResponse) {
        $response->send();
    } else {
        echo (string) $response;
    }

    if (count($this->middleware) > 0) {
        $this->callTerminableMiddleware($response);
    }
}
```

The trait's run() method is called from the front controller (public/index.php). The first line dispatches the request, expecting a response back. If you view the source for the *RoutesRequests::dispatch()* method, you will see a try/catch where exceptions are caught and handled (Listing 6-11).

Listing 6-11. Partial Source of Lumen's Application::dispatch() Method

```
try {
    return $this->sendThroughPipeline($this->middleware, function () use ($method,
$pathInfo) {
        if (isset($this->routes[$method.$pathInfo])) {
            return $this->handleFoundRoute([true, $this->routes[$method.$pathInfo]
['action'], []]);
        }

        return $this->handleDispatcherResponse(
            $this->createDispatcher()->dispatch($method, $pathInfo)
        );
    });
} catch (Exception $e) {
    return $this->sendExceptionToHandler($e);
} catch (Throwable $e) {
    return $this->sendExceptionToHandler($e);
}
```

Application exceptions are caught and then *sendExceptionToHandler()* is called. The sendExceptionToHandler() appears as shown in Listing 6-12 (at the time of writing) in the RegistersExceptionHandlers trait.

Listing 6-12. The Application::sendExceptionToHandler() Method

```
/**
 * Send the exception to the handler and return the response.
 *
 * @param  \Throwable  $e
 * @return Response
 */
protected function sendExceptionToHandler($e)
{
    $handler = $this->resolveExceptionHandler();

    if ($e instanceof Error) {
        $e = new FatalThrowableError($e);
    }

    $handler->report($e);

    return $handler->render($this->make('request'), $e);
}
```

The exception handler is resolved from the container on the first line, and is an instance of *app/Exceptions/Handler.php*. The handler instance from the container is responsible for rendering the exception. Lumen uses a contract (https://laravel.com/docs/5.2/contracts), specifically the *Illuminate\Contracts\Debug\ExceptionHandler*, to bind the container to the application's handler. The *bootstrap/app.php* binds the application handler to the ExceptionHandler contract (Listing 6-13).

Listing 6-13. The Exception Handler Contract in bootstrap/app.php

```
41  $app->singleton(
42      Illuminate\Contracts\Debug\ExceptionHandler::class,
43      App\Exceptions\Handler::class
44  );
```

The Application class will resolve the Handler class in app/Exceptions/Handler.php. Listing 6-14 shows the *Handler::render()* method.

Listing 6-14. The Exception Handler Render Method

```
39  /**
40   * Render an exception into an HTTP response.
41   *
42   * @param \Illuminate\Http\Request $request
43   * @param \Exception $e
44   * @return \Illuminate\Http\Response
45   */
46  public function render($request, Exception $e)
47  {
48      return parent::render($request, $e);
49  }
```

The application handler defers to the parent class to render out the exception. The parent of the application Handler is the Lumen framework Handler, which you can find at *vendor/laravel/lumen-framework/src/Exceptions/Handler.php*. I'll leave it to you to investigate the source if you want, but basically the default Handler uses the Symfony Debug component (http://symfony.com/doc/current/components/debug.html) ExceptionHandler class to send a response.

JSON Exceptions

Now that you understand a bit about how Lumen calls the app/Exception/Handler, you are going to update the Handler::render() method to respond with JSON instead of HTML when appropriate (Listing 6-15).

Listing 6-15. Checking to See if the User Wants a JSON Response

```
40  /**
41   * Render an exception into an HTTP response.
42   *
43   * @param \Illuminate\Http\Request $request
44   * @param \Exception $e
45   * @return \Illuminate\Http\Response
46   */
47  public function render($request, Exception $e)
48  {
49      if ($request->wantsJson() && !($e instanceof ValidationException)) {
50          $response = [
51              'message' => (string) $e->getMessage(),
52              'status' => 400
53          ];
54
55          if ($e instanceof HttpException) {
56              $response['message'] = Response::$statusTexts[$e->getStatusCode()];
57              $response['status'] = $e->getStatusCode();
58          }
59
60          if ($this->isDebugMode()) {
61              $response['debug'] = [
62                  'exception' => get_class($e),
63                  'trace' => $e->getTrace()
64              ];
65          }
66
67          return response()->json(['error' => $response], $response['status']);
68      }
69
70      return parent::render($request, $e);
71  }
72
73  /**
74   * Determine if the application is in debug mode.
75   *
76   * @return Boolean
77   */
78  public function isDebugMode()
```

```
79  {
80      return (Boolean) env('APP_DEBUG');
81  }
```

You need to import Response at the top of your Handler class or you will get a fatal error (Listing 6-16).

Listing 6-16. Importing the Response Class

```php
<?php

namespace App\Exceptions;

use Exception;
use Symfony\Component\HttpFoundation\Response;
// ...

class Handler extends ExceptionHandler
```

Let's break down the changes you made to the render method:

- $request->wantsJson() checks if the user has "json" in the Accept header.

- You skip ValidationException, allowing the parent handler to handle validation exceptions.

- If the user doesn't want JSON, skip and call parent::render() like the original method.

- If the user wants JSON, you start building the response array, which will be the returned JSON data.

- You start out with the default exception message and a status code of 400 Bad Request for generic errors.

- If the exception is an instance of Symfony\Component\HttpKernel\Exception\ HttpException, change the message and status code of the exception (i.e. status=404, message=Not Found).

- If debug mode is enabled, add the exception class and the stack trace.

- Finally, return a JSON response with the assembled data.

Try your new handler logic out in the console with curl (Listing 6-17).

Listing 6-17. Exception Response With Debugging Disabled for Brevity

```
# vagrant@homestead:~/Code/bookr$
$ curl -H"Accept: application/json" http://bookr.app/foo/bar

HTTP/1.0 404 Not Found
Host: localhost:8000
Connection: close
X-Powered-By: PHP/5.6.13
Cache-Control: no-cache
Date: Sun, 25 Oct 2015 06:37:31 GMT
Content-Type: application/json

{"error":{"message":"Not Found","status":404}}
```

If you have debugging turned on, your response will have more data. You should check what happens if you don't send the Accept header (Listing 6-18).

Listing 6-18. Response Example for a Missing Route

```
# vagrant@homestead:~/Code/bookr$
$ curl -I http://bookr.app/foo/bar

HTTP/1.1 404 Not Found
Server: nginx/1.9.7
Content-Type: text/html; charset=UTF-8
Connection: keep-alive
Cache-Control: no-cache, private
date: Wed, 06 Jan 2016 04:28:54 GMT
```

You have not asked for JSON, so the handler defers to the parent class. You can make the determination to always respond with JSON in your own applications, but for now you will keep your check and fall back to the default. The approach you've taken to send a JSON response for exceptions is basic, but your approach is good enough to get started. Eventually, you might want to build your own handler(s) for handling exceptions that you can reuse on multiple projects. Start simple, and add complexity when you need it.

You could have started writing tests before this change, but I thought it was more important to show you how the handler works under the hood and see the results of your modifications first.

Testing the Exception Handler

You have an exception handler that can respond to JSON, but you need to write tests to make sure it behaves as you expect. You will write unit tests for the handler, and your existing API tests will cover integration tests.

A really useful library for unit testing is a mocking library called Mockery (http://docs.mockery.io/en/latest/), which will help you mock dependencies with relative ease. Mockery is not a requirement for Lumen so you need to install it with Composer (Listing 6-19).

Listing 6-19. Requiring Mockery

```
# vagrant@homestead:~/Code/bookr$
$ composer require --dev mockery/mockery:~0.9.4
```

Now let's create your Handler unit test file (Listing 6-20).

Listing 6-20. Creating the HandlerTest File

```
# vagrant@homestead:~/Code/bookr$
$ mkdir -p tests/app/Exceptions
$ touch tests/app/Exceptions/HandlerTest.php
```

Add the following code in Listing 6-21 to the new HandlerTest.php file.

Listing 6-21. The HandlerTest File (tests/app/Exceptions/HandlerTest.php)

```
1  <?php
2
3  namespace Tests\App\Exceptions;
4
```

```
5   use TestCase;
6   use \Mockery as m;
7   use App\Exceptions\Handler;
8   use Illuminate\Http\Request;
9   use Illuminate\Http\JsonResponse;
10
11  class HandlerTest extends TestCase
12  {
13
14  }
```

The following is a list of things you need to test based on the code you've written in the
Handler::render() method:

- It responds with HTML when json *is not* requested.

- It responds with json when json *is* requested.

- It provides a default status code for non-HTTP exceptions.

- It provides common HTTP status codes for HTTP exceptions.

- It provides debug information when debugging is *enabled*.

- It skips debugging information when debugging is *disabled*.

Your first test (Listing 6-22) will ensure the application responds with HTML when JSON is not
requested. Mockery makes mocking dependencies a breeze.

Listing 6-22. Testing That the API Responds with HTML When JSON Is Not Accepted

```
13  /** @test **/
14  public function it_responds_with_html_when_json_is_not_accepted()
15  {
16      // Make the mock a partial, you only want to mock the `isDebugMode` method
17      $subject = m::mock(Handler::class)->makePartial();
18      $subject->shouldNotReceive('isDebugMode');
19
20      // Mock the interaction with the Request
21      $request = m::mock(Request::class);
22      $request->shouldReceive('wantsJson')->andReturn(false);
23
24      // Mock the interaction with the exception
25      $exception = m::mock(\Exception::class, ['Error!']);
26      $exception->shouldNotReceive('getStatusCode');
27      $exception->shouldNotReceive('getTrace');
28      $exception->shouldNotReceive('getMessage');
29
30      // Call the method under test, this is not a mocked method.
31      $result = $subject->render($request, $exception);
32
33      // Assert that `render` does not return a JsonResponse
34      $this->assertNotInstanceOf(JsonResponse::class, $result);
35  }
```

You mock the class under test (App\Exceptions\Handler) as a partial mock (http://docs.mockery.io/en/latest/reference/partial_mocks.html). This allows you to mock certain methods, but the other methods respond normally. In your case, you want to control the return of the *isDebugMode* method you created. Mocking isDebugMode allows you to assert that it was never called! The expectation declaration shouldNotReceive means that the mocked method should never receive a call (http://docs.mockery.io/en/latest/reference/expectations.html).

You mock Illuminate\Http\Request and control the flow of the render method by instructing that wantsJson returns false. If wantsJson returns false, the entire block will be skipped and thus Handler::isDebugMode() will not be called. You can see how simple mocks make controlling the flow of the method under test.

The last mock you create before calling $subject->render() is an \Exception. Note in the m::mock() call that you pass an array of constructor arguments (m::mock('ClassName', [arg1,arg2])). Like the partial mock, you set up three shouldNotRecieve expectations for the exception mock: getStatusCode, getTrace, and getMessage.

Lastly, you actually call $subject->render($request, $exception);. You use a PHP assertion to make sure that the render method did not return an instance of the JsonResponse class. Note that because you partially mocked the subject of this test, the render method responds and works normally.

Now that you have an understanding of the test, let's run the first test (Listing 6-23).

Listing 6-23. Running the First Handler Unit Test

```
# vagrant@homestead:~/Code/bookr$
$ phpunit --filter=it_responds_with_html_when_json_is_not_accepted

OK (1 test, 1 assertion)
```

Everything passed, but all that work for one assertion!? Fortunately, Mockery provides a way to make expectations count as assertions in PHPUnit. Open up the base TestCase class found in tests/TestCase.php and add the following code in Listing 6-24.

Listing 6-24. Mockery's PHPUnit Integration Trait (Partial Source)

```
1   <?php
2
3   use Mockery\Adapter\Phpunit\MockeryPHPUnitIntegration;
4
5   class TestCase extends Laravel\Lumen\Testing\TestCase
6   {
7       use MockeryPHPUnitIntegration;
8       // …
9   }
```

Now you should get more assertions (Listing 6-25).

Listing 6-25. Running Tests After Adding the Mockery PHPUnit Trait

```
# vagrant@homestead:~/Code/bookr$
$ phpunit --filter=it_responds_with_html_when_json_is_not_accepted

OK (1 test, 6 assertions)
```

Great, you want your hard work and commitment to writing tests mean something. I personally don't know if I would write all those mocks without the assertion count payoff!

MOCKING

Mocking is an invaluable tool in your testing arsenal. It forces you to think about good code design. Mocking the interactions a class has with other dependencies helps you detect complicated code and hard-to-test code. A class with many dependencies can become difficult to mock, which might mean that you should refactor, or perhaps you are mocking things that don't need to be mocked.

Mocking is an easy enough concept to understand, but practical use is an art that takes practice. Don't give up on using mocking in your tests; the concepts will eventually click! I encourage you to read through the whole Mockery documentation and practice mocking.

The phpspec (http://phpspec.readthedocs.org/en/latest/) library is another good library that uses mocks for tests. In this book, I will stick to PHPUnit + Mockery, but phpspec is an excellent choice too!

You've covered the test for what happens when your app is rendering an exception response but the user doesn't want JSON back. Now you are going to test the JSON response when the user *wants* JSON (Listing 6-26).

Listing 6-26. Testing That the API Responds with JSON on an Exception

```php
37  /** @test */
38  public function it_responds_with_json_for_json_consumers()
39  {
40      $subject = m::mock(Handler::class)->makePartial();
41      $subject
42          ->shouldReceive('isDebugMode')
43          ->andReturn(false);
44
45      $request = m::mock(Request::class);
46      $request
47          ->shouldReceive('wantsJson')
48          ->andReturn(true);
49
50      $exception = m::mock(\Exception::class, ['Doh!']);
51      $exception
52          ->shouldReceive('getMessage')
53          ->andReturn('Doh!');
54
55      /** @var JsonResponse $result */
56      $result = $subject->render($request, $exception);
57      $data = $result->getData();
58
59      $this->assertInstanceOf(JsonResponse::class, $result);
60      $this->assertObjectHasAttribute('error', $data);
61      $this->assertAttributeEquals('Doh!', 'message', $data->error);
62      $this->assertAttributeEquals(400, 'status', $data->error);
63  }
```

The mocks in your latest test are very similar to the first handler test, but this time you mock your method under test to go into the if ($request->wantsJson()) { logic. Inside the if ($request->wantsJson()) { statement there are calls that you need to mock that should receive. The $exception mock should receive a call to getMessage and return "Doh!" since that is the parameter you passed to the $exception mock constructor.

The $exception is not an instance of Symfony\Component\HttpKernel\Exception\HttpException so your test will use the default status code and message from the exception. You then assert that the method under test returns an instance of Illuminate\Http\JsonResponse. Finally, you assert the response body for the correct keys, values, and status code.

A couple more tests and you can call your exception response handler good. The next test needs to import a few classes to the top of your HandlerTest class (Listing 6-27).

Listing 6-27. Adding a Few HTTP Exception Classes (tests/app/Exceptions/HandlerTest.php)

```php
<?php

namespace Tests\App\Exceptions;

// ...
use Symfony\Component\HttpKernel\Exception\NotFoundHttpException;
use Symfony\Component\HttpKernel\Exception\AccessDeniedHttpException;

class HandlerTest extends TestCase
```

And now the final test for the Handler.php class. This test ensures that classes extending from HttpException will respond with the matching HTTP request status code and message (Listing 6-28).

Listing 6-28. Testing HTTP Exception Responses

```php
67  /** @test */
68  public function it_provides_json_responses_for_http_exceptions()
69  {
70      $subject = m::mock(Handler::class)->makePartial();
71      $subject
72          ->shouldReceive('isDebugMode')
73          ->andReturn(false);
74
75      $request = m::mock(Request::class);
76      $request->shouldReceive('wantsJson')->andReturn(true);
77
78      $examples = [
79          [
80              'mock' => NotFoundHttpException::class,
81              'status' => 404,
82              'message' => 'Not Found'
83          ],
84          [
85              'mock' => AccessDeniedHttpException::class,
86              'status' => 403,
87              'message' => 'Forbidden'
88          ]
```

```
 89        ];
 90
 91        foreach ($examples as $e) {
 92            $exception = m::mock($e['mock']);
 93            $exception->shouldReceive('getMessage')->andReturn(null);
 94            $exception->shouldReceive('getStatusCode')->andReturn($e['status']);
 95
 96            /** @var JsonResponse $result */
 97            $result = $subject->render($request, $exception);
 98            $data = $result->getData();
 99
100            $this->assertEquals($e['status'], $result->getStatusCode());
101            $this->assertEquals($e['message'], $data->error->message);
102            $this->assertEquals($e['status'], $data->error->status);
103        }
104    }
```

The $subject and $request mocks should look familiar at this point. After mocking and setting expectations, the test creates an array of $examples that you will loop over to test a few exceptions that extend from the HttpException class. The foreach loop mocks each example and sets mockery expectations. Each loop will do the following:

- Set shouldReceive expectation for getMessage and getStatusCode.

- The $subject->render() call is made on the partially mocked test subject.

- Make PHPUnit assertions about the response status and message keys.

You are at a point where you should run tests before moving on (Listing 6-29).

Listing 6-29. Running the Handler Tests and the Full Test Suite

```
# vagrant@homestead:~/Code/bookr$
$ phpunit --filter=HandlerTest

OK (3 tests, 25 assertions)

$ phpunit

OK (16 tests, 57 assertions)
```

Before you call it good, let's refactor the BooksController@show method to not catch exceptions from the Book::findOrFail() method call now that your handler can respond to exceptions. Listing 6-30 shows the current version of the @show method.

Listing 6-30. Current BooksController@show Method

```
24    /**
25     * GET /books/{id}
26     * @param integer $id
27     * @return mixed
28     */
29    public function show($id)
30    {
```

```
31      try {
32          return Book::findOrFail($id);
33      } catch (ModelNotFoundException $e) {
34          return response()->json([
35              'error' => [
36                  'message' => 'Book not found'
37              ]
38          ], 404);
39      }
40  }
```

Let's remove the try/catch to see how your App\Exceptions\Handler::render() method handles the findOrFail() call (Listing 6-31).

Listing 6-31. Removing try/catch From the BooksController@show Method

```
24  /**
25   * GET /books/{id}
26   * @param integer $id
27   * @return mixed
28   */
29  public function show($id)
30  {
31      return Book::findOrFail($id);
32  }
```

Now try making a request to an invalid record (Listing 6-32).

Listing 6-32. Making a Request for an Invalid Book

```
# vagrant@homestead:~/Code/bookr$
$ curl -i -H"Accept: application/json" http://bookr.app/books/5555

HTTP/1.1 400 Bad Request
Server: nginx/1.9.7
Content-Type: application/json
Transfer-Encoding: chunked
Connection: keep-alive
Cache-Control: no-cache
Date: Wed, 06 Jan 2016 05:00:35 GMT

{"error":{"message":"No query results for model [App\\Book].","status":400}}
```

It looks like your Handler.php adjustments are working, but a 400 is not exactly the right response for a ModelNotFoundException. If you run phpunit, now you will get a failure; your test suite has helped you avoid a bug! Let's make one last adjustment to your Handler::render() method (Listing 6-33) to account for a ModelNotFoundException.

Listing 6-33. Additional Check for ModelNotFoundException

```
49  if ($e instanceof HttpException) {
50      $response['message'] = Response::$statusTexts[$e->getStatusCode()];
```

```
51        $response['status'] = $e->getStatusCode();
52    } else if ($e instanceof ModelNotFoundException) {
53        $response['message'] = Response::$statusTexts[Response::HTTP_NOT_FOUND];
54        $response['status'] = Response::HTTP_NOT_FOUND;
55    }
```

Try your request again and then run your test suite (Listing 6-34).

Listing 6-34. Making a Request After Changing the Handler

```
# vagrant@homestead:~/Code/bookr$
$ curl -i -H"Accept: application/json" http://bookr.app/books/5555

HTTP/1.1 404 Not Found
Server: nginx/1.9.7
Content-Type: application/json
Transfer-Encoding: chunked
Connection: keep-alive
Cache-Control: no-cache
Date: Wed, 06 Jan 2016 05:07:21 GMT

{"error":{"message":"Not Found","status":404}}
```

Much better! Let's see if your tests are passing now (Listing 6-35).

Listing 6-35. Running the Entire Test Suite

```
# vagrant@homestead:~/Code/bookr$
$ phpunit

There was 1 failure:

1) Tests\App\Http\Controllers\BooksControllerTest::show_should_fail_when_the_book_id_does_
not_exist
Invalid JSON was returned from the route. Perhaps an exception was thrown?
…

FAILURES!
Tests: 16, Assertions: 56, Failures: 1.
```

Your failing test claims that you have invalid JSON. It makes sense because your test is not asking for JSON with Accept: application/json and the return parent::render($request, $e); part of your handler is returning a 404 HTML response. If you look at the test, the message you are looking for is "Book not found", but you can actually update the handler to use the 404 message and status, so you need to change your seeJson() assertion (Listing 6-36).

Listing 6-36. Fixing the Broken BooksController@show Test

```
49  /** @test **/
50  public function show_should_fail_when_the_book_id_does_not_exist()
51  {
52      $this
```

```
53            ->get('/books/99999', ['Accept' => 'application/json'])
54            ->seeStatusCode(404)
55            ->seeJson([
56                'message' => 'Not Found',
57                'status' => 404
58            ]);
59  }
```

The $this->get() method can pass an array of headers; the Accept header will trigger your Handler::response() JSON logic. Next, you changed the seeJson check to match the ModelNotFoundException response message and status; you gain more consistent 404 messages by allowing the Handler to deal with them. Run the test suite again (Listing 6-37) to see if you are back to green!

Listing 6-37. Running the Full Test Suite

```
# vagrant@homestead:~/Code/bookr$
$ phpunit

OK (16 tests, 57 assertions)
```

Much better! You added more logic to your Handler class to deal with the ModelNotFoundException so you need to account for the added code in your test suite. You will add the ModelNotFoundException to your array of examples that you loop through by modifying an existing test (Listing 6-38).

Listing 6-38. Adding the ModelNotFoundException to Your $examples Array

```
73  /** @test */
74  public function it_provides_json_responses_for_http_exceptions()
75  {
76      $subject = m::mock(Handler::class)->makePartial();
77      $subject
78          ->shouldReceive('isDebugMode')
79          ->andReturn(false);
80
81      $request = m::mock(Request::class);
82      $request->shouldReceive('wantsJson')->andReturn(true);
83
84      $examples = [
85          [
86              'mock' => NotFoundHttpException::class,
87              'status' => 404,
88              'message' => 'Not Found'
89          ],
90          [
91              'mock' => AccessDeniedHttpException::class,
92              'status' => 403,
93              'message' => 'Forbidden'
94          ],
95          [
96              'mock' => ModelNotFoundException::class,
97              'status' => 404,
98              'message' => 'Not Found'
```

```
 99            ]
100       ];
101
102       foreach ($examples as $e) {
103           $exception = m::mock($e['mock']);
104           $exception->shouldReceive('getMessage')->andReturn(null);
105           $exception->shouldReceive('getStatusCode')->andReturn($e['status']);
106
107           /** @var JsonResponse $result */
108           $result = $subject->render($request, $exception);
109           $data = $result->getData();
110
111           $this->assertEquals($e['status'], $result->getStatusCode());
112           $this->assertEquals($e['message'], $data->error->message);
113           $this->assertEquals($e['status'], $data->error->status);
114       }
115  }
```

You need to import the ModelNotFoundException class (Listing 6-39) and run the test suite (Listing 6-40).

Listing 6-39. Importing ModelNotFoundException to Your HandlerTest Class

```
<?php

namespace Tests\App\Exceptions;

// ...
use Illuminate\Database\Eloquent\ModelNotFoundException;

class HandlerTest extends TestCase
{
    // ...
}
```

Listing 6-40. Running the Full Test Suite

```
# vagrant@homestead:~/Code/bookr$
$ phpunit

OK (16 tests, 62 assertions)
```

Adding a check for the ModelNotFoundException was fairly easy! Your Handler is in good shape. You now have test database migrations and factories working and a better exception response handler class.

ℹ Git commit: Handle Exceptions with a JSON Response

d5e41d7 (https://bitbucket.org/paulredmond/apress-bookr/commits/d5e41d7)

Listing 6-40 contains the final Handler file in full and Listing 6-40 contains the final HandlerTest file in full.

Listing 6-41. Final Handler.php File

```php
<?php

namespace App\Exceptions;

use Exception;
use Symfony\Component\HttpFoundation\Response;
use Illuminate\Validation\ValidationException;
use Illuminate\Auth\Access\AuthorizationException;
use Illuminate\Database\Eloquent\ModelNotFoundException;
use Symfony\Component\HttpKernel\Exception\HttpException;
use Laravel\Lumen\Exceptions\Handler as ExceptionHandler;

class Handler extends ExceptionHandler
{
    /**
     * A list of the exception types that should not be reported.
     *
     * @var array
     */
    protected $dontReport = [
        AuthorizationException::class,
        HttpException::class,
        ModelNotFoundException::class,
        ValidationException::class,
    ];

    /**
     * Report or log an exception.
     *
     * This is a great spot to send exceptions to Sentry, Bugsnag, etc.
     *
     * @param  \Exception  $e
     * @return void
     */
    public function report(Exception $e)
    {
        parent::report($e);
    }

    /**
     * Render an exception into an HTTP response.
     *
     * @param \Illuminate\Http\Request $request
     * @param \Exception $e
     * @return \Illuminate\Http\Response
     */
    public function render($request, Exception $e)
    {
        if ($request->wantsJson() && !($e instanceof ValidationException)) {
```

```php
        $response = [
            'message' => (string) $e->getMessage(),
            'status' => 400
        ];

        if ($e instanceof HttpException) {
            $response['message'] = Response::$statusTexts[$e->getStatusCode()];
            $response['status'] = $e->getStatusCode();
        } else if ($e instanceof ModelNotFoundException) {
            $response['message'] = Response::$statusTexts[Response::HTTP_NOT_FOUND];
            $response['status'] = Response::HTTP_NOT_FOUND;
        }

        if ($this->isDebugMode()) {
            $response['debug'] = [
                'exception' => get_class($e),
                'trace' => $e->getTrace()
            ];
        }

        return response()->json(['error' => $response], $response['status']);
    }

    return parent::render($request, $e);
}

/**
 * Determine if the application is in debug mode.
 *
 * @return Boolean
 */
public function isDebugMode()
{
    return (Boolean) env('APP_DEBUG');
}
}
```

Listing 6-42. Final HandlerTest.php

```php
<?php

namespace Tests\App\Exceptions;

use TestCase;
use \Mockery as m;
use App\Exceptions\Handler;
use Illuminate\Http\Request;
use Illuminate\Http\JsonResponse;
use Symfony\Component\HttpKernel\Exception\NotFoundHttpException;
use Symfony\Component\HttpKernel\Exception\AccessDeniedHttpException;
use Illuminate\Database\Eloquent\ModelNotFoundException;
```

```php
class HandlerTest extends TestCase
{
    /** @test **/
    public function it_responds_with_html_when_json_is_not_accepted()
    {
        // Make the mock a partial, you only want to mock the `isDebugMode` method
        $subject = m::mock(Handler::class)->makePartial();
        $subject->shouldNotReceive('isDebugMode');

        // Mock the interaction with the Request
        $request = m::mock(Request::class);
        $request->shouldReceive('wantsJson')->andReturn(false);

        // Mock the interaction with the exception
        $exception = m::mock(\Exception::class, ['Error!']);
        $exception->shouldNotReceive('getStatusCode');
        $exception->shouldNotReceive('getTrace');
        $exception->shouldNotReceive('getMessage');

        // Call the method under test, this is not a mocked method.
        $result = $subject->render($request, $exception);

        // Assert that `render` does not return a JsonResponse
        $this->assertNotInstanceOf(JsonResponse::class, $result);
    }

    /** @test */
    public function it_responds_with_json_for_json_consumers()
    {
        $subject = m::mock(Handler::class)->makePartial();
        $subject
            ->shouldReceive('isDebugMode')
            ->andReturn(false);

        $request = m::mock(Request::class);
        $request
            ->shouldReceive('wantsJson')
            ->andReturn(true);

        $exception = m::mock(\Exception::class, ['Doh!']);
        $exception
            ->shouldReceive('getMessage')
            ->andReturn('Doh!');

        /** @var JsonResponse $result */
        $result = $subject->render($request, $exception);
        $data = $result->getData();
```

```php
        $this->assertInstanceOf(JsonResponse::class, $result);
        $this->assertObjectHasAttribute('error', $data);
        $this->assertAttributeEquals('Doh!', 'message', $data->error);
        $this->assertAttributeEquals(400, 'status', $data->error);
    }

    /** @test */
    public function it_provides_json_responses_for_http_exceptions()
    {
        $subject = m::mock(Handler::class)->makePartial();
        $subject
            ->shouldReceive('isDebugMode')
            ->andReturn(false);

        $request = m::mock(Request::class);
        $request->shouldReceive('wantsJson')->andReturn(true);

        $examples = [
            [
                'mock' => NotFoundHttpException::class,
                'status' => 404,
                'message' => 'Not Found'
            ],
            [
                'mock' => AccessDeniedHttpException::class,
                'status' => 403,
                'message' => 'Forbidden'
            ],
            [
                'mock' => ModelNotFoundException::class,
                'status' => 404,
                'message' => 'Not Found'
            ]
        ];

        foreach ($examples as $e) {
            $exception = m::mock($e['mock']);
            $exception->shouldReceive('getMessage')->andReturn(null);
            $exception->shouldReceive('getStatusCode')->andReturn($e['status']);

            /** @var JsonResponse $result */
            $result = $subject->render($request, $exception);
            $data = $result->getData();

            $this->assertEquals($e['status'], $result->getStatusCode());
            $this->assertEquals($e['message'], $data->error->message);
            $this->assertEquals($e['status'], $data->error->status);
        }
    }
}
```

Conclusion

Your API now responds to exceptions more intelligently, and API consumers will get better feedback when things go wrong. Along the way, you worked on

- Defining model factories
- Using a dedicated test database
- Installing and using Mockery
- Customizing the App\Exceptions\Handler response
- Understanding how Lumen responds to exceptions

I hope you spend more time on your own playing with Mockery; it's a wonderful mocking library. Mocking takes time and practice but is well worth the effort.

CHAPTER 7

Leveling Up Responses

Your API responses work fine, but at the moment they don't scale very well. You need to make them more consistent across all endpoints by using conventions, as well as anticipate adding things like pagination to your response. If you've consumed a few APIs, you have probably noticed that response data formats vary between each API. Understanding each API format can be challenging enough, but add inconsistencies between endpoints within the same API and it can be a frustrating user experience.

Your current API response for all books looks something like Listing 7-1.

Listing 7-1. The GET /books JSON Response

```
[{
    "id": 1,
    "title": "War of the Worlds",
    "description": "A science fiction masterpiece about Martians invading London",
    "author": "H. G. Wells",
    "created_at": "2015-10-21 06:54:33",
    "updated_at": "2015-10-21 06:54:33"
}, {
    "id": 2,
    "title": "A Wrinkle in Time",
    "description": "A young girl goes on a mission to save her father who has gone missing
after working on a mysterious project called a tesseract.",
    "author": "Madeleine L'Engle",
    "created_at": "2015-10-21 06:54:33",
    "updated_at": "2015-10-21 06:54:33"
}]
```

The data format not *bad* per se, but what if you want to add metadata like pagination? Where will it go? It's easy to see how quickly your current response will crumble. Plus, right now each controller is responsible for formatting its response.

Introducing Fractal

I believe that the response handling code is one of the most critical parts of an API, and so you need to offload the responsibility from the controller to a service that the controller can use. You could write the code from scratch on your own, but Fractal (http://fractal.thephpleague.com/) provides a good (and flexible) solution for us. Fractal describes itself as follows:

© Paul Redmond 2016
P. Redmond, *Lumen Programming Guide*, DOI 10.1007/978-1-4842-2187-7_7

Fractal provides a presentation and transformation layer for complex data output, the like found in RESTful APIs, and works really well with JSON. Think of this as a view layer for your JSON/YAML/etc.

When building an API it is common for people to just grab stuff from the database and pass it to json_encode(). This might be passable for "trivial" APIs but if they are in use by the public, or used by mobile applications then this will quickly lead to inconsistent output.

Sounds exactly like what you need! Out of the box you can quickly get a format like that shown in Listing 7-2.

Listing 7-2. Example JSON Response Using Fractal

```
{
    "data": [{
        "id": 1,
        "title": "War of the Worlds",
        "description": "A science fiction masterpiece about Martians invading London",
        "author": "H. G. Wells",
        "created_at": "2015-10-21 06:54:33",
        "updated_at": "2015-10-21 06:54:33"
}, {
        "id": 2,
        "title": "A Wrinkle in Time",
        "description": "A young girl goes on a mission to save her father who has gone
        missing after working on a mysterious project called a tesseract.",
        "author": "Madeleine L'Engle",
        "created_at": "2015-10-21 06:54:33",
        "updated_at": "2015-10-21 06:54:33"
    }]
}
```

With the response content in a "data" key, you can add other things to the response without mixing it in with the book data. Fractal encourages good data design, and responses will be consistent across the API.

You need to install Fractal with Composer and then configure it so you can use it in your controllers. Various libraries exist to even integrate Fractal, but you are going to roll your own. Sometimes rolling your own is better than adding a dependency. Using Fractal is simple enough to use that you don't need to use a Laravel/Lumen integration.

I try to keep application dependencies to a minimum and invest in dependencies where it counts. You add complexity to your application with each new dependency and you increase the size of your application. Always weigh the value of using a vendor vs. rolling your own. In your case, Fractal makes sense and provides a good value for data transformation; but by rolling your own service provider to integrate Fractal you will learn (if you haven't used them in Laravel) how to write services.

First Version of API Response Formatting

Let's get to work on your first version of refactoring response formatting. You could start integrating Fractal immediately, but that's not an iterative approach. First, you will write test specifications and make the minimum change needed to support your response changes. Once you have the tests in place, you will be ready to make the move to the Fractal library.

You will cover the BooksController@index route test first (Listing 7-3).

Listing 7-3. Updating the BooksController@index Test

```
18   /** @test **/
19   public function index_should_return_a_collection_of_records()
20   {
21       $books = factory('App\Book', 2)->create();
22
23       $this->get('/books');
24       $expected = [
25           'data' => $books->toArray()
26       ];
27
28       $this->seeJsonEquals($expected);
29   }
```

You remove the foreach loop and use the *Collection::toArray()* method to create the expected JSON response. You check the data with seeJsonEquals() to make sure your response matches the actual response.

You should have a failing test now (Listing 7-4).

Listing 7-4. Failing PHPUnit Test

```
# vagrant@homestead:~/Code/bookr$
$ phpunit


1) Tests\App\Http\Controllers\BooksControllerTest::index_should_return_a_collect\
ion_of_records
Failed asserting that two strings are equal.
--- Expected
+++ Actual
@@ @@
-'{"data":[{"author":"Dortha Hodkiewicz"...
+'[{"author":"Dortha Hodkiewicz",...

/home/vagrant/Code/bookr/vendor/laravel/lumen-framework/src/Testing/CrawlerTrait\
.php:338
/home/vagrant/Code/bookr/tests/app/Http/Controllers/BooksControllerTest.php:28


FAILURES!
Tests: 16, Assertions: 61, Failures: 1.
```

Getting your test back to green is achieved by changing your return from a model collection to an array with a data key (Listing 7-5). After your change, the test suite should be back to green (Listing 7-6).

Listing 7-5. BooksController@index Data Implementation

```
15   /**
16    * GET /books
17    * @return array
18    */
19   public function index()
20   {
21       return ['data' => Book::all()->toArray()];
22   }
```

Listing 7-6. Passing PHPUnit Test for BooksController@index

```
# vagrant@homestead:~/Code/bookr$
$ phpunit

OK (16 tests, 61 assertions)
```

Next, update the BooksController@show test (Listing 7-7).

Listing 7-7. Updating the BooksController@show Test

```
31  /** @test **/
32  public function show_should_return_a_valid_book()
33  {
34      $book = factory('App\Book')->create();
35      $expected = [
36          'data' => $book->toArray()
37      ];
38      $this
39          ->get("/books/{$book->id}")
40          ->seeStatusCode(200)
41          ->seeJsonEquals($expected);
42  }
```

Your modified test now expects the book data to be inside the data key. Let's make sure your test fails now (Listing 7-8).

Listing 7-8. Failing PHPUnit Test for the BooksController@show Route

```
# vagrant@homestead:~/Code/bookr$
$ phpunit

1) Tests\App\Http\Controllers\BooksControllerTest::show_should_return_a_valid_bo\
ok
Failed asserting that two strings are equal.
--- Expected
+++ Actual
@@ @@
-'{"data":{"author":"Dr. Wyman Brown"...
+'{"author":"Dr. Wyman Brown"...

/home/vagrant/Code/bookr/vendor/laravel/lumen-framework/src/Testing/CrawlerTrait\
.php:338
/home/vagrant/Code/bookr/tests/app/Http/Controllers/BooksControllerTest.php:41

FAILURES!
Tests: 16, Assertions: 56, Failures: 1.
```

Getting your test passing with the minimum amount of code is similar to your BooksController@index change (Listing 7-9).

Listing 7-9. Getting the BooksController@show Route Back to Green

```
24  /**
25   * GET /books/{id}
26   * @param integer $id
27   * @return mixed
28   */
29  public function show($id)
30  {
31      return ['data' => Book::findOrFail($id)->toArray()];
32  }
```

The code change in Listing 7-10 gets your suite passing again.

Listing 7-10. Passing Tests After Updating BooksController@show

```
# vagrant@homestead:~/Code/bookr$
$ phpunit

OK (16 tests, 56 assertions)
```

The remaining routes are store and the update. In the original BooksController@store method you cheated a little bit and responded with {"created": true}, but let's return the new record data instead (Listing 7-11).

Listing 7-11. Updating the BooksController@store Response

```
71  /** @test */
72  public function store_should_save_new_book_in_the_database()
73  {
74      $this->post('/books', [
75          'title' => 'The Invisible Man',
76          'description' => 'An invisible man is trapped in the terror of his own
            creation',
77          'author' => 'H. G. Wells'
78      ]);
79
80      $body = json_decode($this->response->getContent(), true);
81      $this->assertArrayHasKey('data', $body);
82
83      $data = $body['data'];
84      $this->assertEquals('The Invisible Man', $data['title']);
85      $this->assertEquals(
86          'An invisible man is trapped in the terror of his own creation',
87          $data['description']
88      );
89      $this->assertEquals('H. G. Wells', $data['author']);
90      $this->assertTrue($data['id'] > 0, 'Expected a positive integer, but did not see
        one.');
91      $this->seeInDatabase('books', ['title' => 'The Invisible Man']);
92  }
```

Your failing test confirms that you are ready to get the test back to green (Listing 7-12).

Listing 7-12. Failing BooksController@store Test

```
# vagrant@homestead:~/Code/bookr$
$ phpunit

There was 1 failure:

1) Tests\App\Http\Controllers\BooksControllerTest::store_should_save_new_book_in\
_the_database
Failed asserting that an array has the key 'data'.

/home/vagrant/Code/bookr/tests/app/Http/Controllers/BooksControllerTest.php:78

FAILURES!
Tests: 16, Assertions: 55, Failures: 1.
```

The implementation swaps out the *"created": true* JSON with the newly created book data (Listing 7-13).

Listing 7-13. Updating the BooksController@store Method

```
34  /**
35   * POST /books
36   * @param Request $request
37   * @return \Symfony\Component\HttpFoundation\Response
38   */
39  public function store(Request $request)
40  {
41      $book = Book::create($request->all());
42
43      return response()->json(['data' => $book->toArray()], 201, [
44          'Location' => route('books.show', ['id' => $book->id])
45      ]);
46  }
```

Your suite should be fully passing again after your code change (Listing 7-14).

Listing 7-14. Passing BooksController@store Test

```
# vagrant@homestead:~/Code/bookr$
$ phpunit

OK (16 tests, 60 assertions)
```

The BooksController@update test is next. Update the code as shown in Listing 7-15 before writing the test to illustrate a caveat of using seeJson().

Listing 7-15. Updating the BooksController@update Method

```
48  /**
49   * PUT /books/{id}
50   * @param Request $request
51   * @param $id
52   * @return mixed
```

94

```
53    */
54    public function update(Request $request, $id)
55    {
56        try {
57            $book = Book::findOrFail($id);
58        } catch (ModelNotFoundException $e) {
59            return response()->json([
60                'error' => [
61                    'message' => 'Book not found'
62                ]
63            ], 404);
64        }
65
66        $book->fill($request->all());
67        $book->save();
68
69        return ['data' => $book->toArray()];
70    }
```

You've made a code change, and you should expect your tests to fail now (Listing 7-16), but they don't!

Listing 7-16. Running Tests After Changing BooksController@update. Will They Fail?

```
# vagrant@homestead:~/Code/bookr$
$ phpunit

OK (16 tests, 60 assertions)
```

The controller change did not cause your tests to fail—not good. You've introduced a breaking change to the API that your tests failed to catch. Your test does some response checking with seeJson, but it doesn't check the integrity of the JSON response. The seeJson() method checks *fragments* of JSON but not the location of the data. Be careful when you are writing tests to ensure the response format carefully. The seeJson() method is not to blame; you need to test for the data key (Listing 7-17).

Listing 7-17. Checking for the Data Key in the Response

```
110    /** @test **/
111    public function update_should_only_change_fillable_fields()
112    {
113        $book = factory('App\Book')->create([
114            'title' => 'War of the Worlds',
115            'description' => 'A science fiction masterpiece about Martians invading
                London',
116            'author' => 'H. G. Wells',
117        ]);
118
119        $this->notSeeInDatabase('books', [
120            'title' => 'The War of the Worlds',
121            'description' => 'The book is way better than the movie.',
122            'author' => 'Wells, H. G.'
123        ]);
124
```

```
125        $this->put("/books/{$book->id}", [
126            'id' => 5,
127            'title' => 'The War of the Worlds',
128            'description' => 'The book is way better than the movie.',
129            'author' => 'Wells, H. G.'
130        ]);
131
132        $this
133            ->seeStatusCode(200)
134            ->seeJson([
135                'id' => 1,
136                'title' => 'The War of the Worlds',
137                'description' => 'The book is way better than the movie.',
138                'author' => 'Wells, H. G.',
139            ])
140            ->seeInDatabase('books', [
141                'title' => 'The War of the Worlds'
142            ]);
143
144        // Verify the data key in the response
145        $body = json_decode($this->response->getContent(), true);
146        $this->assertArrayHasKey('data', $body);
147 }
```

At the end of the test you check the response body for the existence of the data key. If you revert the controller change you did first, you should now get a failing test (Listing 7-18).

Listing 7-18. Testing Results of Reverting the BooksController@update Route

```
# vagrant@homestead:~/Code/bookr$
$ phpunit

There was 1 failure:

1) Tests\App\Http\Controllers\BooksControllerTest::update_should_only_change_fil\
lable_fields
Failed asserting that an array has the key 'data'.
...

FAILURES!
Tests: 16, Assertions: 62, Failures: 1.
```

The test suite should be fully passing again. If you reverted the BooksController@update method to see the test fail, put the change back (Listing 7-19).

Listing 7-19. Fully Passing Test Suite

```
# vagrant@homestead:~/Code/bookr$
$ phpunit

OK (16 tests, 62 assertions)
```

ⓘ Git commit: Contain Book Responses in a `data` Attribute

9ded4b6 (https://bitbucket.org/paulredmond/apress-bookr/commits/9ded4b6)

The Fractal Response Class

Now that your tests are passing again, you are free to start refactoring code or adding new features. I could end the chapter now, but experience says that changing arrays to include a `data` key like you've done isn't going to scale very well. It does afford you passing tests and gives you the green light to refactor and make sure your tests still pass. As mentioned at the beginning of the chapter, you are going to lean on the Fractal library for handling your response data.

The first step is installing the Fractal (`http://fractal.thephpleague.com/`) library as a composer dependency (Listing 7-20).

Listing 7-20. Installing Fractal with Composer

```
# vagrant@homestead:~/Code/bookr$
$ composer require league/fractal=^0.13.0
```

You will take the following steps to refactor responses:

- Create a transformer (`http://fractal.thephpleague.com/transformers/`) for the Book model.

- Create a dedicated Fractal service to transform models.

- Create a service provider (`https://lumen.laravel.com/docs/5.2/providers`) to define the Fractal service.

- Use the service in the `BooksController` to return responses.

The Book Transformer

The first step is creating a transformer for the Book model. Transformers in Fractal are responsible for transforming data into an array format. Your application will pass Eloquent models into transformers, and the transformer will be responsible for formatting the model data into an array. You will see shortly how this works in your controllers, but first, you will write a test-driven Book transformer.

Create the transformer test class (Listing 7-21).

Listing 7-21. Creating the BookTransformerTest.php Test

```
# vagrant@homestead:~/Code/bookr$
$ mkdir -p tests/app/Transformer/
$ touch tests/app/Transformer/BookTransformerTest.php
```

Listing 7-22 shows the skeleton of your implementation class.

Listing 7-22. The BookTransformerTest Class Skeleton

```php
1   <?php
2
3   namespace Tests\App\Transformer;
4
5   use TestCase;
6   use App\Book;
7   use App\Transformer\BookTransformer;
8   use League\Fractal\TransformerAbstract;
9   use Laravel\Lumen\Testing\DatabaseMigrations;
10
11  class BookTransformerTest extends TestCase
12  {
13      use DatabaseMigrations;
14
15      /** @test **/
16      public function it_can_be_initialized()
17      {
18          $subject = new BookTransformer();
19          $this->assertInstanceOf(TransformerAbstract::class, $subject);
20      }
21  }
```

I like to write an initialization test for unit tests. I find that starting with a simple initialization test gets me past the mental hurdle of starting to write tests for a class, and I can start building off of that first test that just gets my foot in the door.

What happens if you run this test without creating the class (Listing 7-23)?

Listing 7-23. First Test Run For The BookTransforerTest

```
# vagrant@homestead:~/Code/bookr$
$ phpunit --filter=BookTransformerTest

There was 1 error:

1) Tests\App\Transformer\BookTransformerTest::it_can_be_initialized
Error: Class 'App\Transformer\BookTransformer' not found

/home/vagrant/Code/bookr/tests/app/Transformer/BookTransformerTest.php:18

FAILURES!
Tests: 1, Assertions: 0, Errors: 1.
```

Obviously, you haven't defined the BookTransformer yet, but it's nice that PHPUnit can keep us honest; to get the initialization test passing you must define the class (Listing 7-24).

Listing 7-24. Creating the BookTransformer Class

```
# vagrant@homestead:~/Code/bookr$
$ mkdir -p app/Transformer
$ touch app/Transformer/BookTransformer.php
```

Define the BookTransformer Class

```php
1   <?php
2
3   namespace App\Transformer;
4
5   use League\Fractal\TransformerAbstract;
6
7   class BookTransformer extends TransformerAbstract
8   {
9
10  }
```

Fractal transformers extend the *League\Fractal\TransformerAbstract* class provided by Fractal. All your transformers should extend this class.

Now that you have your BookTransformer class, your test should pass now (Listing 7-25).

Listing 7-25. The Initializable Test Passes

```
# vagrant@homestead:~/Code/bookr$
$ phpunit --filter=BookTransformerTest

OK (1 test, 1 assertion)
```

Ok, now you are ready to write your next test describing how the BookTransformer should transform a Book model (Listing 7-26). Transforming model data will allow all controllers rendering book data to use a consistent transformation.

Listing 7-26. Test to Transform a Book Model

```php
22  /** @test **/
23  public function it_transforms_a_book_model()
24  {
25      $book = factory(Book::class)->create();
26      $subject = new BookTransformer();
27
28      $transform = $subject->transform($book);
29
30      $this->assertArrayHasKey('id', $transform);
31      $this->assertArrayHasKey('title', $transform);
32      $this->assertArrayHasKey('description', $transform);
33      $this->assertArrayHasKey('author', $transform);
34      $this->assertArrayHasKey('created_at', $transform);
35      $this->assertArrayHasKey('updated_at', $transform);
36  }
```

You can see the missing method you have not defined in the transformer—the transform() method. The test passes a model from the factory that exists in the database, and then asserts that the model has all the keys you expect a book response to contain. The book must exist in the database because your transformer is transforming existing records, including the id attribute.

You are ready to write the BookTransformer::transform() implementation. The transform method allows you to define a public data interface of the book model while the internal details are hidden. This means that your internal logic can change but the API consumer continues to get the same data interface (Listing 7-27).

Listing 7-27. Writing the BookTransformer::transform() Method

```php
1   <?php
2
3   namespace App\Transformer;
4
5   use App\Book;
6   use League\Fractal\TransformerAbstract;
7
8   class BookTransformer extends TransformerAbstract
9   {
10      /**
11       * Transform a Book model into an array
12       *
13       * @param Book $book
14       * @return array
15       */
16      public function transform(Book $book)
17      {
18          return [
19              'id'          => $book->id,
20              'title'       => $book->title,
21              'description' => $book->description,
22              'author'      => $book->author,
23              'created'     => $book->created_at->toIso8601String(),
24              'updated'     => $book->updated_at->toIso8601String(),
25          ];
26      }
27  }
```

Note that the created and updated keys do not match your database column. What is really cool about using Fractal transformers is abstracting the API format from the database schema when it makes sense. In this case, is it necessary to change created_at into created? Probably not, but it serves as an illustration of how you can change the background implementation details and *continue to provide consistent data transformation* to the API user.

As an example, say that when a new book is created in the database you immediately offer it for sale in your online store. Imagine that the application needs to display how long ago the title was released in a relative format (Listing 7-28).

Listing 7-28. Example Transformation

```php
1   return [
2       'id' => $book->id,
3       'title' => $book->title,
4       'description' => $book->description,
5       'author' => $book->author,
6       'created' => $book->created_at->toIso8601String(),
7       'updated' => $book->updated_at->toIso8601String(),
8       'released' => $book->created_at->diffForHumans()
9   ]
```

In this example, the released key is tied to created_at field and uses Carbon's (http://carbon.nesbot.com/) diffForHumans() method to provide a relative date. In the future, you could change the 'released' key to use a 'published' datetime column from the database and the implementation details would be invisible to consumers. Note that the *created_at* and *updated_at* properties in the example are also Carbon instances.

DATE MUTATORS

Eloquent automatically provides a Carbon instance for created_at and updated_at, but you can configure your model to provide Carbon for other fields. See the "Date Mutators" section (https://laravel.com/docs/5.2/eloquent-mutators#date-mutators) in the Laravel documentation.

Next, you need to run your implementation to see if it satisfies your test (Listing 7-29).

Listing 7-29. Runing the BookTransformer Test

```
# vagrant@homestead:~/Code/bookr$
$ phpunit --filter=BookTransformerTest::it_transforms_a_book_model

There was 1 failure:

1) Tests\App\Transformer\BookTransformerTest::it_transforms_a_book_model
Failed asserting that an array has the key 'created_at'.

/home/vagrant/Code/bookr/tests/app/Transformer/BookTransformerTest.php:34

FAILURES!
Tests: 1, Assertions: 6, Failures: 1.
```

Whoops! Your test was looking for created_at but you designed your transformer to use created. Let's fix the test to match your transformer (Listing 7-30) and run the test again.

Listing 7-30. Fixing the BookTransformerTest to Match BookTransformer::transform()

```
34  $this->assertArrayHasKey('created', $transform);
35  $this->assertArrayHasKey('updated', $transform);
```

With your created and updated key assertions, let's run your test again (Listing 7-31).

Listing 7-31. Running PHPUnit Test for the BookTransfomer

```
# vagrant@homestead:~/Code/bookr$
$ phpunit --filter=BookTransformerTest::it_transforms_a_book_model

OK (1 test, 7 assertions)
```

The Fractal Response Class

It's time to move on to your Fractal response class. If you look at the Fractal documentation for a simple transformer example (http://fractal.thephpleague.com/simple-example/), you will see that you need a League\Fractal\Manager class. You could use the manager class directly in your controllers, but let's provide a service for the Fractal manager.

You will call your service *App\Http\Response\FractalResponse* and start by writing some tests for it (Listing 7-32).

Listing 7-32. Setting Up the FractalResponse Files

```
# vagrant@homestead:~/Code/bookr$
$ mkdir -p app/Http/Response
$ touch app/Http/Response/FractalResponse.php
$ mkdir -p tests/app/Http/Response
$ touch tests/app/Http/Response/FractalResponseTest.php
```

Write the class initialization test first (Listing 7-33).

Listing 7-33. Test for FractalResponse Initialization

```
1   <?php
2
3   namespace Tests\App\Http\Response;
4
5   use TestCase;
6   use App\Http\Response\FractalResponse;
7
8   class FractalResponseTest extends TestCase
9   {
10      /** @test **/
11      public function it_can_be_initialized()
12      {
13          $this->assertInstanceOf(FractalResponse::class, new FractalResponse());
14      }
15  }
```

Running the test will fail at this point. Listing 7-34 shows the initial class skeleton to get it passing again.

Listing 7-34. Initial FractalResponse Skeleton Class

```
1   <?php
2
3   namespace App\Http\Response;
4
5   class FractalResponse
6   {
7       public function __construct()
8       {
9
10      }
11  }
```

The FractalResponse constructor will have a few dependencies: a *League\Fractal\Manager* instance and a DataArraySerializer (http://fractal.thephpleague.com/serializers/#dataarrayserializer) instance.

Serializers provide structure around your data without affecting transformers—in your case, that means wrapping your transformer output in a "data" property using the DataArraySerializer. The manager sets the serializer by calling setSerializer() and passing a serializer instance. Serializers extend from the *League\Fractal\Serializer\SerializerAbstract* class so you can even write your unit tests against the abstract implementation!

Let's flesh out your FractalResponse initialization dependencies in a test (Listing 7-35).

Listing 7-35. Testing the FractalResponse with a Manager Dependency

```php
1   <?php
2
3   namespace Tests\App\Http\Response;
4
5   use TestCase;
6   use Mockery as m;
7   use League\Fractal\Manager;
8   use App\Http\Response\FractalResponse;
9   use League\Fractal\Serializer\SerializerAbstract;
10
11  class FractalResponseTest extends TestCase
12  {
13      /** @test **/
14      public function it_can_be_initialized()
15      {
16          $manager = m::mock(Manager::class);
17          $serializer = m::mock(SerializerAbstract::class);
18
19          $manager
20              ->shouldReceive('setSerializer')
21              ->with($serializer)
22              ->once()
23              ->andReturn($manager);
24
25          $fractal = new FractalResponse($manager, $serializer);
26          $this->assertInstanceOf(FractalResponse::class, $fractal);
27      }
28  }
```

The whole class is provided for clarity. Note the use of Mockery's *shouldReceive* method, which sets an expectation that FractalResponse calls setSerializer once. The test mocks SerializerAbstract and expects that the manager will receive a call to setSerializer with the mock. The last part of test asserts the FractalResponse class was successfully initialized.

It's time to ensure that your new test fails (Listing 7-36).

Listing 7-36. Testing Initialization of FractalResponse

```
# vagrant@homestead:~/Code/bookr$
$ phpunit --filter=FractalResponseTest
```

There was 1 error:

```
1) Tests\App\Http\Response\FractalResponseTest::it_can_be_initialized
Mockery\Exception\InvalidCountException: Method setSerializer(object(Mockery_7_L\
eague_Fractal_Serializer_SerializerAbstract)) from Mockery_6_League_Fractal_Manager should
be called
exactly 1 times but called 0 times.
```

```
/home/vagrant/Code/bookr/vendor/mockery/mockery/library/Mockery/CountValidator/Exact.php:37
/home/vagrant/Code/bookr/vendor/mockery/mockery/library/Mockery/Expectation.php:271
/home/vagrant/Code/bookr/vendor/mockery/mockery/library/Mockery/ExpectationDirector.php:120
/home/vagrant/Code/bookr/vendor/mockery/mockery/library/Mockery/Container.php:297
/home/vagrant/Code/bookr/vendor/mockery/mockery/library/Mockery/Container.php:282
/home/vagrant/Code/bookr/vendor/mockery/mockery/library/Mockery.php:142
/home/vagrant/Code/bookr/vendor/mockery/mockery/library/Mockery/Adapter/Phpunit/
MockeryPHPUnitIntegration.php:24
```

```
FAILURES!
Tests: 1, Assertions: 2, Errors: 1.
```

You will notice that Mockery expected setSerializer() to be called once, but you haven't introduced the manager and serializer parameters in the constructor. Now you are ready to write out your implementation (Listing 7-37).

Listing 7-37. FractalResponse Defines the Manager and Serializer Dependencies

```php
1   <?php
2
3   namespace App\Http\Response;
4
5   use League\Fractal\Manager;
6   use League\Fractal\Serializer\SerializerAbstract;
7
8   class FractalResponse
9   {
10      /**
11       * @var Manager
12       */
13      private $manager;
14
15      /**
16       * @var SerializerAbstract
17       */
18      private $serializer;
19
20      public function __construct(Manager $manager, SerializerAbstract $serializer)
21      {
22          $this->manager = $manager;
23          $this->serializer = $serializer;
24          $this->manager->setSerializer($serializer);
25      }
26  }
```

Your constructor type hints SerializerAbstract, which allows you to accept any instance that extends the abstract class so you can swap it out whenever you wish.

The FractalResponse class is not very useful right now; you are ready to add a few methods that controllers can use to create response data. You know, based on your BooksController, that you need to support serializing collections and individual records. You will define two public methods, *FractalResponse::item()* and *FractalResponse::collection()*, which will use Resources (http://fractal.thephpleague.com/resources/) to transform the data and convert it into an array.

Listing 7-38 is an example of how you will use your service.

Listing 7-38. Example FractalResponse Method Usage

```
// BooksController::show()
return $this->fractal->item($book, new BookTransformer());

// BooksController::index()
return $this->fractal->collection($books, new BookTransformer());
```

You will start with the FractalResponse::item() method first. The basic usage of Fractal to return an item might look like Listing 7-39.

Listing 7-39. Example Usage of Fractal Manager Item

```
$data = ['bar' => 'bar'];
$manager = new \League\Fractal\Manager();
$item = new \League\Fractal\Resource\Item($data, function (array $data) {
    return [
        'foo' => $data['bar']
    ];
});

$manager->createData($item)->toArray();
```

In this code, you create a Manager instance and an Item resource. The manager calls createData(), which returns an instance of *League\Fractal\Scope*, and then you chain a toArray() call on the scope. This simple example illustrates using a Closure but you will pass a transformer object in your implementation.

With that in mind, write a test for your FractalResponse::item() method (Listing 7-40).

Listing 7-40. Test for the FractalResponse::item() Method

```
29  /** @test **/
30  public function it_can_transform_an_item()
31  {
32      // Transformer
33      $transformer = m::mock('League\Fractal\TransformerAbstract');
34
35      // Scope
36      $scope = m::mock('League\Fractal\Scope');
37      $scope
38          ->shouldReceive('toArray')
39          ->once()
40          ->andReturn(['foo' => 'bar']);
41
```

```
42        // Serializer
43        $serializer = m::mock('League\Fractal\Serializer\SerializerAbstract');
44
45        $manager = m::mock('League\Fractal\Manager');
46        $manager
47            ->shouldReceive('setSerializer')
48            ->with($serializer)
49            ->once();
50
51        $manager
52            ->shouldReceive('createData')
53            ->once()
54            ->andReturn($scope);
55
56        $subject = new FractalResponse($manager, $serializer);
57        $this->assertInternalType(
58            'array',
59            $subject->item(['foo' => 'bar'], $transformer)
60        );
61   }
```

This is a pretty long test, so let's break it down:

- You mock a transformer that the item method will accept (BookTransformer).

- You mock a Scope object that will be returned from the Manager::createData() method call.

- You mock the serializer to initialize your class.

- You mock the manager class, which should receive a call to createdData and setSerializer.

- Finally, you initialize the class under test and assert that the item method returns the internal type array.

I must say, it's pretty neat when tests help design how you write your implementation. Now that you have a failing test (you can run it on your own) you are ready to write some code (Listing 7-41).

Listing 7-41. The FractalResponse::item() Implementation

```php
1    <?php
2
3    namespace App\Http\Response;
4
5    use League\Fractal\Manager;
6    use League\Fractal\Resource\Item;
7    use League\Fractal\TransformerAbstract;
8    use League\Fractal\Serializer\SerializerAbstract;
9
10   class FractalResponse
11   {
12       /**
13        * @var Manager
```

```
14      */
15     private $manager;
16
17     /**
18      * @var SerializerAbstract
19      */
20     private $serializer;
21
22     public function __construct(Manager $manager, SerializerAbstract $serializer)
23     {
24         $this->manager = $manager;
25         $this->serializer = $serializer;
26         $this->manager->setSerializer($serializer);
27     }
28
29     public function item($data, TransformerAbstract $transformer, $resourceKey = null)
30     {
31         $resource = new Item($data, $transformer, $resourceKey);
32
33         return $this->manager->createData($resource)->toArray();
34     }
35 }
```

The item() method accepts the data to be transformed, a transformer (BookTransformer), and a resource key. You will not be using the resource key, but you want to support the full League\Fractal\Resource\Item API. You create a new League\Fractal\Resource\Item instance and pass it to the manager's createData method. The createData method returns a League\Fractal\Scope instance and you call toArray to return array data from the League\Fractal\Scope instance.

ℹ️ You can read about resource keys in the official Fractal serializer (http://fractal.thephpleague.com/serializers/) documentation

---

You are ready to run the tests after your first stab at the implementation (Listing 7-42).

Listing 7-42. Testing the FractalResponse::item() Implementation

```
# vagrant@homestead:~/Code/bookr$
$ phpunit

OK (20 tests, 75 assertions)
```

You can move on to your collection method test. The *FractalResponse::collection()* method is very similar to the item method, so I won't spend much time on it. You will be passing the collection method an *Illuminate\Database\Eloquent\Collection* to iterate over the collection and transform each item. Listing 7-43 shows the test for the collection method.

Listing 7-43. Initial Test for the FractalResponse::collection() Method

```
63  /** @test **/
64  public function it_can_transform_a_collection()
65  {
66      $data = [
67          ['foo' => 'bar'],
```

```
68              ['fizz' => 'buzz'],
69          ];
70
71          // Transformer
72          $transformer = m::mock('League\Fractal\TransformerAbstract');
73
74          // Scope
75          $scope = m::mock('League\Fractal\Scope');
76          $scope
77              ->shouldReceive('toArray')
78              ->once()
79              ->andReturn($data);
80
81          // Serializer
82          $serializer = m::mock('League\Fractal\Serializer\SerializerAbstract');
83
84          $manager = m::mock('League\Fractal\Manager');
85          $manager
86              ->shouldReceive('setSerializer')
87              ->with($serializer)
88              ->once();
89
90          $manager
91              ->shouldReceive('createData')
92              ->once()
93              ->andReturn($scope);
94
95          $subject = new FractalResponse($manager, $serializer);
96          $this->assertInternalType(
97              'array',
98              $subject->collection($data, $transformer)
99          );
100 }
```

This test is nearly identical to your *FractalResponseTest::it_can_transform_an_item()* test. The only difference is that you are calling the collection method instead. You could merge the item and collection tests into one, but let's leave them separate for clarity.

Listing 7-44 shows the implementation for FractalResponse::collection().

Listing 7-44. The FractalResponse::collection() Implementation

```php
1   <?php
2
3   namespace App\Http\Response;
4
5   use League\Fractal\Manager;
6   use League\Fractal\Resource\Item;
7   use League\Fractal\TransformerAbstract;
8   use League\Fractal\Resource\Collection;
9   use League\Fractal\Serializer\SerializerAbstract;
10
11  class FractalResponse
```

```
12  {
13      /**
14       * @var Manager
15       */
16      private $manager;
17
18      /**
19       * @var SerializerAbstract
20       */
21      private $serializer;
22
23      public function __construct(Manager $manager, SerializerAbstract $serializer)
24      {
25          $this->manager = $manager;
26          $this->serializer = $serializer;
27          $this->manager->setSerializer($serializer);
28      }
29
30      public function item($data, TransformerAbstract $transformer, $resourceKey = null)
31      {
32          $resource = new Item($data, $transformer, $resourceKey);
33
34          return $this->manager->createData($resource)->toArray();
35      }
36
37      public function collection($data, TransformerAbstract $transformer, $resourceKey =
        null)
38      {
39          $resource = new Collection($data, $transformer, $resourceKey);
40
41          return $this->manager->createData($resource)->toArray();
42      }
43  }
```

The collection endpoint initializes a League\Fractal\Resource\Collection instance, but everything else is exactly the same. Both the item and collection methods duplicate creating the data and converting it to an array. All tests should be passing, so you are now able to refactor out the duplication (Listing 7-45).

Listing 7-45. Refactoring FractalResponse::item() and FractalResponse::collection()

```
1   <?php
2
3   namespace App\Http\Response;
4
5   use League\Fractal\Manager;
6   use League\Fractal\Resource\Item;
7   use League\Fractal\TransformerAbstract;
8   use League\Fractal\Resource\Collection;
9   use League\Fractal\Resource\ResourceInterface;
10  use League\Fractal\Serializer\SerializerAbstract;
11
12  class FractalResponse
```

```
13  {
14      /**
15       * @var Manager
16       */
17      private $manager;
18
19      /**
20       * @var SerializerAbstract
21       */
22      private $serializer;
23
24      public function __construct(Manager $manager, SerializerAbstract $serializer)
25      {
26          $this->manager = $manager;
27          $this->serializer = $serializer;
28          $this->manager->setSerializer($serializer);
29      }
30
31      public function item($data, TransformerAbstract $transformer, $resourceKey = null)
32      {
33          return $this->createDataArray(
34              new Item($data, $transformer, $resourceKey)
35          );
36      }
37
38      public function collection($data, TransformerAbstract $transformer, $resourceKey =
    null)
39      {
40          return $this->createDataArray(
41              new Collection($data, $transformer, $resourceKey)
42          );
43      }
44
45      private function createDataArray(ResourceInterface $resource)
46      {
47          return $this->manager->createData($resource)->toArray();
48      }
49  }
```

After your refactor, you should run the test suite again to make sure all tests still pass (Listing 7-46).

Listing 7-46. Making Sure Tests Still Pass After the Refactoring

```
# vagrant@homestead:~/Code/bookr$
$ phpunit

OK (21 tests, 79 assertions)
```

You didn't do anything ground-breaking, but you did consolidated duplicate code while using your passing tests to refactor. Refactoring is an important part of the test-driven process because the goal is to get tests passing with minimal code, and then improve the minimal code while keeping tests passing.

ⓘ Git commit: Add FractalResponse Class

f1123c8 (https://bitbucket.org/paulredmond/apress-bookr/commits/f1123c8)

Fractal Response Service

The FractalResponse class is ready to be used in your BooksController. What is really cool is that you wrote the implementation in isolation, but the tests provide a good degree of confidence that it will work. Writing it in isolation also has the benefit of helping you resist the temptation to start integrating before fully testing.

How should you go about integrating the FractalResponse class in your controllers? One option would be to create an instance of FractalResponse in the controller, as shown in Listing 7-47.

Listing 7-47. One Option: Using the FractalResponse Object in the Controller

```
1  public function __construct() {
2      // ...
3      $this->fractal = new FractalResponse($manager, $serializer);
4  }
```

Constructing a new instance of the FractalResponse in the controller means that you also need to create an instance of the manager and serializer, and pass them to the FractalResponse constructor. Doing this by hand each time you need them sounds like a bad time.

A facade would work, and that is definitely a viable option (Listing 7-48).

Listing 7-48. Using the Façade Option

```
1  // An individual book
2  return FractalResponse::item($book, new BookTransformer());
3
4  // A collection of books
5  return FractalResponse::collection($books, new BookTransformer());
```

In this book you will not use either option; instead you will define a Service Provider (https://lumen.laravel.com/docs/5.2/providers) to resolve a fully initialized FractalResponse instance anywhere you need it. Laravel provides a powerful and easy-to-use service container (https://laravel.com/docs/5.2/container) that you will use to define a FractalResponse service.

Service providers are used to bootstrap the application by registering service container bindings (among other things) which can be resolved from the service container. This means that you need to define a service for the FractalResponse class that you can resolve out of the container.

In Lumen, providers are configured in the *bootstrap/app.php* file. Listing 7-49 shows what the section looks like by default at the time of writing.

Listing 7-49. Boilerplate Service Provider Configuration

```
70  /*
71  |--------------------------------------------------------------------------
72  | Register Service Providers
73  |--------------------------------------------------------------------------
74  |
```

```
75  | Here you will register all of the application's service providers which
76  | are used to bind services into the container. Service providers are
77  | totally optional, so you are not required to uncomment this line.
78  |
79  */
80
81  // $app->register(App\Providers\AppServiceProvider::class);
82  // $app->register(App\Providers\AuthServiceProvider::class);
83  // $app->register(App\Providers\EventServiceProvider::class);
```

As you can see, the framework provides an *AppServiceProvider* class that you could use to register application services. You will create your own service provider class because you will benefit from learning how to create one, but more commonly you would use the AppServiceProvider to define your application services.

Let's start by creating your new service provider class (Listing 7-50).

Listing 7-50. Creating the FractalServiceProvider Class

```
# vagrant@homestead:~/Code/bookr$
$ touch app/Providers/FractalServiceProvider.php
```

Add the code in Listing 7-51 to the newly created file.

Listing 7-51. A Skeleton FractalServiceProvider Class

```php
1   <?php
2
3   namespace App\Providers;
4
5   use Illuminate\Support\ServiceProvider;
6
7   class FractalServiceProvider extends ServiceProvider
8   {
9       public function register()
10      {
11
12      }
13
14      public function boot()
15      {
16
17      }
18  }
```

Service providers can be defined anywhere you want; however, let's use the convention provided in Lumen, which is under the *App\Providers* namespace. Service providers must define a *register()* method. The sole purpose of the `register` method is to bind things to the service container.

The boot method is called after all other services have been registered, and is optional. One example of using the boot method is loading configuration that your provider needs. You don't need to use boot in the *FractalServiceProvider*, but it was included for awareness. I will not delve into the full ServiceProvider API; read the service provider documentation (`https://lumen.laravel.com/docs/5.2/providers`) and browse the source code to learn more.

With a bit of background behind us, let's register your service (Listing 7-52).

Listing 7-52. Defining the FractalResponse Service

```php
1   <?php
2
3   namespace App\Providers;
4
5   use League\Fractal\Manager;
6   use App\Http\Response\FractalResponse;
7   use Illuminate\Support\ServiceProvider;
8   use League\Fractal\Serializer\DataArraySerializer;
9
10  class FractalServiceProvider extends ServiceProvider
11  {
12      public function register()
13      {
14          // Bind the DataArraySerializer to an interface contract
15          $this->app->bind(
16              'League\Fractal\Serializer\SerializerAbstract',
17              'League\Fractal\Serializer\DataArraySerializer'
18          );
19
20          $this->app->bind(FractalResponse::class, function ($app) {
21              $manager = new Manager();
22              $serializer = $app['League\Fractal\Serializer\SerializerAbstract'];
23
24              return new FractalResponse($manager, $serializer);
25          });
26
27          $this->app->alias(FractalResponse::class, 'fractal');
28      }
29  }
```

The first thing the register method does is bind the *DataArraySerializer* implementation to the abstract serializer. When you type-hint *League\Fractal\Serializer\SerializerAbstract* the container will resolve League\Fractal\Serializer\DataArraySerializer for you. Binding is powerful because when you code to an interface you can change the implementation in the provider, and classes consuming the service will not know the difference.

Secondly, you define your FractalResponse service. The $this->app->bind() call accepts the abstract name, and the second argument can be a concrete implementation (like your DataArraySerializer class) or a Closure. When you pass a Closure, it accepts your application instance ($app) as an argument. In the closure, you construct a League\Fractal\Manager instance and reference the SerializerAbstract from the container, which was the contract you bound to the DataArraySerializer. Lastly, you create and return the FractalResponse instance.

The last thing you do in the register method is call $this->app->alias(), which will alias your service to a shorter name when you ask for it from the container. The alias is a convenient short name to the service but is not required.

You can now access your service in a few ways (Listing 7-53).

Listing 7-53. Different Ways to Resolve the FractalResponse Service

```php
$fractal = app('App\Http\Response\FractalResponse');
$fractal = \App::make('App\Http\Response\FractalResponse');
```

```
// Using the alias you defined:
$fractal = app('fractal');

// Or via constructor hinting for the classes the container resolves
class MyController extends Controller
{
    public function __construct(App\Http\Response\FractalResponse $fractal)
    {
        $this->fractal = $fractal;
    }
}
```

For your particular use case, you will use the constructor to easily provide all of your controllers with the FractalResponse service.

The next step in finishing the service provider is registering the provider in your application. Open the bootstrap/app.php file and add the code in Listing 7-54.

Listing 7-54. Registering the FractalServiceProvider

```
81  // $app->register(App\Providers\AppServiceProvider::class);
82  // $app->register(App\Providers\AuthServiceProvider::class);
83  // $app->register(App\Providers\EventServiceProvider::class);
84
85  $app->register(\App\Providers\FractalServiceProvider::class);
```

You can now resolve the FractalResponse class from the service container, and you are ready to integrate the service into your BooksController class in the next section. Onward!

Integrating the Fractal Response Service

Your final task is integrating the FractalResponse service. You could make each controller resolve the service out of the container, but you want to provide consistency across all your responses. The *App\Http\Controllers\ Controller* class sounds like a good place to resolve the service because all controllers extend from it. Edit *app/Http/Controllers/Controller.php* and add the code from Listing 7-55 for your controllers to use.

Listing 7-55. Integrating the FractalResponse Service in the Base Controller

```
1   <?php
2
3   namespace App\Http\Controllers;
4
5   use App\Http\Response\FractalResponse;
6   use Laravel\Lumen\Routing\Controller as BaseController;
7   use League\Fractal\TransformerAbstract;
8
9   class Controller extends BaseController
10  {
11      /**
12       * @var FractalResponse
13       */
14      private $fractal;
```

```
15
16      public function __construct(FractalResponse $fractal)
17      {
18          $this->fractal = $fractal;
19      }
20
21      /**
22       * @param $data
23       * @param TransformerAbstract $transformer
24       * @param null $resourceKey
25       * @return array
26       */
27      public function item($data, TransformerAbstract $transformer, $resourceKey = null)
29      {
30          return $this->fractal->item($data, $transformer, $resourceKey);
31      }
32
33      /**
34       * @param $data
35       * @param TransformerAbstract $transformer
36       * @param null $resourceKey
37       * @return array
38       */
39      public function collection($data, TransformerAbstract $transformer, $resourceKey =
        null)
41      {
42          return $this->fractal->collection($data, $transformer, $resourceKey);
43      }
44  }
```

The constructor method type-hints the FractalResponse argument that the service container will resolve automatically when initializing the controller. The item and collection methods are pass-through methods to the FractalResponse service. You could make the methods more generic like respondWithItem and take care of the response, but what you have is good enough for now. You can refactor when you sense duplication and brittle code.

Let's try your first integration with the BooksController. Be sure to add *use App\Transformer\ BookTransformer;* and *extends Controller* to start using the base application controller at the top of *app/Http/Controllers/BooksController.php* (Listing 7-56).

Listing 7-56. Using the FractalResponse Service in the BooksController

```
1   <?php
2
3   namespace App\Http\Controllers;
4
5   use App\Book;
6   use Illuminate\Http\Request;
7   use App\Transformer\BookTransformer;
8   use Illuminate\Database\Eloquent\ModelNotFoundException;
9
10  /**
11   * Class BooksController
```

```
12    * @package App\Http\Controllers
13    */
14   class BooksController extends Controller
15   {
16       /**
17        * GET /books
18        * @return array
19        */
20       public function index()
21       {
22           return $this->collection(Book::all(), new BookTransformer());
23       }
24       // ...
25   }
```

Importantly, the BooksController is now extending the base Controller class found in the same folder. **Don't forget to extend this controller now**, because you need it to inherit the collection and item methods you just wrote! The BooksController@index method calls the App\Http\ Controller::collection() method and passes the Eloquent collection and the BookTransformer as parameters. The method returns an array that will resemble the JSON response in Listing 7-57.

Listing 7-57. The /books Response Using the FractalResponse Service

```
{
    "data": [
        {
            "author": "H. G. Wells",
            "created": "2015-10-21T06:54:33+0000",
            "description": "A science fiction masterpiece about Martians invading London",
            "id": 1,
            "title": "War of the Worlds",
            "updated": "2015-10-21T06:54:33+0000"
        },
        {
            "author": "Madeleine L'Engle",
            "created": "2015-10-21T06:54:33+0000",
            "description": "A young girl goes on a mission to save her father who has gone
            missing after working on a mysterious project called a tesseract.",
            "id": 2,
            "title": "A Wrinkle in Time",
            "updated": "2015-10-21T06:54:33+0000"
        }
    ]
}
```

Let's run a test to see if your integration is working (Listing 7-58).

Listing 7-58. Test Failure After Integrating Fractal

```
# vagrant@homestead:~/Code/bookr$
$ phpunit
```

```
There was 1 failure:

1) Tests\App\Http\Controllers\BooksControllerTest::index_should_return_a_collection_of_
records
Failed asserting that two strings are equal.
...
```

It looks like your response test doesn't match the response from the controller. If you recall, the BooksControllerTest test was updated earlier when you added the data key (Listing 7-59).

Listing 7-59. Your Index Test for a Collection of Books

```
/** @test **/
public function index_should_return_a_collection_of_records()
{
    $books = factory('App\Book', 2)->create();

    $this->get('/books');

    $expected = [
        'data' => $books->toArray()
    ];

    $this->seeJsonEquals($expected);
}
```

The $books->toArray() method will do the equivalent of (string) $book->created_at to the date, but your new transformer is using $book->created_at->toIso8601String(). The transformer is also defining a created property but your test is expecting a created_at property. Let's fix the test to pass again (Listing 7-60).

Listing 7-60. Changing the Test to Assert the BookTransformer Correctly

```
18  /** @test **/
19  public function index_should_return_a_collection_of_records()
20  {
21      $books = factory('App\Book', 2)->create();
22
23      $this->get('/books');
24
25      $content = json_decode($this->response->getContent(), true);
26      $this->assertArrayHasKey('data', $content);
27
28      foreach ($books as $book) {
29          $this->seeJson([
30              'id' => $book->id,
31              'title' => $book->title,
32              'description' => $book->description,
33              'author' => $book->author,
34              'created' => $book->created_at->toIso8601String(),
35              'updated' => $book->updated_at->toIso8601String(),
36          ]);
37      }
38  }
```

After getting the /books response, you check for the data key and then loop through the factory models to ensure they are all in the response correctly. With your change in place, you will see if the tests pass now (Listing 7-61).

Listing 7-61. Running the Test Suite

```
# vagrant@homestead:~/Code/bookr$
$ phpunit

OK (21 tests, 92 assertions)
```

The BooksController@show method is next (Listing 7-62).

Listing 7-62. Updating BooksController@show to Use Fractal

```
25  /**
26   * GET /books/{id}
27   * @param integer $id
28   * @return mixed
29   */
30  public function show($id)
31  {
32      return $this->item(Book::findOrFail($id), new BookTransformer());
33  }
```

The @show method is using the inherited Controller::item() method you built earlier. You are refactoring at this point so you should expect your tests to pass. If not, you need to fix them before moving on (Listing 7-63).

Listing 7-63. Running the Test Suite after Refactoring BooksController@show

```
# vagrant@homestead:~/Code/bookr$
$ phpunit

There was 1 failure:

1) Tests\App\Http\Controllers\BooksControllerTest::show_should_return_a_valid_book
Failed asserting that two strings are equal.
```

Darn! If you have a keen eye, you can see that you have the same issue in the BooksController@show test that you just fixed for the BooksController@index test (Listing 7-64).

Listing 7-64. Updating the BooksController@show Test

```
40  /** @test **/
41  public function show_should_return_a_valid_book()
42  {
43      $book = factory('App\Book')->create();
44
45      $this
46          ->get("/books/{$book->id}")
47          ->seeStatusCode(200);
48
```

```
49        // Get the response and assert the data key exists
50        $content = json_decode($this->response->getContent(), true);
51        $this->assertArrayHasKey('data', $content);
52        $data = $content['data'];
53
54        // Assert the Book Properties match
55        $this->assertEquals($book->id, $data['id']);
56        $this->assertEquals($book->title, $data['title']);
57        $this->assertEquals($book->description, $data['description']);
58        $this->assertEquals($book->author, $data['author']);
59        $this->assertEquals($book->created_at->toIso8601String(), $data['created']);
60        $this->assertEquals($book->updated_at->toIso8601String(), $data['created']);
61  }
```

Your test now asserts each property instead of the whole model data all at once. With this change, and more granular checking, let's see if the tests are passing now (Listing 7-65).

Listing 7-65. Running the Test Suite

```
# vagrant@homestead:~/Code/bookr$
$ phpunit

OK (21 tests, 98 assertions)
```

Your next refactor is the BooksController@store method (Listing 7-66).

Listing 7-66. Refactoring BooksController@store to Use Fractal

```
35  /**
36   * POST /books
37   * @param Request $request
38   * @return \Symfony\Component\HttpFoundation\Response
39   */
40  public function store(Request $request)
41  {
42      $book = Book::create($request->all());
43      $data = $this->item($book, new BookTransformer());
44
45      return response()->json($data, 201, [
46          'Location' => route('books.show', ['id' => $book->id])
47      ]);
48  }
```

Nothing in this example that you haven't seen before, so let's run the tests (Listing 7-67).

Listing 7-67. Running the Test Suite

```
# vagrant@homestead:~/Code/bookr$
$ phpunit

OK (21 tests, 98 assertions)
```

Your tests pass, but you should review them to make sure they still cover everything. If you look at the *store_should_save_new_book_in_the_database* test, notice that it doesn't check for the *created* or *updated* field. You can either provide extra assertions to check, or you can rely on the *BookTransformer::it_transforms_a_book_model()* test to ensure that this works correctly. Your test is an integration test, so let's add the additional checks. You cannot guarantee at this point that the BookTransformer is being used.

You have one problem, though: if you assert the value of created and updated, how do you know what to expect? These fields are populated dynamically when the book is created. Lucky for us, Lumen uses the Carbon (http://carbon.nesbot.com/) library to work with dates in Eloquent.

If you browse the Carbon documentation or the API, you will find the *Carbon::setTestNow()* method; you need to mock the time so you know what to expect! Mocking Carbon makes testing dates really easy!

In preparation to updating your test, you need to add a *setUp* and *tearDown* method so you can test dates in each test and then reset Carbon afterwards (Listing 7-68).

Listing 7-68. Mocking Carbon in the BooksControllerTest Class (Partial Source)

```php
1  <?php
2
3  namespace Tests\App\Http\Controllers;
4
5  use TestCase;
6  use Carbon\Carbon;
7  use Illuminate\Foundation\Testing\DatabaseMigrations;
8
9  class BooksControllerTest extends TestCase
10 {
11     use DatabaseMigrations;
12
13     public function setUp()
14     {
15         parent::setUp();
16
17         Carbon::setTestNow(Carbon::now('UTC'));
18     }
19
20     public function tearDown()
21     {
22         parent::tearDown();
23
24         Carbon::setTestNow();
25     }
26     // ...
27 }
```

At the top of your BooksControllerTest you import Carbon with use Carbon\Carbon;. You override the setUp and tearDown methods (see https://phpunit.de/manual/current/en/fixtures.html) to mock Carbon.

Calling Carbon::setTestNow(Carbon::now('UTC')); will mock your tests to use the current time. Once the test is over, you call Carbon::setTestNow(); in the tearDown method to reset Carbon to its normal behavior.

Now that you've mocked Carbon, you can write your test expectations (Listing 7-69).

Listing 7-69. Updating the BooksController@store Test to Assert Created and Updated Values

```
104  /** @test **/
105  public function store_should_save_new_book_in_the_database()
106  {
107      $this->post('/books', [
108          'title' => 'The Invisible Man',
109          'description' => 'An invisible man is trapped in the terror of his own
                 creation',
110          'author' => 'H. G. Wells'
111      ]);
112
113      $body = json_decode($this->response->getContent(), true);
114      $this->assertArrayHasKey('data', $body);
115
116      $data = $body['data'];
117      $this->assertEquals('The Invisible Man', $data['title']);
118      $this->assertEquals(
119          'An invisible man is trapped in the terror of his own creation',
120          $data['description']
121      );
122      $this->assertEquals('H. G. Wells', $data['author']);
123      $this->assertTrue($data['id'] > 0, 'Expected a positive integer, but did not see
             one.');
124
125      $this->assertArrayHasKey('created', $data);
126      $this->assertEquals(Carbon::now()->toIso8601String(), $data['created']);
127      $this->assertArrayHasKey('updated', $data);
128      $this->assertEquals(Carbon::now()->toIso8601String(), $data['updated']);
129
130      $this->seeInDatabase('books', ['title' => 'The Invisible Man']);
131  }
```

Near the end of the test you assert that the response has the created and updated keys, and you use carbon to make sure the dates are in ISO 8601 (http://www.iso.org/iso/home/standards/iso8601.htm) format.

Let's make sure your new assertions pass (Listing 7-70).

Listing 7-70. Running the Entire Test Suite

```
# vagrant@homestead:~/Code/bookr$
$ phpunit

OK (21 tests, 102 assertions)
```

And your tests all pass! You are on the final method refactor and then you are done. The BooksController@update method will be similar to the store method (Listing 7-71).

Listing 7-71. Refactoring BooksController@update

```
50   /**
51    * PUT /books/{id}
52    * @param Request $request
```

```
53    * @param $id
54    * @return mixed
55    */
56   public function update(Request $request, $id)
57   {
58       try {
59           $book = Book::findOrFail($id);
60       } catch (ModelNotFoundException $e) {
61           return response()->json([
62               'error' => [
63                   'message' => 'Book not found'
64               ]
65           ], 404);
66       }
67
68       $book->fill($request->all());
69       $book->save();
70
71       return $this->item($book, new BookTransformer());
72   }
```

The only change here is returning a transformed model. Let's check the test (Listing 7-72).

Listing 7-72. Running the Test Suite

```
# vagrant@homestead:~/Code/bookr$
$ phpunit

OK (21 tests, 102 assertions)
```

And you are still green!

Next, add response checks and assert the dates in the *update_should_only_change_fillable_fields* test (Listing 7-73).

Listing 7-73. Adding Additional Checks for BooksController@update

```
150   /** @test **/
151   public function update_should_only_change_fillable_fields()
152   {
153       $book = factory('App\Book')->create([
154           'title' => 'War of the Worlds',
155           'description' => 'A science fiction masterpiece about Martians invading
                London',
156           'author' => 'H. G. Wells',
157       ]);
158
159       $this->notSeeInDatabase('books', [
160           'title' => 'The War of the Worlds',
161           'description' => 'The book is way better than the movie.',
162           'author' => 'Wells, H. G.'
163       ]);
164
```

```
165     $this->put("/books/{$book->id}", [
166         'id' => 5,
167         'title' => 'The War of the Worlds',
168         'description' => 'The book is way better than the movie.',
169         'author' => 'Wells, H. G.'
170     ]);
171
172     $this
173         ->seeStatusCode(200)
174         ->seeJson([
175             'id' => 1,
176             'title' => 'The War of the Worlds',
177             'description' => 'The book is way better than the movie.',
178             'author' => 'Wells, H. G.',
179         ])
180         ->seeInDatabase('books', [
181             'title' => 'The War of the Worlds'
182         ]);
183
184     $body = json_decode($this->response->getContent(), true);
185     $this->assertArrayHasKey('data', $body);
186
187     $data = $body['data'];
188     $this->assertArrayHasKey('created', $data);
189     $this->assertEquals(Carbon::now()->toIso8601String(), $data['created']);
190     $this->assertArrayHasKey('updated', $data);
191     $this->assertEquals(Carbon::now()->toIso8601String(), $data['updated']);
192 }
```

At the end of the test method you added assertions for the created and updated values, just like in your last test. Time for the moment of truth: running the whole suite one last time (Listing 7-74).

Listing 7-74. Running the Test Suite

```
# vagrant@homestead:~/Code/bookr$
$ phpunit

OK (21 tests, 106 assertions)
```

ℹ Git commit: Integrate the FractalResponse Service

845f27e (https://bitbucket.org/paulredmond/apress-bookr/commits/845f27e)

Conclusion

You've had a long journey in this chapter, but now you have a decent way to generate consistent responses in your app. Along the way you learned

- How to write the minimum amount of code to get tests to pass

- To refactor *only* after getting tests to pass

- How to create and install a service provider

- How to use the service container

- The basics of the Fractal library

At this point I encourage you to read more about the service container (`https://lumen.laravel.com/docs/5.2/container`) and service providers (`https://lumen.laravel.com/docs/5.2/providers`) in the official documentation. The container and providers are related concepts that you will use frequently when you develop Lumen applications.

CHAPTER 8

Validation

Your /books API is going smoothly up to this point, but your tests and controllers assume that *good* data is being submitted. Your application doesn't protect against bad data (and empty data) being saved to the database; specifically, the BooksController@store and BooksController@update methods happily save bad data.

You will focus your efforts on validating data submitted to the /books API using the validation (https://lumen.laravel.com/docs/5.2/validation) tools provided by Lumen. You will write tests for your validation logic; this will provide you with a good foundation of how write validation tests in your own applications.

First Attempt at Validation

You will start out with basic validation and then iteratively add features as you go. Like always, you create tests first.

What validation rules do you need? Validation is a combination of business logic and security practices. For example, in your /books API, all books should be required to have a title. For your purposes, the database schema doesn't allow null values, and you intend to make the title, description, and author fields required. If these fields are present, you will consider them valid.

Let's start by creating a new integration test file (Listing 8-1) and the skeleton class (Listing 8-2) with a few basic tests for validation.

Listing 8-1. Creating the Test Class

```
# vagrant@homestead:~/Code/bookr$
$ touch tests/app/Http/Controllers/BooksControllerValidationTest.php
```

Listing 8-2. The Skeleton BooksControllerValidationTest Class

```
1   <?php
2
3   namespace Tests\App\Http\Controllers;
4
5   use TestCase;
6   use Illuminate\Http\Response;
7   use Laravel\Lumen\Testing\DatabaseMigrations;
8
9   class BooksControllerValidationTest extends TestCase
10  {
11      use DatabaseMigrations;
12
13      /** @test **/
```

© Paul Redmond 2016
P. Redmond, *Lumen Programming Guide*, DOI 10.1007/978-1-4842-2187-7_8

```
14      public function it_validates_required_fields_when_creating_a_new_book()
15      {
16
17      }
18
19      /** @test **/
20      public function it_validates_requied_fields_when_updating_a_book()
21      {
22
23      }
24  }
```

Take note of the imported Illuminate\Http\Response class that you will use to test expected response codes. You also import the DatabaseMigrations trait to test existing database records and insert new ones.

Start writing your first test, making sure that your BooksController@store method validates required fields before creating a new book (Listing 8-3).

Listing 8-3. Writing Validation Assertions for the BooksController@store Method

```
13  /** @test **/
14  public function it_validates_required_fields_when_creating_a_new_book()
15  {
16      $this->post('/books', [], ['Accept' => 'application/json']);
17
18      $this->assertEquals(Response::HTTP_UNPROCESSABLE_ENTITY, $this->response-
        >getStatusCode());
19
20      $body = json_decode($this->response->getContent(), true);
21
22      $this->assertArrayHasKey('title', $body);
23      $this->assertArrayHasKey('description', $body);
24      $this->assertArrayHasKey('author', $body);
25
26      $this->assertEquals(["The title field is required."], $body['title']);
27      $this->assertEquals(["The description field is required."], $body['description']);
28      $this->assertEquals(["The author field is required."], $body['author']);
29  }
```

Your first test tries to create a new book without sending any data; you expect to receive a *422 Unprocessable Entity* status code from the failed validation. Next, you decode the JSON response and assert that certain validation errors are present in the response. The validator formats error messages into an array for each field. Now run your first failing validation test (Listing 8-4).

Listing 8-4. Running the Test Suite

```
# vagrant@homestead:~/Code/bookr$
$ phpunit --filter=it_validates_required_fields_when_creating_a_new_book

There was 1 failure:

1) Tests\App\Http\Controllers\BooksControllerValidationTest::it_validates_required_fields_
when_creating_a_new_book
Failed asserting that 201 matches expected 422.
```

bookr/tests/app/Http/Controllers/BooksControllerValidationTest.php:18

FAILURES!
Tests: 1, Assertions: 1, Failures: 1.

The API responds with a *201 Created* status code which you expect when valid data is submitted, but you expect failure because the data submitted is invalid. With the failed test you are ready to integrate your validation logic in the controller (Listing 8-5).

Listing 8-5. The Validation Implementation for Creating a Book

```
35   /**
36    * POST /books
37    *
38    * @param Request $request
39    * @return \Illuminate\Http\JsonResponse
40    */
41   public function store(Request $request)
42   {
43       $this->validate($request, [
44           'title' => 'required',
45           'description' => 'required',
46           'author' => 'required'
47       ]);
48
49       $book = Book::create($request->all());
50       $data = $this->item($book, new BookTransformer());
51
52       return response()->json($data, 201, [
53           'Location' => route('books.show', ['id' => $book->id])
54       ]);
55   }
```

The first line of the controller calls the *validate()* method, which accepts an *Illuminate\Http\ Request* instance and an array of validation rules mapped to the request data. You validate the request using the required rule, which means the field must be present. If the validate() method fails, it will throw an *HttpResponseException* with the 422 Unprocessable Entity status code, which is what your test expects.

THE VALIDATE METHOD

The validate() method comes from the *Laravel\Lumen\Routing\ProvidesConvenienceMethods* trait provided by the base Laravel\Lumen\Routing\Controller class.

Read the validation documentation (https://laravel.com/docs/5.2/validation#available-validation-rules) to find a complete list of all the validation rules Lumen supports out of the box, as well as how to create your own custom rules.

Next, test your implementation to see if it succeeds (Listing 8-6).

Listing 8-6. Testing the BooksController@store Validation Implementation

```
# vagrant@homestead:~/Code/bookr$
$ phpunit --filter=it_validates_required_fields_when_creating_a_new_book

OK (1 test, 7 assertions)
```

Add the same basic validation to the BooksController@update method before doing some refactoring and improvements (Listing 8-7).

Listing 8-7. Writing the Validation Test for the BooksController@update Method

```
31  /** @test **/
32  public function it_validates_validates_passed_fields_when_updating_a_book()
33  {
34      $book = factory(\App\Book::class)->create();
35
36      $this->put("/books/{$book->id}", [], ['Accept' => 'application/json']);
37
38      $this->assertEquals(Response::HTTP_UNPROCESSABLE_ENTITY, $this->response-
        >getStatusCode());
39
40      $body = json_decode($this->response->getContent(), true);
41
42      $this->assertArrayHasKey('title', $body);
43      $this->assertArrayHasKey('description', $body);
44      $this->assertArrayHasKey('author', $body);
45
46      $this->assertEquals(["The title field is required."], $body['title']);
47      $this->assertEquals(["The description field is required."], $body['description']);
48      $this->assertEquals(["The author field is required."], $body['author']);
49  }
```

This test creates a valid record in the database and attempts a PUT request with no data. Running the tests will give an error similar to the first validation test (Listing 8-8).

Listing 8-8. Running the Test Suite

```
# vagrant@homestead:~/Code/bookr$
$ phpunit

There was 1 failure:

1) Tests\App\Http\Controllers\BooksControllerValidationTest::it_validates_valida\
tes_passed_fields_when_updating_a_book
Failed asserting that 200 matches expected 422.

/home/vagrant/Code/bookr/tests/app/Http/Controllers/BooksControllerValidationTest.php:38

FAILURES!
Tests: 23, Assertions: 114, Failures: 1.
```

The BooksController@update implementation is identical to the BooksController@create method (Listing 8-9).

Listing 8-9. Implementing Validation in the BooksController@update Method

```
57  /**
58   * PUT /books/{id}
59   *
60   * @param Request $request
61   * @param $id
62   * @return mixed
63   */
64  public function update(Request $request, $id)
65  {
66      try {
67          $book = Book::findOrFail($id);
68      } catch (ModelNotFoundException $e) {
69          return response()->json([
70              'error' => [
71                  'message' => 'Book not found'
72              ]
73          ], 404);
74      }
75
76      $this->validate($request, [
77          'title' => 'required',
78          'description' => 'required',
79          'author' => 'required'
80      ]);
81
82      $book->fill($request->all());
83      $book->save();
84
85      return $this->item($book, new BookTransformer());
86  }
```

Next, you should run your test to see if you are back to green again (Listing 8-10).

Listing 8-10. Running the BooksController@update Validation Test

```
# vagrant@homestead:~/Code/bookr$
$ phpunit

OK (23 tests, 120 assertions)
```

With passing tests you've provided basic validation for books. Your validation code is ready to be expanded to include more rules and tests to ensure your validation continues to work as expected.

More Validation Constraints

The second validation rule is limiting the length of the book title. The database is constrained to 255 characters so you will write your application to match. You will test a few scenarios, including "just long enough" and "just too long." Add the tests in Listing 8-11 to the BooksControllerValidationTest file.

Listing 8-11. Testing the "Title Is Too Long" Scenario

```php
51  /** @test **/
52  public function title_fails_create_validation_when_just_too_long()
53  {
54  // Creating a book
55  $book = factory(\App\Book::class)->make();
56  $book->title = str_repeat('a', 256);
57
58  $this->post("/books", [
59      'title' => $book->title,
60      'description' => $book->description,
61      'author' => $book->author,
62  ], ['Accept' => 'application/json']);
63
64  $this
65      ->seeStatusCode(Response::HTTP_UNPROCESSABLE_ENTITY)
66      ->seeJson([
67          'title' => ["The title may not be greater than 255 characters."]
68      ])
69      ->notSeeInDatabase('books', ['title' => $book->title]);
70  }
71
72  /** @test **/
73  public function title_fails_update_validation_when_just_too_long()
74  {
75  // Updating a book
76  $book = factory(\App\Book::class)->create();
77  $book->title = str_repeat('a', 256);
78
79  $this->put("/books/{$book->id}", [
80      'title' => $book->title,
81      'description' => $book->description,
82      'author' => $book->author
83  ], ['Accept' => 'application/json']);
84
85  $this
86      ->seeStatusCode(Response::HTTP_UNPROCESSABLE_ENTITY)
87      ->seeJson([
88          'title' => ["The title may not be greater than 255 characters."]
89      ])
90      ->notSeeInDatabase('books', ['title' => $book->title]);
91  }
```

In the first test, the *factory(\App\Book::class)->make()* method was introduced. When you call ->make() from the factory instead of ->create() it gives you an unsaved model that is not persisted in the database. Both tests make the title just too long to pass validation in order to test the threshold of failure. The error message is asserted and you also assert that a record with the invalid title is not in the database.

You need to wire up the controller changes to match these tests (Listing 8-12 and Listing 8-13). At this point you should run tests, which will fail because the validation will still pass.

Listing 8-12. Adding Max Validation to BooksController@create

```
43  $this->validate($request, [
44      'title' => 'required|max:255',
45      'description' => 'required',
46      'author' => 'required'
47  ]);
```

Listing 8-13. Adding Max Validation to BooksController@update

```
76  $this->validate($request, [
77      'title' => 'required|max:255',
78      'description' => 'required',
79      'author' => 'required'
80  ]);
```

Validation rules are separated by the pipe | character, thus, title is required and max:255 length. Now see if your new validation rules pass (Listing 8-14).

Listing 8-14. Running the Test Suite

```
# vagrant@homestead:~/Code/bookr$
$ phpunit

OK (25 tests, 126 assertions)
```

The next two tests, shown in Listing 8-15, will assert that validation passes when you have exactly 255 characters.

Listing 8-15. Testing That Validation Passes with a Title of Exactly 255 Characters

```
93   /** @test **/
94   public function title_passes_create_validation_when_exactly_max()
95   {
96       // Creating a new Book
97       $book = factory(\App\Book::class)->make();
98       $book->title = str_repeat('a', 255);
99
100      $this->post("/books", [
101          'title' => $book->title,
102          'description' => $book->description,
103          'author' => $book->author,
104      ], ['Accept' => 'application/json']);
105
106      $this
107          ->seeStatusCode(Response::HTTP_CREATED)
108          ->seeInDatabase('books', ['title' => $book->title]);
109  }
110
111  /** @test **/
112  public function title_passes_update_validation_when_exactly_max()
113  {
114      // Updating a book
```

```
115      $book = factory(\App\Book::class)->create();
116      $book->title = str_repeat('a', 255);
117
118      $this->put("/books/{$book->id}", [
119          'title' => $book->title,
120          'description' => $book->description,
121          'author' => $book->author
122      ], ['Accept' => 'application/json']);
123
124      $this
125          ->seeStatusCode(Response::HTTP_OK)
126          ->seeInDatabase('books', ['title' => $book->title]);
127  }
```

The BooksControllerTest class already covers creating a valid book, so you only assert the correct status code, which means validation passed. Last, you check that a new record exists in the database. At this point, your tests should all be passing (Listing 8-16), but if the maximum value changes, your tests will fail, indicating business rules around your title length. These tests will guide developers in understanding the business rules around data.

Listing 8-16. Running the Test Suite

```
# vagrant@homestead:~/Code/bookr$
$ phpunit

OK (27 tests, 130 assertions)
```

You now have additional *max:255* validation for the title that's working. As you can see, validation is really easy in Lumen, but it can also handle more complex rules. Your data is not complicated at the moment so a few built-in validation rules will suffice.

Custom Validation Messages

Lumen has good validation messages out of the box, but I will show you how you can customize them if needed. You will use the description field as an example.

The first thing to do is update your tests to match the new error message you want to use. The validation test for BooksController@create should look Listing 8-17 and Listing 8-18 now.

Listing 8-17. Test for Custom Description Validation Message for BooksController@create

```
13  /** @test **/
14  public function it_validates_required_fields_when_creating_a_new_book()
15  {
16      $this->post('/books', [], ['Accept' => 'application/json']);
17
18      $this->assertEquals(Response::HTTP_UNPROCESSABLE_ENTITY, $this->response-
        >getStatusCode());
19
20      $body = json_decode($this->response->getContent(), true);
21
22      $this->assertArrayHasKey('title', $body);
```

```
23        $this->assertArrayHasKey('description', $body);
24        $this->assertArrayHasKey('author', $body);
25
26        $this->assertEquals(["The title field is required."], $body['title']);
27        $this->assertEquals(
28            ["Please provide a description."],
29            $body['description']
30        );
31        $this->assertEquals(["The author field is required."], $body['author']);
32    }
```

Listing 8-18. Test for Custom Description Validation Message for BooksController@update

```
34    /** @test **/
35    public function it_validates_validates_passed_fields_when_updating_a_book()
36    {
37        $book = factory(\App\Book::class)->create();
38
39        $this->put("/books/{$book->id}", [], ['Accept' => 'application/json']);
40
41        $this->assertEquals(Response::HTTP_UNPROCESSABLE_ENTITY, $this->response-
          >getStatusCode());
42
43        $body = json_decode($this->response->getContent(), true);
44
45        $this->assertArrayHasKey('title', $body);
46        $this->assertArrayHasKey('description', $body);
47        $this->assertArrayHasKey('author', $body);
48
49        $this->assertEquals(["The title field is required."], $body['title']);
50        $this->assertEquals(
51            ["Please provide a description."],
52            $body['description']
53        );
54        $this->assertEquals(["The author field is required."], $body['author']);
55    }
```

The only thing you needed to change was the custom error message for the description field, but the entire test cases are provided for clarity.

At this point, the tests are failing, and you are ready to implement your custom message. The `Controller::validate()` method accepts an optional third argument, which is an associative array of custom validation messages. You can define them with the pattern *'attribute.<rule>' => <message>* to override a specific field (Listing 8-19 and Listing 8-20).

Listing 8-19. Adding the Custom Validation Method for the Description

```
43    $this->validate($request, [
44        'title' => 'required|max:255',
45        'description' => 'required',
46        'author' => 'required'
47    ], [
48        'description.required' => 'Please provide a :attribute.'
49    ]);
```

Listing 8-20. Adding the Custom Description Message for BooksController@update

```
78  $this->validate($request, [
79      'title' => 'required|max:255',
80      'description' => 'required',
81      'author' => 'required'
82  ], [
83      'description.required' => 'Please provide a :attribute.'
84  ]);
```

You added a custom message for the description's `required` validation rule. The validator understands certain placeholders like `:attribute`, which will be resolved to the word "description". If you were to pass `'required' => 'Please fill out the :attribute.'` the custom message would apply to all fields being validated with the required rule.

It's time to run your test suite one last time and see if the new custom message worked (Listing 8-21).

Listing 8-21. Running the Test Suite

```
# vagrant@homestead:~/Code/bookr$
$ phpunit

OK (27 tests, 130 assertions)
```

Other Approaches

Admittedly, this validation chapter is barebones, and you might be scratching your head wondering if validation logic even belongs in the controller. Shouldn't the model be responsible for validating data? Not surprisingly, there are differing opinions about where validation should be covered: in the controller or the model within Model-View-Controller (MVC).

I try to take a pragmatic approach. In your API thus far, is validation making your controller too complex? Nope. Is the controller processing user input from a request? Yes. The controller is a fine place for validation logic, in my opinion. The key is to keep your code simple; you can always refactor later.

That being said, I will touch briefly on another technique used in Laravel (and thus Lumen): validation in models. For example, Dayle Rees wrote about one approach to move validation into models (`https://daylerees.com/trick-validation-within-models/`). Other notable frameworks (such as Rails) also integrate validation rules in the model layer.

In your case, you also *have* duplicated logic by validating in controller methods. Isn't that bad? In my opinion, it *can* be, but at this point in your API, I would argue that creating a base model and moving validation logic into your Book model would be a premature optimization and more complex than your simple validation rules. Plus, you have validation tests for both endpoints. I encourage you to solve this problem however you feel fits your style; just try to avoid premature optimization and doing it for the sake of doing it. Lumen is flexible enough to allow you to come up with your own approach.

Conclusion

You breezed through adding basic API validation. At this point, I encourage you to read through the validation documentation (`https://lumen.laravel.com/docs/5.2/validation`) to become more familiar with the available built-in validation rules and making your own custom rules. You should have a good foundation for writing validation rules and tests to ensure your APIs respond to invalid data in a useful way. Validation not only helps keep bad data out of the database, it provides API consumers helpful information when bad data is submitted to the application.

ⓘ Git commit: Add Book API Validation

d4144f0 (`https://bitbucket.org/paulredmond/apress-bookr/commits/d4144f0`)

## CHAPTER 9

Authors

So far your /books endpoint provides an author column on the books database table. Making authors a string field on the books table was intentional so that you could focus on other primary concepts of building your API, but now you are ready to create proper author data and provide API endpoints for author data.

This chapter will cover the following:

- Creating the authors database schema

- Creating a relationship between book data and authors

- Creating API endpoints for author information

- Modifying your /books endpoint to use new author data

The Authors Database Schema

Creating the authors database table involves a few migrations:

1. Create a new authors database table.

2. Associate authors and books.

3. Remove the deprecated author column on the books table.

You will start by creating the new authors database table. If you remember when you created the books table you have an artisan command to create migration scripts (Listing 9-1).

Listing 9-1. Creating the Authors Database Migration

```
# vagrant@homestead:~/Code/bookr$
$ php artisan make:migration create_authors_table --create=authors
```

Add the columns shown in Listing 9-2 to the up() method.

Listing 9-2. The Authors Table Migration

```
8   /**
9    * Run the migrations.
10   *
11   * @return void
12   */
13   public function up()
14   {
```

```
15      Schema::create('authors', function (Blueprint $table) {
16          $table->increments('id');
17          $table->string('name');
18          $table->enum('gender', ['male', 'female']);
19          $table->text('biography');
20          $table->timestamps();
21      });
22  }
```

This time around I will move at a quicker pace, so you might want to review your original migration of the books table.

The up migration might be the first time you've seen the *$table->text()* method and *$table->enum()* in a migration:

- The text() method is the TEXT equivalent for the database.

- The enum() method is equivalent to a relational database ENUM field.

You can go ahead and run the migration to try it out (Listing 9-3).

Listing 9-3. Running the Database Migration

```
# vagrant@homestead:~/Code/bookr$
$ php artisan migrate:refresh
Rolled back: 2015_12_29_234835_create_books_table
Migrated: 2015_12_29_234835_create_books_table
Migrated: 2016_01_20_050526_create_authors_table
```

Keep in mind that commands like `migrate:refresh` will remove data from the database, but this is a good thing in development because you can depend on seed data to quickly get a repeatable development environment.

The next migration will define the database association between the books table and the `authors` table. Because you are using Eloquent you have access to the following types of relationships:

- One-to-one

- One-to-many

- Many-to-many

- Has-many-through

- Polymorphic relationships

- Many-to-many polymorphic relationships

You can read more about model relationships (https://laravel.com/docs/5.2/eloquent-relationships) in the Laravel documentation. You will pick one-to-many, although a many-to-many relationship might be better suited if you are allowing multiple authors.

For the purposes of your API, a book will only have *one* author, and you will define that relationship with a new migration (Listing 9-4).

Listing 9-4. Making the Migration to Associate Books and Authors

```
# vagrant@homestead:~/Code/bookr$
$ php artisan make:migration \
associate_books_with_authors --table=books
```

Your API is not in production yet, so you could modify the original books migration that creates the books table. Changing the existing migration is much cleaner when you are developing a new application; if your application is already in production, you must create another migration. You are creating a new migration in this case so that you can get familiar with how to write migrations for a production API that already has production data.

This migration is a little trickier than your previous experience with migrations (Listing 9-5).

Listing 9-5. The Migration to Associate Authors and Books

```php
1   <?php
2
3   use Illuminate\Database\Schema\Blueprint;
4   use Illuminate\Database\Migrations\Migration;
5
6   class AssociateBooksWithAuthors extends Migration
7   {
8       /**
9        * Run the migrations.
10       *
11       * @return void
12       */
13      public function up()
14      {
15          Schema::table('books', function (Blueprint $table) {
16
17              // Create the author_id column as an unsigned integer
18              $table->integer('author_id')->after('id')->unsigned();
19
20              // Create a basic index for the author_id column
21              $table->index('author_id');
22
23              // Create a foreign key constraint and cascade on delete.
24              $table
25                  ->foreign('author_id')
26                  ->references('id')
27                  ->on('authors')
28                  ->onDelete('cascade');
29          });
30      }
31
32      /**
33       * Reverse the migrations.
34       *
35       * @return void
36       */
37      public function down()
38      {
39          Schema::table('books', function (Blueprint $table) {
40              // Drop the foreign key first
41              $table->dropForeign('books_author_id_foreign');
42
43              // Now drop the basic index
```

```
44              $table->dropIndex('books_author_id_index');
45
46              // Lastly, now it's safe to drop the column
47              $table->dropColumn('author_id');
48          });
49      }
50  }
```

I will start by explaining the up method:

- Create an unsigned integer column author_id *after* the id column.

- Add a basic index to the author_id column.

- Add a foreign key associated with the authors.id column.

- The foreign key should cascade on delete.

The down method looks simple but is actually a little trickier:

- You *must* drop the foreign key first.

- You then *must* drop the index.

- Finally, you are safe to drop the author_id column.

A migration should be able to be applied and rolled back without error cleanly. You will try out applying and rolling back to make sure your migration is working as expected (Listing 9-6).

Listing 9-6. Making Sure Migrations Can Be Applied and Rolled Back

```
# vagrant@homestead:~/Code/bookr$
$ php artisan migrate:refresh
Rolled back: 2016_07_31_195159_associate_books_with_authors
Rolled back: 2016_07_31_194721_create_authors_table
Rolled back: 2016_07_28_232137_create_books_table
Migrated: 2016_07_28_232137_create_books_table
Migrated: 2016_07_31_194721_create_authors_table
Migrated: 2016_07_31_195159_associate_books_with_authors
```

Now that you have a working migration, you need to update your seed data for the books table and create a new factory for authors. First, you need an Eloquent model for authors (Listing 9-7).

Listing 9-7. Creating the Author Model File

```
# vagrant@homestead:~/Code/bookr$
$ touch app/Author.php
```

Your Author model will look like Listing 9-8.

Listing 9-8. The Author Model Class

```
1  <?php
2
3  namespace App;
4
5  use Illuminate\Database\Eloquent\Model;
```

```
6
7   class Author extends Model
8   {
9       /**
10       * The attributes that are mass assignable
11       *
12       * @var array
13       */
14      protected $fillable = ['name', 'biography', 'gender'];
15
16      public function books()
17      {
18          return $this->hasMany(Book::class);
19      }
20  }
```

The $fillable property was introduced in the Book model and defines mass-assignable columns. Next, you define a books() method that has the one-to-many relationship with the Book model. The hasMany method takes the Book model class name. By convention, the Author model will use author_id on the books table to look up associations.

Next, you need to adjust your Book model to include the authors association (Listing 9-9).

Listing 9-9. The Book Model Association with Authors

```
1   <?php
2
3   namespace App;
4
5   use Illuminate\Database\Eloquent\Model;
6
7   class Book extends Model
8   {
9       /**
10       * The attributes that are mass assignable
11       *
12       * @var array
13       */
14      protected $fillable = ['title', 'description', 'author'];
15
16      public function author()
17      {
18          return $this->belongsTo(Author::class);
19      }
20  }
```

By convention, the belongsTo method sets up the association with the Author model and Eloquent will take the author_id and find the author record with the Author.id field. You can tweak the foreign key name as the second argument in belongsTo, but let's follow the naming conventions that automatically take care of it.

The Eloquent relationships (https://laravel.com/docs/5.2/eloquent-relationships) documentation explains in detail how you can customize model associations and how to use them.

With the one-to-many association in place, Eloquent can load data about the associated models, as shown in Listing 9-10.

Listing 9-10. Example of Using Eloquent Associations

```
$book = Book::find(1);
echo $book->author->name;

$author = Author::find(1);
foreach ($author->books as $book) {
    echo $book->title;
}
```

The models are ready to go, and you have your schema migration working! Now you need to add a new factory definition for authors and update the seed data. Start by adding the factory definition to database/factories/ModelFactory.php (Listing 9-11).

Listing 9-11. The Author Model Factory

```
31  $factory->define(App\Author::class, function ($faker) {
32      return [
33          'name' => $faker->name,
34          'biography' => join(" ", $faker->sentences(rand(3, 5))),
35          'gender' => rand(1, 6) % 2 === 0 ? 'male' : 'female'
36      ];
37  });
```

The biography key uses the $faker->sentences() method from the Faker\Provider\Lorem provider. The $faker->sentences() method takes an integer for the first parameter, which determines how many sentences will be generated. You use a random number between 3 and 5 sentences and join the array with an empty space (" "). The gender key can either be male or female and you use the modulus operator to randomly pick male or female. An even random number will be male, and an odd number will be female.

Next, you will put your new factory to work by using it to seed book and author data. You will modify the database/seeds/BooksTableSeeder.php to use your model association (Listing 9-12).

Listing 9-12. Seed Author and Book Data

```
1   <?php
2
3   use Carbon\Carbon;
4   use Illuminate\Database\Seeder;
5   use Illuminate\Database\Eloquent\Model;
6
7   class BooksTableSeeder extends Seeder
8   {
9       /**
10       * Run the database seeds.
11       *
12       * @return void
13       */
14      public function run()
15      {
```

```
16          factory(App\Author::class, 10)->create()->each(function ($author) {
17              $booksCount = rand(1, 5);
18
19              while ($booksCount > 0) {
20                  $author->books()->save(factory(App\Book::class)->make());
21                  $booksCount--;
22              }
23          });
24      }
25  }
```

The modified BooksTableSeeder is not complicated; it creates 10 authors and then iterates over each record with a Closure callback. Inside the each callback you get a random $booksCount integer to determine how many books an author will have. The while loop is used to keep creating new books for the author until the $bookCount is 0.

Feel free to purge your database and run the seeder again to try it out (Listing 9-13).

Listing 9-13. Purging the Database and Applying the Modified BooksTableSeeder

```
# vagrant@homestead:~/Code/bookr$
$ php artisan migrate:refresh
$ php artisan db:seed
```

Keep in mind that if your application were in production, you would need to migrate the data *and* the schema. Since you are in early development you don't need to worry about losing data in the database.

You have one final migration that will remove the authors column in the database (Listing 9-14).

Listing 9-14. Migration to Remove the Authors Column from the Books Table

```
# vagrant@homestead:~/Code/bookr$
$ php artisan make:migration \
remove_books_authors_column --table=books
```

The migration will drop the author column on up and add it back on down. Like I mentioned, if this application were in production you might have to find all the authors and migrate them over to the new authors table inside the up method. The down callback would reverse the effects of migrating the authors column to a new table. Again, since you are in early development, you could also just remove this column from the original books migration. I want to provide you with more exposure to database migrations, so let's use a new migration to demonstrate dropping a column via a migration.

Listing 9-15 shows a simple migration for removing the author column.

Listing 9-15. Cleaning Up the Author Column on the books Table

```
1   <?php
2
3   use Illuminate\Database\Schema\Blueprint;
4   use Illuminate\Database\Migrations\Migration;
5
6   class RemoveBooksAuthorsColumn extends Migration
7   {
8       /**
9        * Run the migrations.
```

```
10        *
11        * @return void
12        */
13       public function up()
14       {
15           Schema::table('books', function (Blueprint $table) {
16               $table->dropColumn('author');
17           });
18       }
19
20       /**
21        * Reverse the migrations.
22        *
23        * @return void
24        */
25       public function down()
26       {
27           Schema::table('books', function (Blueprint $table) {
28               $table->string('author');
29           });
30       }
31   }
```

Time to run the migration and see what happens (Listing 9-16).

Listing 9-16. Refreshing the Database Migrations

```
# vagrant@homestead:~/Code/bookr$
$ php artisan migrate:refresh
Rolled back: 2016_07_31_195159_associate_books_with_authors
Rolled back: 2016_07_31_194721_create_authors_table
Rolled back: 2016_07_28_232137_create_books_table
Migrated: 2016_07_28_232137_create_books_table
Migrated: 2016_07_31_194721_create_authors_table
Migrated: 2016_07_31_195159_associate_books_with_authors
Migrated: 2016_07_31_201317_remove_books_authors_column
```

You will get errors now if you run php artisan db:seed after running the migration to remove the authors column from the books table. You need to fix the db seeder, which is now broken due to the database migration (Listing 9-17).

Listing 9-17. The Broken Database Seeder

```
# vagrant@homestead:~/Code/bookr$
$ php artisan db:seed
...
[PDOException]
  SQLSTATE[42S22]: Column not found: 1054 Unknown column 'author' in 'field list'
...
```

To fix the seeder you need to remove the author key in the Book factory. Open the database/factories/ModelFactory.php file and locate the Book factory (Listing 9-18).

Listing 9-18. Removing the Author Key from the Book Factory

```
21  $factory->define(App\Book::class, function ($faker) {
22      $title = $faker->sentence(rand(3, 10));
23
24      return [
25          'title' => substr($title, 0, strlen($title) - 1),
26          'description' => $faker->text,
27      ];
28  });
```

Now you can refresh seed data successfully (Listing 9-19).

Listing 9-19. Successfully Seeding the Database

```
# vagrant@homestead:~/Code/bookr$
$ php artisan migrate:refresh
...
$ php artisan db:seed
```

That wraps up your database schema and migration. You have a new authors table and you've cleaned up migrations and database seeding. At this point, the tests will blow up, so you need to find out what broke and fix it.

Fixing Broken Tests

You need to fix the tests that are failing as the result of schema changes. Although fixing broken tests isn't the most glamorous part of programming, it's nice to know that your test suite catches broken code before you ship it.

Since you just changed your database schema, it makes sense that various tests adding database records would break since you removed the authors column from the books table. You have a validation requirement of an author name in your PUT /books and POST /books endpoints too, which doesn't exist in your schema.

If you inspect the BooksControllerTest you will see this factory call a few times:

```
$books = factory('App\Book', 2)->create();
```

Similar to the BooksTableSeeder change you made in this chapter, various tests will need to create an author and then associate that author with a book. It makes sense to create a method to avoid boilerplate code everywhere. Add the code in Listing 9-20 to the tests/TestCase.php from which your tests extend.

Listing 9-20. A Book Factory Method in tests/TestCase.php

```
54  /**
55   * Convenience method for creating a book with an author
56   *
57   * @param int $count
58   * @return mixed
59   */
60  protected function bookFactory($count = 1)
61  {
62      $author = factory(\App\Author::class)->create();
```

```
63      $books = factory(\App\Book::class, $count)->make();
64
65      if ($count === 1) {
66          $books->author()->associate($author);
67          $books->save();
68      } else {
69          $books->each(function ($book) use ($author) {
70              $book->author()->associate($author);
71              $book->save();
72          });
73      }
74
75      return $books;
76  }
```

The bookFactory method is creating an author in the database. Next, the method calls make() to populate a Book model instance that is not yet saved in the database. The author_id column is required by a foreign key constraint so you need to call make() so you can attach the author_id before inserting the record in the database. The if statement checks to see how many books should be created. If only one book needs to be created, you attach the author to the book; otherwise you loop through each book and attach the author to all books.

Now that you have a convenient way of creating books and authors in the test database, you need to determine which tests need fixing. The easiest way to do that is to run the whole phpunit suite and go through each error one by one. As you find an error, you update it and run the test in isolation until it passes. You then move on to the next error, and so on, until you get back to green.

I will spare you the output from all of the failures, but the first one you will work on is this error (Listing 9-21).

Listing 9-21. PHPUnit Error Output

```
Tests\App\Http\Controllers\BooksControllerTest::store_should_save_new_book_in_the_database
PHPUnit_Framework_Exception: Argument #2 (No Value) of PHPUnit_Framework_Assert:\
:assertArrayHasKey() must be a array or ArrayAccess

bookr/tests/app/Http/Controllers/BooksControllerTest.php:108
```

The BooksController@store method is obviously breaking. Let's find out what's happening (Listing 9-22).

Listing 9-22. Temporarily Dump the $body Variable

```
104  /** @test **/
105  public function store_should_save_new_book_in_the_database()
106  {
107      $this->post('/books', [
108          'title' => 'The Invisible Man',
109          'description' => 'An invisible man is trapped in the terror of his own
                 creation',
110          'author' => 'H. G. Wells'
111      ]);
112
113      $body = json_decode($this->response->getContent(), true);
114      dd($body, $this->response->getStatusCode());
115      // ....
116  }
```

146

The dd() function is a convenience function for dumping the variable and exiting the program. Listing 9-23 shows the output you will receive when you run the test now.

Listing 9-23. Debugging the Failing Test

```
# vagrant@homestead:~/Code/bookr$
$ phpunit --filter=store_should_save_new_book_in_the_database

null
500
```

The response body is null and the status code is 500. Weird! You should comb the logs and see what you can find. Clear out the storage/logs/lumen.log file and run the test again. You should see something like Listing 9-24.

Listing 9-24. Test Error in storage/logs/lumen.log

```
[2016-07-31 20:37:28] lumen.ERROR: PDOException: SQLSTATE[42S22]: Column not found: 1054
Unknown column 'author' in 'field list' in /Users/paul/Code/laravel-valet/bookr/vendor/
illuminate/database/Connection.php:441
```

The BooksController@store method is trying to insert an author column that no longer exists in the books table. You could remove it from your test to get the next error, but I want to show you another issue here: the Book model has defined author as a fillable field. You need to remove the field that is invalid now (Listing 9-25).

Listing 9-25. Updating the app/Book.php Fillable Fields

```
 9  /**
10   * The attributes that are mass assignable
11   *
12   * @var array
13   */
14  protected $fillable = ['title', 'description'];
```

If you run your test again, you will get a different error (Listing 9-26).

Listing 9-26. A PDOException Error in storage/logs/lumen.log

```
[2016-07-31 20:38:17] lumen.ERROR: PDOException: SQLSTATE[23000]: Integrity constraint
violation: 1452 Cannot add or update a child row: a foreign key constraint fails (`bookr_
testing`.`books`, CONSTRAINT `books_author_id_foreign` FOREIGN KEY (`author_id`) REFERENCES
`authors` (`id`) ON DELETE CASCADE) in /Users/paul/Code/laravel-valet/bookr/vendor/
illuminate/database/Connection.php:441
```

Now the BooksController@store method is failing because of a missing foreign key constraint; you are not passing a proper author_id in the request. You are creating a book so you just need to generate a valid author in your test (Listing 9-27).

Listing 9-27. Updating the Test to Pass an Author ID

```
104  /** @test **/
105  public function store_should_save_new_book_in_the_database()
```

```
107  {
107        $author = factory(\App\Author::class)->create([
108            'name' => 'H. G. Wells'
109        ]);
110
111        $this->post('/books', [
112            'title' => 'The Invisible Man',
113            'description' => 'An invisible man is trapped in the terror of his own
                creation',
114            'author_id' => $author->id
115        ], ['Accept' => 'application/json']);
116
117        $body = json_decode($this->response->getContent(), true);
118
119        $this->assertArrayHasKey('data', $body);
120
121        $data = $body['data'];
122        $this->assertEquals('The Invisible Man', $data['title']);
123        $this->assertEquals(
124            'An invisible man is trapped in the terror of his own creation',
125            $data['description']
126        );
127        $this->assertEquals('H. G. Wells', $data['author']);
128        $this->assertTrue($data['id'] > 0, 'Expected a positive integer, but did not see
                one.');
129
130        $this->assertArrayHasKey('created', $data);
131        $this->assertEquals(Carbon::now()->toIso8601String(), $data['created']);
132        $this->assertArrayHasKey('updated', $data);
133        $this->assertEquals(Carbon::now()->toIso8601String(), $data['updated']);
134
135        $this->seeInDatabase('books', ['title' => 'The Invisible Man']);
136  }
```

Run the test again (Listing 9-28).

Listing 9-28. Running Your Failing Test Again

```
# vagrant@homestead:~/Code/bookr$
$ phpunit --filter=store_should_save_new_book_in_the_database

There was 1 failure:

1) Tests\App\Http\Controllers\BooksControllerTest::store_should_save_new_book_in_the_
database
Failed asserting that an array has the key 'data'.

/home/vagrant/Code/bookr/tests/app/Http/Controllers/BooksControllerTest.php:119

FAILURES!
Tests: 1, Assertions: 1, Failures: 1.
```

You're still getting errors, so let's investigate the response (Listing 9-29).

Listing 9-29. Debugging the Failing Test (Partial Code)

```
104   /** @test **/
105   public function store_should_save_new_book_in_the_database()
106   {
107       $author = factory(\App\Author::class)->create([
108           'name' => 'H. G. Wells'
109       ]);
110
111       $this->post('/books', [
112           'title' => 'The Invisible Man',
113           'description' => 'An invisible man is trapped in the terror of his own
                  creation',
114           'author_id' => $author->id
115       ], ['Accept' => 'application/json']);
116
117       $body = json_decode($this->response->getContent(), true);
118       dd($body);
119       // …
```

The output should be something like Listing 9-30.

Listing 9-30. Output from Debugging the Failing Test

```
# vagrant@homestead:~/Code/bookr$
$ phpunit --filter=store_should_save_new_book_in_the_database

array:1 [
  "author" => array:1 [
    0 => "The author field is required."
  ]
]
```

You have a failed validation constraint for the author column that is no longer valid since you removed the authors column. You need to replace it with a validation rule for a valid author_id (Listing 9-31).

Listing 9-31. Updating Validation in BooksController@store

```
43    $this->validate($request, [
44        'title' => 'required|max:255',
45        'description' => 'required',
46        'author_id' => 'required|exists:authors,id'
47    ], [
48        'description.required' => 'Please fill out the :attribute.'
49    ]);
```

You've replaced author with author_id and you are using the exists validation rule that ensures an author record exist in the authors table. The exists validation in this case reads like this: *exists:<table>,<column>*. If you omit the column, it will use the field associated with the validation rule, in this case author_id. At this point, running the test again will still fail (see if you can figure out why on your own).

149

You haven't changed the controller to set the author_id property on the model, although you are passing it at this point in the failing test. You need to allow this field to be fillable (Listing 9-32).

Listing 9-32. Making the author_id Field Mass-Assignable

```
 9  /**
10   * The attributes that are mass assignable
11   *
12   * @var array
13   */
14  protected $fillable = ['title', 'description', 'author_id'];
```

Now your controller should be able to populate the author_id field when it calls $book = Book::create($request->all());. Let's run your test again and see (Listing 9-33).

Listing 9-33. Running the Test After Making author_id Fillable

```
# vagrant@homestead:~/Code/bookr$
$ phpunit --filter=store_should_save_new_book_in_the_database

There was 1 failure:

1) Tests\App\Http\Controllers\BooksControllerTest::store_should_save_new_book_in_the_
database
Array (…) does not match expected type "string".

bookr/tests/app/Http/Controllers/BooksControllerTest.php:121
```

It looks like your save is now succeeding, but your assertions are not matching up anymore. The response should look something like Listing 9-34 now if you call dd().

Listing 9-34. Dumped Response from the Test

```
array:1 [
  "data" => array:6 [
    "id" => 1
    "title" => "The Invisible Man"
    "description" => "An invisible man is trapped in the terror of his own creation"
    "author" => array:6 [
      "id" => 1
      "name" => "H. G. Wells"
      "gender" => "female"
      "biography" => "Ut quis doloremque dolorem eaque. Repellendus et dolor eos doloribus.
Velit omnis alias ut fugiat molestias ab velit."
      "created_at" => "2015-11-21 16:32:34"
      "updated_at" => "2015-11-21 16:32:34"
    ]
    "created" => "2015-11-21T16:32:34+0000"
    "updated" => "2015-11-21T16:32:34+0000"
  ]
]
```

Whoops, the BookTransformer is now outputting the entire author record instead of just the author name. Later on in the book you will change the way responses include author data, but for now let's just keep your API the same. You can now use the associated author model to pass the author name (Listing 9-35).

Listing 9-35. Updating the BookTransformer::transform() Method

```
10   /**
11    * Transform a Book model into an array
12    *
13    * @param Book $book
14    * @return array
15    */
16   public function transform(Book $book)
17   {
18       return [
19           'id'          => $book->id,
20           'title'       => $book->title,
21           'description' => $book->description,
22           'author'      => $book->author->name,
23           'created'     => $book->created_at->toIso8601String(),
24           'updated'     => $book->updated_at->toIso8601String(),
25       ];
26   }
```

Run your test again after the transformer change (Listing 9-36). If you have any dd() calls in your test, don't forget to remove them!

Listing 9-36. Running the Test After Updating the BookTransformer

```
# vagrant@homestead:~/Code/bookr$
$ phpunit --filter=store_should_save_new_book_in_the_database
OK (1 test, 10 assertions)
```

You had to do considerable amount of investigating for a simple change, but it was a good exercise to get more familiar with debugging failing tests. You are ready to move on to the *update_should_only_change_fillable_fields* failing test, shown in Listing 9-37.

Listing 9-37. Failing Test for Updating Fillable Fields

```
Tests\App\Http\Controllers\BooksControllerTest::update_should_only_change_fillable_fields
Illuminate\Database\QueryException: SQLSTATE[42S22]: Column not found: 1054 Unknown column
'author' in 'field list'…
```

This error looks familiar. The BooksController@update and accompanying tests are still using the author parameter. You will start by updating the test to look like Listing 9-38.

Listing 9-38. Fixes for the update_should_only_change_fillable_fields Test

```
153   /** @test **/
154   public function update_should_only_change_fillable_fields()
155   {
156       $book = $this->bookFactory();
157
```

```
158        $this->notSeeInDatabase('books', [
159            'title' => 'The War of the Worlds',
160            'description' => 'The book is way better than the movie.',
161        ]);
162
163        $this->put("/books/{$book->id}", [
164            'id' => 5,
165            'title' => 'The War of the Worlds',
166            'description' => 'The book is way better than the movie.'
167        ], ['Accept' => 'application/json']);
168
169        $this
170            ->seeStatusCode(200)
171            ->seeJson([
172                'id' => 1,
173                'title' => 'The War of the Worlds',
174                'description' => 'The book is way better than the movie.'
175            ])
176            ->seeInDatabase('books', [
177                'title' => 'The War of the Worlds'
178            ]);
179
180        $body = json_decode($this->response->getContent(), true);
181        $this->assertArrayHasKey('data', $body);
182
183        $data = $body['data'];
184        $this->assertArrayHasKey('created', $data);
185        $this->assertEquals(Carbon::now()->toIso8601String(), $data['created']);
186        $this->assertArrayHasKey('updated', $data);
187        $this->assertEquals(Carbon::now()->toIso8601String(), $data['updated']);
188    }
```

It is a good idea to remove changing the author from the test and focus on updating the book. Now that you have a separate database table for authors, you should make a separate test for changing the author. You should also remove the author column from the notSeeInDatabase and the $this->seeJson() assertion (Listing 9-39).

Listing 9-39. Running the Test After Updating

```
# vagrant@homestead:~/Code/bookr$
$ phpunit --filter=update_should_only_change_fillable_fields

There was 1 failure:

1) Tests\App\Http\Controllers\BooksControllerTest::update_should_only_change_fil\
lable_fields
Failed asserting that 422 matches expected 200.
```

It looks like you are getting a validation error from your missing author parameter. Let's change the validation rule to match the BooksController@update change you just made (Listing 9-40).

Listing 9-40. Updating Validation for BooksController@update

```
$this->validate($request, [
    'title' => 'required|max:255',
    'description' => 'required',
    'author_id' => 'exists:authors,id'
], [
    'description.required' => 'Please fill out the :attribute.'
]);
```

An important difference between BooksController@update and BooksController@store validation is that you don't use the require rule on update. You only check that the records exist in the authors table if the field is present and allow the endpoint to optionally change the author. Now, let's see if your change makes the test pass (Listing 9-41).

Listing 9-41. Running the Test After Updating Validation

```
# vagrant@homestead:~/Code/bookr$
$ phpunit --filter=update_should_only_change_fillable_fields

OK (1 test, 11 assertions)
```

Moving on, the next error from the suite is from the *destroy_should_remove_a_valid_book* test (Listing 9-42).

Listing 9-42. The Next Error from Your Test Suite

```
1) Tests\App\Http\Controllers\BooksControllerTest::destroy_should_remove_a_valid_book
Illuminate\Database\QueryException: SQLSTATE[23000]: Integrity constraint violation: 1452
Cannot add or update a child row: a foreign key constraint fails
```

The test's factory() call fails because of the foreign key constraint. Fixing this test is a one-line change using your new bookFactory() method (Listing 9-43).

Listing 9-43. Fixing the Failing BooksController@destroy Test

```
208    /** @test **/
209    public function destroy_should_remove_a_valid_book()
210    {
211        $book = $this->bookFactory();
212
213        $this
214            ->delete("/books/{$book->id}")
215            ->seeStatusCode(204)
216            ->isEmpty();
217
218        $this->notSeeInDatabase('books', ['id' => $book->id]);
219    }
```

Let's see if your destroy test passes after your change (Listing 9-44).

Listing 9-44. Running the Test After Updating BooksController@destroy

```
# vagrant@homestead:~/Code/bookr$
$ phpunit --filter=destroy_should_remove_a_valid_book

OK (1 test, 2 assertions)
```

You've fixed a few individual tests. Now run the entire suite to see what remains (Listing 9-45).

Listing 9-45. The Next Error from the Test Suite

```
Tests\App\Http\Controllers\BooksControllerValidationTest::it_validates_required_fields_when_
updating_a_book
Illuminate\Database\QueryException: SQLSTATE[23000]: Integrity constraint violation: 1452
Cannot add or update a child row: a foreign key constraint fails
```

This error comes from *tests/app/Http/Controllers/BooksControllerValidationTest.php* and looks like another factory failure (Listing 9-46).

Listing 9-46. Updating the Test to Use the bookFactory() Method

```php
/** @test **/
public function it_validates_required_fields_when_updating_a_book()
{
    $book = $this->bookFactory();

    $this->put("/books/{$book->id}", [], ['Accept' => 'application/json']);
    $this->assertEquals(Response::HTTP_UNPROCESSABLE_ENTITY, $this->response-
>getStatusCode());
    $body = json_decode($this->response->getContent(), true);

    $this->assertArrayHasKey('title', $body);
    $this->assertArrayHasKey('description', $body);

    $this->assertEquals(["The title field is required."], $body['title']);
    $this->assertEquals(["Please provide a description."], $body['description']);
}
```

You replace the factory() call with the bookFactory() method and remove a few assertions for the authors validation. That should be enough to get the test passing again (Listing 9-47).

Listing 9-47. Running the Validation Test

```
# vagrant@homestead:~/Code/bookr$
$ phpunit --filter=it_validates_required_fields_when_updating_a_book

OK (1 test, 5 assertions)
```

You are getting the same foreign key errors in various places so let's bulk-update tests that are using the original factory() call and see what remains afterwards. Let's start with the *tests/app/Http/Controllers/BooksControllerValidationTest.php* file (Listing 9-48).

Listing 9-48. Replacing All factory() Calls in the Validation Test File

```
/** @test **/
public function title_fails_create_validation_when_just_too_long()
{
    // Creating a book
    $book = $this->bookFactory();
    //...
}

/** @test **/
public function title_fails_update_validation_when_just_too_long()
{
    // Updating a book
    $book = $this->bookFactory();
    // ...
}

/** @test **/
public function title_passes_create_validation_when_exactly_max()
{
    // Creating a new Book
    $book = $this->bookFactory();
    // ...
}

/** @test **/
public function title_passes_update_validation_when_exactly_max()
{
    // Updating a book
    $book = $this->bookFactory();
    // ...
}
```

Next, you will update the tests/app/Http/Controllers/BooksControllerTest.php file (Listing 9-49).

Listing 9-49. Replacing All factory() Calls in BooksControllerTest

```
/** @test **/
public function index_should_return_a_collection_of_records()
{
    $books = $this->bookFactory(2);
    // ...
}

/** @test **/
public function show_should_return_a_valid_book()
{
    $book = $this->bookFactory();
    // ...
}
```

The BooksController@index test creates two books since you are testing for a collection of records.

Hopefully the foreign key errors are behind you. Let's see what failures you have remaining in the BooksControllerValidationTest (Listing 9-50).

Listing 9-50. Remaining Validation Test Failures

```
# vagrant@homestead:~/Code/bookr$
$ phpunit tests/app/Http/Controllers/BooksControllerValidationTest.php

There were 2 failures:

1) Tests\App\Http\Controllers\BooksControllerValidationTest::it_validates_requir\
ed_fields_when_creating_a_new_book
Failed asserting that an array has the key 'author'.

/home/vagrant/Code/bookr/tests/app/Http/Controllers/BooksControllerValidationTest.php:24

2) Tests\App\Http\Controllers\BooksControllerValidationTest::title_passes_create_validation_
when_exactly_max
Failed asserting that 422 matches expected 201.

/home/vagrant/Code/bookr/vendor/laravel/lumen-framework/src/Testing/CrawlerTrait.php:412
/home/vagrant/Code/bookr/tests/app/Http/Controllers/BooksControllerValidationTest.php:107

FAILURES!
Tests: 6, Assertions: 20, Failures: 2.
```

It looks like you have a failed assertion for a key you are no longer providing and a *422* response code, which means you have some validation errors when you don't expect them.

The first fix is simply removing an assertion for the author key and removing the author validation message check. Listing 9-51 shows what the BooksControllerValidationTest should look like after you remove the author checks.

Listing 9-51. Removing Author Test Assertions

```
13  /** @test **/
14  public function it_validates_required_fields_when_creating_a_new_book()
15  {
16      $this->post('/books', [], ['Accept' => 'application/json']);
17
18      $this->assertEquals(Response::HTTP_UNPROCESSABLE_ENTITY, $this->response-
        >getStatusCode());
19
20      $body = json_decode($this->response->getContent(), true);
21
22      $this->assertArrayHasKey('title', $body);
23      $this->assertArrayHasKey('description', $body);
24
25      $this->assertEquals(["The title field is required."], $body['title']);
26      $this->assertEquals(
27          ["Please provide a description."],
28          $body['description']
29      );
30  }
```

The second failure in BooksControllerValidationTest happens because the author_id is a required field (Listing 9-52).

Listing 9-52. Fixing the BooksController@create Exactly Max Validation Test

```
90   /** @test **/
91   public function title_passes_create_validation_when_exactly_max()
92   {
93       // Creating a new Book
94       $book = $this->bookFactory();
95       $book->title = str_repeat('a', 255);
96       $this->post("/books", [
97           'title' => $book->title,
98           'description' => $book->description,
99           'author_id' => $book->author->id, // Pass a valid author
100      ], ['Accept' => 'application/json']);
101
102      $this
103          ->seeStatusCode(Response::HTTP_CREATED)
104          ->seeInDatabase('books', ['title' => $book->title]);
105  }
```

Next, there are some instances of 'author' => $book->author you need to replace with a valid author_id in BooksControllerValidationTest. The first test is when the title is just too long when trying to create a book (Listing 9-53).

Listing 9-53. Adding the author_id Field to the POST Request

```
48   /** @test **/
49   public function title_fails_create_validation_when_just_too_long()
50   {
51       // Creating a book
52       $book = $this->bookFactory();
53       $book->title = str_repeat('a', 256);
54
55       $this->post("/books", [
56           'title' => $book->title,
57           'description' => $book->description,
58           'author_id' => $book->author->id,
59       ], ['Accept' => 'application/json']);
60
61       $this
62           ->seeStatusCode(Response::HTTP_UNPROCESSABLE_ENTITY)
63           ->seeJson([
64               'title' => ["The title may not be greater than 255 characters."]
65           ])
66           ->notSeeInDatabase('books', ['title' => $book->title]);
67   }
```

The second place you need to send an author id is when updating a title with a PUT request (Listing 9-54).

Listing 9-54. Adding the author_id Field to the PUT Request

```
69   /** @test **/
70   public function title_fails_update_validation_when_just_too_long()
71   {
72       // Updating a book
73       $book = $this->bookFactory();
74       $book->title = str_repeat('a', 256);
75
76       $this->put("/books/{$book->id}", [
77           'title' => $book->title,
78           'description' => $book->description,
79           'author_id' => $book->author->id,
80       ], ['Accept' => 'application/json']);
81
82       $this
83           ->seeStatusCode(Response::HTTP_UNPROCESSABLE_ENTITY)
84           ->seeJson([
85               'title' => ["The title may not be greater than 255 characters."]
86           ])
87           ->notSeeInDatabase('books', ['title' => $book->title]);
88   }
```

The final author id replacement is when the title passes validation with exactly the maximum characters allowed (Listing 9-55).

Listing 9-55. Adding the author_id Field to the PUT Request

```
108  /** @test **/
109  public function title_passes_update_validation_when_exactly_max()
110  {
111      // Updating a book
112      $book = $this->bookFactory();
113      $book->title = str_repeat('a', 255);
114
115      $this->put("/books/{$book->id}", [
116          'title' => $book->title,
117          'description' => $book->description,
118          'author_id' => $book->author->id,
119      ], ['Accept' => 'application/json']);
120
121      $this
122          ->seeStatusCode(Response::HTTP_OK)
123          ->seeInDatabase('books', ['title' => $book->title]);
124  }
```

After making these author changes, you can run all the tests in the BooksControllerValidationTest class (Listing 9-56).

Listing 9-56. Running the Tests for BooksControllerValidationTest

```
# vagrant@homestead:~/Code/bookr$
$ phpunit tests/app/Http/Controllers/BooksControllerValidationTest.php

OK (6 tests, 20 assertions)
```

You are starting to see the light at the end of the refactor tunnel! Run your test suite and see what remains (Listing 9-57).

Listing 9-57. Running the Full Test Suite After Your Fixes

```
# vagrant@homestead:~/Code/bookr$
$ phpunit

There were 3 failures:
...

FAILURES!
Tests: 27, Assertions: 104, Errors: 1, Failures: 3.
```

I've only provided partial error output, but if you inspect the "Unable to find JSON fragment" error closely you will notice that the response includes all author data from the Author model. You need to update your test to check the author's name (Listing 9-58).

Listing 9-58. Using Author Model in the Assertion of the author Property

```php
/** @test **/
public function index_should_return_a_collection_of_records()
{
    $books = $this->bookFactory(2);

    $this->get('/books');

    $content = json_decode($this->response->getContent(), true);
    $this->assertArrayHasKey('data', $content);

    foreach ($books as $book) {
        $this->seeJson([
            'id' => $book->id,
            'title' => $book->title,
            'description' => $book->description,
            'author' => $book->author->name, // Check the author's name
            'created' => $book->created_at->toIso8601String(),
            'updated' => $book->updated_at->toIso8601String(),
        ]);
    }
}
```

Next, verify that your change fixed the test (Listing 9-59).

Listing 9-59. Testing the BooksController@index Test

```
# vagrant@homestead:~/Code/bookr$
$ phpunit --filter=index_should_return_a_collection_of_records

OK (1 test, 13 assertions)
```

Now run phpunit again to get the last two failures (Listing 9-60).

Listing 9-60. Getting the Next PHPUnit Failure

```
# vagrant@homestead:~/Code/bookr$
$ phpunit
...
There were 2 failures:

FAILURES!
Tests: 27, Assertions: 115, Errors: 1, Failures: 2.
```

You're getting closer! The next error looks like an invalid comparison of the Author model. Looking at the *show_should_return_a_valid_book* test closely, you need to update the following assertEquals check (Listing 9-61).

Listing 9-61. Fixing the Assertion for the Author's Name

```
/** @test **/
public function show_should_return_a_valid_book()
{
    $book = $this->bookFactory();

    $this
        ->get("/books/{$book->id}")
        ->seeStatusCode(200);

    // Get the response and assert the data key exists
    $content = json_decode($this->response->getContent(), true);
    $this->assertArrayHasKey('data', $content);
    $data = $content['data'];

    // Assert the Book Properties match
    $this->assertEquals($book->id, $data['id']);
    $this->assertEquals($book->title, $data['title']);
    $this->assertEquals($book->description, $data['description']);
    $this->assertEquals($book->author->name, $data['author']);
    $this->assertEquals($book->created_at->toIso8601String(), $data['created']);
    $this->assertEquals($book->updated_at->toIso8601String(), $data['created']);
}
```

Let's see if you fixed the test and what remains to be fixed (Listing 9-62).

Listing 9-62. Running the Test Suite

```
# vagrant@homestead:~/Code/bookr$
$ phpunit

There was 1 failure:
...

FAILURES!
Tests: 27, Assertions: 117, Errors: 1, Failures: 1.
```

The Failed asserting that 302 matches expected 201 message means that the controller is sending a redirect response. You are communicating with JSON clients so you need to send the request with the Accept: application/json header in order to get back a JSON response instead of the default failed validation redirect. Looking at this test, you can see that validation will fail because you need to send an author_id, which is required in BooksController@create, so let's update both now (Listing 9-63).

Listing 9-63. Using the Author Model to Fix the Failing Test

```
138  /** @test */
139  public function store_should_respond_with_a_201_and_location_header_when_successful()
140  {
141      $author = factory(\App\Author::class)->create();
142      $this->post('/books', [
143          'title' => 'The Invisible Man',
144          'description' => 'An invisible man is trapped in the terror of his own
                 creation',
145          'author_id' => $author->id
146      ], ['Accept' => 'application/json']);
147
148      $this
149          ->seeStatusCode(201)
150          ->seeHeaderWithRegExp('Location', '#/books/[\d]+$#');
151  }
```

The individual test passes now (Listing 9-64).

Listing 9-64. Running the PHPUnit Test

```
# vagrant@homestead:~/Code/bookr$
$ phpunit --filter=store_should_respond_with_a_201_and_location_header_when_successful

OK (1 test, 3 assertions)
```

Run your entire suite again and see if you are back to green yet (Listing 9-65).

Listing 9-65. Running the Test Suite

```
# vagrant@homestead:~/Code/bookr$
$ phpunit
```

There was 1 error:

```
1) Tests\App\Transformer\BookTransformerTest::it_transforms_a_book_model
Illuminate\Database\QueryException: SQLSTATE[23000]: Integrity constraint violat\
ion...
```

```
FAILURES!
Tests: 27, Assertions: 117, Errors: 1.
```

One more error and you should be back to green. The error is another foreign key constraint violation in the BooksTransformerTest file. You just need to use the bookFactory() method (Listing 9-66).

Listing 9-66. Updating the Failing BookTransformerTest

```php
22  /** @test **/
23  public function it_transforms_a_book_model()
24  {
25      $book = $this->bookFactory();
26      $subject = new BookTransformer();
27
28      $transform = $subject->transform($book);
29
30      $this->assertArrayHasKey('id', $transform);
31      $this->assertArrayHasKey('title', $transform);
32      $this->assertArrayHasKey('description', $transform);
33      $this->assertArrayHasKey('author', $transform);
34      $this->assertArrayHasKey('created', $transform);
35      $this->assertArrayHasKey('updated', $transform);
36  }
```

You should be completely done and have full passing tests again (Listing 9-67).

Listing 9-67. Running the Test Suite

```
# vagrant@homestead:~/Code/bookr$
$ phpunit

OK (27 tests, 125 assertions)
```

Finally!

Git Commit: Add Author Model Data to Books

b463cc9 (https://bitbucket.org/paulredmond/apress-bookr/commits/b463cc9)

Conclusion

You've successfully refactored your code to use the new authors model. For a minor change, you can see that your test suite took a bit of work to fix. While annoying, good test coverage is a huge time saver in the long run.

The small investment in fixing tests will pay dividends. You can rip out the guts of your code and have confidence that test specifications will lead you to less bugs, and keep business and code requirements documented.

You could have designed your schema with separate tables up front in a real project. Thinking about schema design early is important, but do not over-design your schema up front if it blocks you from developing iteratively. Your string column for the author name was fine to get you going, and you were able to refactor things (somewhat) painlessly. You don't have to finish the application in one sitting and you may get a few things wrong at first.

CHAPTER 10

The /authors API Resource

In this chapter, you are going to build on the last chapter's introduction to the authors table. You will start working on API endpoints for your dedicated Author resource! At this point, you should be familiar with the basics of defining routes and working with controllers. Reference Chapter 4 and Chapter 5 to get a refresher as needed.

The author endpoint will provide API endpoints for getting author details and the books they've authored. Along the way I will show you a really cool feature of Fractal that allows you to include associated transformer data in a response; this means you can easily include book data in author responses if desired.

Your basic API endpoints will look like Listing 10-1.

Listing 10-1. Basic REST /authors Resource

```
GET     /authors        Get all the authors
POST    /authors        Create a new author
GET     /authors/{id}   Get an author's details
PUT     /authors/{id}   Update an author
DELETE  /authors/{id}   Delete an author
```

Before you work on the individual endpoints, let's define all your routes in app/Http/routes.php (Listing 10-2).

Listing 10-2. Defining the Author Routes

```
27  $app->group([
28      'prefix' => '/authors',
29      'namespace' => 'App\Http\Controllers'
30  ], function (\Laravel\Lumen\Application $app) {
31      $app->get('/', 'AuthorsController@index');
32      $app->post('/', 'AuthorsController@store');
33      $app->get('/{id:[\d]+}', 'AuthorsController@show');
34      $app->put('/{id:[\d]+}', 'AuthorsController@update');
35      $app->delete('/{id:[\d]+}', 'AuthorsController@destroy');
36  });
```

The code snippet introduces the $app->group() method, which accepts the following keys: prefix, namespace, and middleware. You need to define the namespace key so the group knows how to locate the AuthorsController and you define a prefix of /authors that all routes in the group will use.

© Paul Redmond 2016
P. Redmond, *Lumen Programming Guide*, DOI 10.1007/978-1-4842-2187-7_10

The GET /authors Endpoint

Your first endpoint will get all authors. You will create an *AuthorTransformer* class that you can use on all author responses. If you recall, in the last chapter you created a factory and database seeder for authors that you can use to write your tests for the /authors endpoints. Time to code.

First up, let's create the files necessary for this whole section (Listing 10-3).

Listing 10-3. Creating the AuthorTransformer Class

```
# vagrant@homestead:~/Code/bookr$
$ touch app/Transformer/AuthorTransformer.php
$ touch tests/app/Transformer/AuthorTransformerTest.php
$ touch app/Http/Controllers/AuthorsController.php
$ touch tests/app/Http/Controllers/AuthorsControllerTest.php
```

The AuthorsTransformer

Let's start with the AuthorTransformerTest class (Listing 10-4).

Listing 10-4. The AuthorTransformerTest Skeleton Class

```php
 1  <?php
 2
 3  namespace Tests\App\Transformer;
 4
 5  use TestCase;
 6  use App\Transformer\AuthorTransformer;
 7  use Laravel\Lumen\Testing\DatabaseMigrations;
 8
 9  class AuthorTransformerTest extends TestCase
10  {
11      use DatabaseMigrations;
12
13      public function setUp()
14      {
15          parent::setUp();
16
17          $this->subject = new AuthorTransformer();
18      }
19      /** @test **/
20      public function it_can_be_initialized()
21      {
22          $this->assertInstanceOf(AuthorTransformer::class, $this->subject);
23      }
24  }
```

Your test file is fairly familiar. As a convenience I've opted to construct the transformer before each test in the setUp() method and assign it to $this->subject.

Next, you create the AuthorTransformer class to get the test passing (Listing 10-5).

Listing 10-5. Creating the AuthorTransformer Class

```php
1   <?php
2
3   namespace App\Transformer;
4
5   use App\Author;
6   use League\Fractal\TransformerAbstract;
7
8   class AuthorTransformer extends TransformerAbstract
9   {
10  }
```

Now that you have the boilerplate code, you need to write tests for your specification. First, the
AuthorTransformer should simply need to be able to transform an Author model in a consistent way that
you expect (Listing 10-6).

Listing 10-6. The Test Specification for the transform() Method

```php
25  /** @test **/
26  public function it_can_transform_an_author()
27  {
28      $author = factory(\App\Author::class)->create();
29
30      $actual = $this->subject->transform($author);
31
32      $this->assertEquals($author->id, $actual['id']);
33      $this->assertEquals($author->name, $actual['name']);
34      $this->assertEquals($author->gender, $actual['gender']);
35      $this->assertEquals($author->biography, $actual['biography']);
36      $this->assertEquals(
37          $author->created_at->toIso8601String(),
38          $actual['created']
39      );
40      $this->assertEquals(
41          $author->updated_at->toIso8601String(),
42          $actual['created']
43      );
44  }
```

Your assertions are straightforward and make sure that the transformer includes all the expected author
properties. Now write the AuthorTransformer::transform() implementation to get the newly written test
to pass (Listing 10-7).

Listing 10-7. Implementing the AuthorTransformer::transform() Method

```php
10  /**
11   * Transform an author model
12   *
13   * @param Author $author
14   * @return array
15   */
```

167

```
16  public function transform(Author $author)
17  {
18      return [
19          'id' => $author->id,
20          'name' => $author->name,
21          'gender' => $author->gender,
22          'biography' => $author->biography,
23          'created' => $author->created_at->toIso8601String(),
24          'updated' => $author->created_at->toIso8601String(),
25      ];
26  }
```

You should have been running tests after writing each test and then after implementing it. Let's make sure you are passing now (Listing 10-8).

Listing 10-8. Running the Test Suite

```
# vagrant@homestead:~/Code/bookr$
$ phpunit

OK (29 tests, 132 assertions)
```

The Author Controller

Now that you have a basic `AuthorTransformer` you will change focus to the `AuthorsController@index` route. Let's write your first test in the `tests/app/Http/Controllers/AuthorsControllerTest.php` file (Listing 10-9).

Listing 10-9. Testing the AuthorsController@index for a 200 Status Code

```
1   <?php
2
3   namespace Tests\App\Http\Controllers;
4
5   use TestCase;
6   use Illuminate\Http\Response;
7   use Laravel\Lumen\Testing\DatabaseMigrations;
8
9   class AuthorsControllerTest extends TestCase
10  {
11      use DatabaseMigrations;
12
13      /** @test **/
14      public function index_responds_with_200_status_code()
15      {
16          $this->get('/authors')->seeStatusCode(Response::HTTP_OK);
17      }
18  }
```

Running the test at this point results in a failing test with a 500 status code because you haven't defined the controller. Add the following controller code in Listing 10-10 to get the test back to green.

Listing 10-10. Defining the AuthorsController

```php
1   <?php
2
3   namespace App\Http\Controllers;
4
5   use App\Author;
6
7   class AuthorsController extends Controller
8   {
9       public function index()
10      {
11      }
12  }
```

Just defining the route and controller method results in a 200 status code. Next, you will write assertions to test that the AuthorsController@index returns a collection of records in the AuthorsControllerTest file (Listing 10-11).

Listing 10-11. Testing That the AuthorsController@index Returns Multiple Records

```php
19  /** @test **/
20  public function index_should_return_a_collection_of_records()
21  {
22      $authors = factory(\App\Author::class, 2)->create();
23
24      $this->get('/authors', ['Accept' => 'application/json']);
25
26      $body = json_decode($this->response->getContent(), true);
27      $this->assertArrayHasKey('data', $body);
28      $this->assertCount(2, $body['data']);
29
30      foreach ($authors as $author) {
31          $this->seeJson([
32              'id' => $author->id,
33              'name' => $author->name,
34              'gender' => $author->gender,
35              'biography' => $author->biography,
36              'created' => $author->created_at->toIso8601String(),
37              'updated' => $author->updated_at->toIso8601String(),
38          ]);
39      }
40  }
```

The test is nearly identical to the same test for the /books route. Next, write the integration and get the test to pass (Listing 10-12).

Listing 10-12. Returning a Collection of Author Records

```php
1   <?php
2
3   namespace App\Http\Controllers;
```

```
 4
 5  use App\Author;
 6  use App\Transformer\AuthorTransformer;
 7
 8  class AuthorsController extends Controller
 9  {
10      public function index()
11      {
12          return $this->collection(
13              Author::all(),
14              new AuthorTransformer()
15          );
16      }
17  }
```

You are starting to reap the benefits of your Fractal integration and returning a consistent response takes no effort!

Let's verify your tests now (Listing 10-13).

Listing 10-13. Running Tests for the AuthorsController

```
# vagrant@homestead:~/Code/bookr$
$ phpunit

OK (31 tests, 147 assertions)
```

The GET /authors/{id} Endpoint

You will continue with your quick pace and knock out the first version of the GET /authors/{id} route. In this route, you want to allow including an author's books, so I will show you a way to easily accomplish this with Fractal.

A Basic Response

Let's start by testing for a basic response you are familiar with from the /books/{id} route (Listing 10-14).

Listing 10-14. Testing the AuthorsController@show Method

```
42  /** @test **/
43  public function show_should_return_a_valid_author()
44  {
45      $book = $this->bookFactory();
46      $author = $book->author;
47
48      $this->get("/authors/{$author->id}", ['Accept' => 'application/json']);
49      $body = json_decode($this->response->getContent(), true);
50      $this->assertArrayHasKey('data', $body);
51
52      $this->seeJson([
53          'id' => $author->id,
```

```
54          'name' => $author->name,
55          'gender' => $author->gender,
56          'biography' => $author->biography,
57          'created' => $author->created_at->toIso8601String(),
58          'updated' => $author->updated_at->toIso8601String(),
59      ]);
60  }
61
62  /** @test **/
63  public function show_should_fail_on_an_invalid_author()
64  {
65      $this->get('/authors/1234', ['Accept' => 'application/json']);
66      $this->seeStatusCode(Response::HTTP_NOT_FOUND);
67
68      $this->seeJson([
69          'message' => 'Not Found',
70          'status' => Response::HTTP_NOT_FOUND
71      ]);
72
73      $body = json_decode($this->response->getContent(), true);
74      $this->assertArrayHasKey('error', $body);
75      $error = $body['error'];
76
77      $this->assertEquals('Not Found', $error['message']);
78      $this->assertEquals(Response::HTTP_NOT_FOUND, $error['status']);
79  }
```

I cheated a little and added two tests, but everything in these tests should be familiar to you already. The implementation for the AuthorsController@show method should cover both tests and get back to green (Listing 10-15).

Listing 10-15. Implementing a Passing AuthorsController@show Method

```
18  public function show($id)
19  {
20      return $this->item(
21          Author::findorFail($id),
22          new AuthorTransformer()
23      );
24  }
```

Including Other Models in the Response

Fractal provides a way to build responses for relationships between transformers. This will allow you to load the Book data for an author without much effort on your part, and provide consistent behavior across your API. You can provide these associations by default, or optionally include them.

How should you go about implementing the inclusion of optional data in your API? A common strategy that you are going to use is to include a query string parameter to instruct the API to provide optional extra data (Listing 10-16).

Listing 10-16. Your Query String Used to Include Extra Data

```
http://bookr.app/authors/1?include=books
```

In order for Fractal to include Book data, you need to add a few things to *app/Http/Response/ FractalResponse.php*. You need a way to get the request query string param include and pass its value to fractal. One way to accomplish this is to pass an instance of *Illuminate\Http\Request* as a dependency of FractalResponse.

First, let's write your tests for updating the FractalResponse to include the Request dependency. You will start by adding the Illuminate\Http\Request dependency throughout the *tests/app/Http/Response/ FractalResponseTest.php* file. The FractalResponseTest class should look Listing 10-17 when you are done.

Listing 10-17. Full FractalResponseTest Source

```php
1   <?php
2
3   namespace Tests\App\Http\Response;
4
5   use TestCase;
6   use Mockery as m;
7   use League\Fractal\Manager;
8   use Illuminate\Http\Request;
9   use App\Http\Response\FractalResponse;
10  use League\Fractal\Serializer\SerializerAbstract;
11
12  class FractalResponseTest extends TestCase
13  {
14      /** @test **/
15      public function it_can_be_initialized()
16      {
17          $manager = m::mock(Manager::class);
18          $serializer = m::mock(SerializerAbstract::class);
19          $request = m::mock(Request::class);
20
21          $manager
22              ->shouldReceive('setSerializer')
23              ->with($serializer)
24              ->once()
25              ->andReturn($manager);
26          $fractal = new FractalResponse($manager, $serializer, $request);
27          $this->assertInstanceOf(FractalResponse::class, $fractal);
28      }
29
30      /** @test **/
31      public function it_can_transform_an_item()
32      {
33          // Request
34          $request = m::mock(Request::class);
35
36          // Transformer
37          $transformer = m::mock('League\Fractal\TransformerAbstract');
38
```

```
39          // Scope
40          $scope = m::mock('League\Fractal\Scope');
41          $scope
42              ->shouldReceive('toArray')
43              ->once()
44              ->andReturn(['foo' => 'bar']);
45
46          // Serializer
47          $serializer = m::mock('League\Fractal\Serializer\SerializerAbstract');
48
49          $manager = m::mock('League\Fractal\Manager');
50          $manager
51              ->shouldReceive('setSerializer')
52              ->with($serializer)
53              ->once();
54
55          $manager
56              ->shouldReceive('createData')
57              ->once()
58              ->andReturn($scope);
59
60          $subject = new FractalResponse($manager, $serializer, $request);
61          $this->assertInternalType(
62              'array',
63              $subject->item(['foo' => 'bar'], $transformer)
64          );
65      }
66
67      /** @test **/
68      public function it_can_transform_a_collection()
69      {
70          $data = [
71              ['foo' => 'bar'],
72              ['fizz' => 'buzz'],
73          ];
74
75          // Request
76          $request = m::mock(Request::class);
77
78          // Transformer
79          $transformer = m::mock('League\Fractal\TransformerAbstract');
80
81          // Scope
82          $scope = m::mock('League\Fractal\Scope');
83          $scope
84              ->shouldReceive('toArray')
85              ->once()
86              ->andReturn($data);
87
88          // Serializer
89          $serializer = m::mock('League\Fractal\Serializer\SerializerAbstract');
```

```
90
91              $manager = m::mock('League\Fractal\Manager');
92              $manager
93                  ->shouldReceive('setSerializer')
94                  ->with($serializer)
95                  ->once();
96
97              $manager
98                  ->shouldReceive('createData')
99                  ->once()
100                 ->andReturn($scope);
101
102             $subject = new FractalResponse($manager, $serializer, $request);
103             $this->assertInternalType(
104                 'array',
105                 $subject->collection($data, $transformer)
106             );
107     }
108 }
```

You've imported the Illuminate\Http\Response class and included it throughout the file in order to initialize an instance with the response. Now you need to update your FractalResponse class to accept the Illuminate Request instance in the constructor (Listing 10-18).

Listing 10-18. Updating FractalResponse to Accept a Request Instance (Partial Source)

```
1   <?php
2
3   namespace App\Http\Response;
4
5   use League\Fractal\Manager;
6   use League\Fractal\Resource\Item;
7   use League\Fractal\TransformerAbstract;
8   use League\Fractal\Resource\Collection;
9   use League\Fractal\Resource\ResourceInterface;
10  use League\Fractal\Serializer\SerializerAbstract;
11  use Illuminate\Http\Request;
12
13  class FractalResponse
14  {
15      /**
16       * @var Manager
17       */
18      private $manager;
19
20      /**
21       * @var SerializerAbstract
22       */
23      private $serializer;
24
25      /**
26       * @var Request
```

```
27       */
28       private $request;
29
30       public function __construct(
31           Manager $manager,
32           SerializerAbstract $serializer,
33           Request $request
34       ) {
35           $this->manager = $manager;
36           $this->serializer = $serializer;
37           $this->manager->setSerializer($serializer);
38           $this->request = $request;
39       }
40       // ...
41   }
```

The code snippet looks like a lot of code; all that is happening here is that you are importing the Illuminate\Http\Response class, type-hinting the constructor argument, and assigning the request. The $request parameter will come from the Service Container.

If you run the test suite now, you will get lots of failures because you've updated your FractalResponse constructor with the Response instance. In order to get back to green, you need to update the *app/Providers/FractalServiceProvider.php* file to pass the response instance from the container into your FractalResponse instance (Listing 10-19).

Listing 10-19. Adding the Request Dependency to the FractalResponse Service

```
12   public function register()
13   {
14       // Bind the DataArraySerializer to an interface contract
15       $this->app->bind(
16           'League\Fractal\Serializer\SerializerAbstract',
17           'League\Fractal\Serializer\DataArraySerializer'
18       );
19
20       $this->app->bind(FractalResponse::class, function ($app) {
21           $manager = new Manager();
22           $serializer = $app['League\Fractal\Serializer\SerializerAbstract'];
23
24           return new FractalResponse($manager, $serializer, $app['request']);
25       });
26
27       $this->app->alias(FractalResponse::class, 'fractal');
28   }
```

The service container has the service $app['request'], which is a service that represents the current request. You simply pass the service into the FractalResponse constructor and now your tests should pass again.

Let's verify if your tests are passing now (Listing 10-20).

Listing 10-20. Running the Test Suite

```
# vagrant@homestead:~/Code/bookr$
$ phpunit

OK (33 tests, 160 assertions)
```

Now that you have the $app['request'] instance in your FractalResponse service you are ready to write a method in the FractalResponse class that parses request includes with the following requirements:

- If an include string is passed, use it to parse includes.

- If a parameter is *not* passed, use the URL *?include=* query param.

The requirements allow you to manually pass the includes, but you will commonly rely on the ?include= query string parameter.

The tests should look something like Listing 10-21.

Listing 10-21. Tests for the FractalResponse::parseIncludes() Method

```
110  /** @test **/
111  public function it_should_parse_passed_includes_when_passed()
112  {
113      $serializer = m::mock(SerializerAbstract::class);
114
115      $manager = m::mock(Manager::class);
116      $manager->shouldReceive('setSerializer')->with($serializer);
117      $manager
118          ->shouldReceive('parseIncludes')
119          ->with('books');
120
121      $request = m::mock(Request::class);
122      $request->shouldNotReceive('query');
123
124      $subject = new FractalResponse($manager, $serializer, $request);
125      $subject->parseIncludes('books');
126  }
127
128  /** @test **/
129  public function it_should_parse_request_query_includes_with_no_arguments()
130  {
131      $serializer = m::mock(SerializerAbstract::class);
132      $manager = m::mock(Manager::class);
133      $manager->shouldReceive('setSerializer')->with($serializer);
134      $manager
135          ->shouldReceive('parseIncludes')
136          ->with('books');
137
138      $request = m::mock(Request::class);
139      $request
140          ->shouldReceive('query')
141          ->with('include', '')
```

```
142              ->andReturn('books');
143
144        (new FractalResponse($manager, $serializer, $request))->parseIncludes();
145  }
```

You have tested both outlined scenarios with mockery. The first test ensures that the passed parameter is used and that the request instance query() method is not called. In the second example, you call parseIncludes() with no arguments and assert that the request object's query method is called and returns a value.

The AuthorsTransformer will now optionally include the books associated with an author when the request query string contains */authors/{id}?include=books*. This is where your eager-loading call in the controller is a good idea: instead of each individual book requiring an extra query, all the author's books are retrieved in a single query.

You are now ready to write the implementation in your FractalResponse service (Listing 10-22).

Listing 10-22. Implementing the FractalResponse::parseIncludes() Method

```
41  /**
42   * Get the includes from the request if none are passed.
43   *
44   * @param null $includes
45   */
46  public function parseIncludes($includes = null)
47  {
48      if (empty($includes)) {
49          $includes = $this->request->query('include', '');
50      }
51
52      $this->manager->parseIncludes($includes);
53  }
```

You've defined the parseIncludes() method right below the constructor. The method checks to see if the $includes parameter has a non-empty value. If it *is* empty, you assign $includes to the request query param ?include. The second parameter in $this->request->query('include', '') is the default if include doesn't exist.

Let's run the FractalResponseTest after adding tests and the implementation and see where things are at (Listing 10-23).

Listing 10-23. Running the FractalResponse Tests

```
# vagrant@homestead:~/Code/bookr$
$ phpunit

OK (35 tests, 166 assertions)
```

The FractalResponse class can now accept the ?include= query parameter and allows the Fractal manager class to parse the passed includes.

The other side of the includes functionality is the AuthorTransformer class and making sure it can transform the books associated with the author.

If you look at the transformers documentation (http://fractal.thephpleague.com/transformers/) (see the "Including Data" section) you will see two class properties that transformers can define: $availableIncludes and $defaultIncludes. The $availableIncludes is used to *optionally* include other transformers, and the $defaultIncludes array automatically includes other transformers. You will opt to use $availableIncludes to include related Book records on demand. Append the test in Listing 10-24 to the *tests/app/Transformer/AuthorTransformerTest.php* file.

Listing 10-24. Test for Transforming an Author's Books

```
46  /** @test **/
47  public function it_can_transform_related_books()
48  {
49      $book = $this->bookFactory();
50      $author = $book->author;
51
52      $data = $this->subject->includeBooks($author);
53      $this->assertInstanceOf(\League\Fractal\Resource\Collection::class, $data);
54  }
```

In order to get your new failing author transformer test passing you need to define the *AuthorTransformer::includeBooks()* method in the file *app/Transformers/AuthorTransformer.php*. Define the following at the top of the AuthorTransformer class (Listing 10-25).

Listing 10-25. The AuthorsTransformer::includeBooks() Method

```
10  protected $availableIncludes = [
11      'books'
12  ];
13
14  public function includeBooks(Author $author)
15  {
16      return $this->collection($author->books, new BookTransformer());
17  }
```

Your transformer should pass now (Listing 10-26).

Listing 10-26. Running All Tests for AuthorTransformer

```
# vagrant@homestead:~/Code/bookr$
$ phpunit

OK (36 tests, 167 assertions)
```

You have one task remaining for this feature—you need to wire it all up in the controller. First, let's create a test to optionally include books in the /author/{id} response in your tests/app/Http/Controllers/AuthorsController.php file (Listing 10-27).

Listing 10-27. Test to Optionally Include Books

```
81  /** @test **/
82  public function show_optionally_includes_books()
83  {
84      $book = $this->bookFactory();
```

```
85         $author = $book->author;
86
87         $this->get(
88             "/authors/{$author->id}?include=books",
89             ['Accept' => 'application/json']
90         );
91
92         $body = json_decode($this->response->getContent(), true);
93
94         $this->assertArrayHasKey('data', $body);
95         $data = $body['data'];
96         $this->assertArrayHasKey('books', $data);
97         $this->assertArrayHasKey('data', $data['books']);
98         $this->assertCount(1, $data['books']['data']);
99
100        // See Author Data
101        $this->seeJson([
102            'id' => $author->id,
103            'name' => $author->name,
104        ]);
105
106        // Test included book Data (the first record)
107        $actual = $data['books']['data'][0];
108        $this->assertEquals($book->id, $actual['id']);
109        $this->assertEquals($book->title, $actual['title']);
110        $this->assertEquals($book->description, $actual['description']);
111        $this->assertEquals(
112            $book->created_at->toIso8601String(),
113            $actual['created']
114        );
115        $this->assertEquals(
116            $book->updated_at->toIso8601String(),
117            $actual['updated']
118        );
119    }
```

This test is long but easy to understand. The test looks similar to the *show_should_return_a_valid_author* test, but you don't need to assert as many author keys in the response because it's already covered. You only do enough to know the author is represented in the response and focus on testing that the books associated with the author are included.

The test will fail if you run it because you haven't told fractal about the *?include=books* part of your test yet, so fractal doesn't know you want to include books (Listing 10-28).

Listing 10-28. Optionally Including Books Test Failure

```
# vagrant@homestead:~/Code/bookr$
$ phpunit

There was 1 failure:

1) Tests\App\Http\Controllers\AuthorsControllerTest::show_optionally_includes_bo\
oks
```

Failed asserting that an array has the key 'books'.

/home/vagrant/Code/bookr/tests/app/Http/Controllers/AuthorsControllerTest.php:96

FAILURES!
Tests: 37, Assertions: 169, Failures: 1.

It would be nice if your controllers just automatically called the parseIncludes() method you built earlier to include related entities. To do this, you can call parseIncludes() in the base controller App\Http\Controllers\Controller.php where you assign $this->fractal in the constructor (Listing 10-29).

Listing 10-29. Calling parseIncludes() in the Base Controller

```
16 public function __construct(FractalResponse $fractal)
17 {
18     $this->fractal = $fractal;
19     $this->fractal->parseIncludes();
20 }
```

The base controller is calling FractalManager::parseIncludes() without passing any arguments and will assign any values in the ?include= query params. You can include multiple with ?include=books,another. Your feature should pass at this point (Listing 10-30).

Listing 10-30. Running the Test Suite

```
# vagrant@homestead:~/Code/bookr$
$ phpunit

OK (37 tests, 178 assertions)
```

After you put in some hard work, your feature works! An example response might look like Listing 10-31.

Listing 10-31. Sample Response for AuthorsController@show With Books

```
{
    "data":{
        "id":1,
        "name":"Jane Doe",
        "gender":"female",
        "biography":"Hello World",
        "created":"2015-11-25T00:13:00+0000",
        "updated":"2015-11-25T00:13:00+0000",
        "books":{
            "data":[
                {
                    "id":1,
                    "title":"Ab beatae dignissimos laudantium aut quod beatae",
                    "description":"Non reprehenderit ut pariatur. Voluptate magni nam ea
                    modi dolores rerum. Molestiae eaque et sunt et.",
                    "author":"Jane Doe",
                    "created":"2015-11-25T00:13:00+0000",
                    "updated":"2015-11-25T00:13:00+0000"
```

```
            }
        ]
    }
  }
}
```

With minimal effort you were able to load related model data into your response in a consistent fashion. Any time you include related entities, consumers can expect the same data patterns and keys.

The POST /authors Endpoint

The last section had many moving parts, but now it's time to slow it down and work on a more focused POST /authors endpoint. You've covered creating a new resource in the POST /books endpoint so most of this will be good review and practice. If you recall the steps taken in the BooksController::store() method, they were as follows:

- Validate the POST data.

- Create a new resource; in this case, a new Author.

- Respond with the new resource and a 201 created status code.

- Provide a Location header with the new location of the resource.

You will start by creating a new resource and responding with a 201, followed by adding on validation and the Location header.

First, you define a successful POST request test in tests/app/Http/Controllers/AuhorsControllerTest.php (Listing 10-32).

Listing 10-32. Test for Creating a New Author

```
121  /** @test **/
122  public function store_can_create_a_new_author()
123  {
124      $postData = [
125          'name' => 'H. G. Wells',
126          'gender' => 'male',
127          'biography' => 'Prolific Science-Fiction Writer',
128      ];
129
130      $this->post('/authors', $postData, ['Accept' => 'application/json']);
131
132      $this->seeStatusCode(201);
133      $data = $this->response->getData(true);
134      $this->assertArrayHasKey('data', $data);
135      $this->seeJson($postData);
136
137      $this->seeInDatabase('authors', $postData);
138  }
```

Here is the initial version of the AuthorsController@store (Listing 10-33).

Listing 10-33. AuthorsController with @store Method Added

```php
1   <?php
2
3   namespace App\Http\Controllers;
4
5   use App\Author;
6   use App\Transformer\AuthorTransformer;
7   use Illuminate\Http\Request;
8
9   class AuthorsController extends Controller
10  {
11      public function index()
12      {
13          return $this->collection(
14              Author::all(),
15              new AuthorTransformer()
16          );
17      }
18
19      public function show($id)
20      {
21          return $this->item(
22              Author::findorFail($id),
23              new AuthorTransformer()
24          );
25      }
26
27      public function store(Request $request)
28      {
29          $author = Author::create($request->all());
30          $data = $this->item($author, new AuthorTransformer());
31
32          return response()->json($data, 201);
33      }
34  }
```

The code should pass the tests after your change (Listing 10-34).

Listing 10-34. Running Tests After Defining the @store Method

```
# vagrant@homestead:~/Code/bookr$
$ phpunit

OK (38 tests, 184 assertions)
```

The next feature you are going to add is validation. For the BooksController you separated your controller validation tests into a separate file. Feel free to do that for the AuthorsController validation tests. The code will still work, but you are going to add these tests in the *tests/app/Http/Controllers/AuthorsControllerTest.php* file (Listing 10-35).

Listing 10-35. Validation Test for the AuthorsController@store Method

```
140  /** @test **/
141  public function store_method_validates_required_fields()
142  {
143      $this->post('/authors', [],
144          ['Accept' => 'application/json']);
145
146      $data = $this->response->getData(true);
147
148      $fields = ['name', 'gender', 'biography'];
149
150      foreach ($fields as $field) {
151          $this->assertArrayHasKey($field, $data);
152          $this->assertEquals(["The {$field} field is required."], $data[$field]);
153      }
154  }
```

Implement the code in Listing 10-36 to get the test passing (Listing 10-37).

Listing 10-36. Adding Validation to AuthorsController@store

```
27  public function store(Request $request)
28  {
29      $this->validate($request, [
30          'name' => 'required',
31          'gender' => 'required',
32          'biography' => 'required'
33      ]);
34
35      $author = Author::create($request->all());
36      $data = $this->item($author, new AuthorTransformer());
37
38      return response()->json($data, 201);
39  }
```

Listing 10-37. Running the Test Suite

```
# vagrant@homestead:~/Code/bookr$
$ phpunit

OK (39 tests, 190 assertions)
```

Next, let's experiment and see what happens if you try to post a value for gender that does not match your enum field of male or female (Listing 10-38).

Listing 10-38. Test for Invalid Gender Data

```
156  /** @test **/
157  public function store_invalidates_incorrect_gender_data()
158  {
159      $postData = [
```

```
160              'name' => 'John Doe',
161              'gender' => 'unknown',
162              'biography' => 'An anonymous author'
163         ];
164
165         $this->post('/authors', $postData, ['Accept' => 'application/json']);
166
167         $this->seeStatusCode(422);
168
169         $data = $this->response->getData(true);
170         $this->assertCount(1, $data);
171         $this->assertArrayHasKey('gender', $data);
172         $this->assertEquals(
173             ["Gender format is invalid: must equal 'male' or 'female'"],
174             $data['gender']
175         );
176  }
```

In this test, you've specified a gender value not allowed in your enum field. You assert that you should only have one validation failure by counting the $data array and then assert the validation message for failed gender validation. Even though you are using an enum field, you get a 201 when you shouldn't (Listing 10-39).

Listing 10-39. Running the Gender Validation Test

```
$ phpunit

There was 1 failure:

1) Tests\App\Http\Controllers\AuthorsControllerTest::store_invalidates_incorrect\
_gender_data
Failed asserting that 201 matches expected 422.

/home/vagrant/Code/bookr/vendor/laravel/lumen-framework/src/Testing/CrawlerTrait.php:412
/home/vagrant/Code/bookr/tests/app/Http/Controllers/AuthorsControllerTest.php:167

FAILURES!
Tests: 40, Assertions: 191, Failures: 1.
```

You will use a regex rule to guarantee a valid gender to get the requirement passing (Listing 10-40).

Listing 10-40. Validating Gender in the AuthorsController@store Method

```
27  public function store(Request $request)
28  {
29      $this->validate($request, [
30          'name' => 'required',
31          'gender' => [
32              'required',
33              'regex:/^(male|female)$/i',
34          ],
35          'biography' => 'required'
36      ], [
```

```
37              'gender.regex' => "Gender format is invalid: must equal 'male' or 'female'"
38        ]);
39
40        $author = Author::create($request->all());
41        $data = $this->item($author, new AuthorTransformer());
42
43        return response()->json($data, 201);
44  }
```

You've added a regular expression validation rule for gender and changed the gender rules to use an array. This is because your regex contains a pipe character, (|), which is what the validator uses to separate rules. Lastly, you add a custom validation message so users of the API will know what values are allowed.

Let's check back in with your test suite and make sure it's green (Listing 10-41).

Listing 10-41. Testing Gender Validation Again

```
# vagrant@homestead:~/Code/bookr$
$ phpunit

OK (40 tests, 194 assertions)
```

The last validation rule you will add before you complete the POST /authors endpoint is length validation for the name field (Listing 10-42).

Listing 10-42. Adding Length Validation Tests for AuthorsController@store

```
178  /** @test **/
179  public function store_invalidates_name_when_name_is_just_too_long()
180  {
181        $postData = [
182            'name' => str_repeat('a', 256),
183            'gender' => 'male',
184            'biography' => 'A Valid Biography'
185        ];
186
187        $this->post('/authors', $postData, ['Accept' => 'application/json']);
188
189        $this->seeStatusCode(422);
190
191        $data = $this->response->getData(true);
192        $this->assertCount(1, $data);
193        $this->assertArrayHasKey('name', $data);
194        $this->assertEquals(
195            ["The name may not be greater than 255 characters."],
196            $data['name']
197        );
198  }
199
200  /** @test **/
201  public function store_is_valid_when_name_is_just_long_enough()
202  {
203        $postData = [
```

```
204            'name' => str_repeat('a', 255),
205            'gender' => 'male',
206            'biography' => 'A Valid Biography'
207        ];
208
209        $this->post('/authors', $postData,
210            ['Accept' => 'application/json']);
211
212        $this->seeStatusCode(201);
213        $this->seeInDatabase('authors', $postData);
214    }
```

The two tests check the same max validation you added for the Book's title column. To get these tests passing you need one-line change (Listing 10-43). Run the tests again (Listing 10-44).

Listing 10-43. Adding Max Name Validation Rule

```
27  public function store(Request $request)
28  {
29      $this->validate($request, [
30          'name' => 'required|max:255',
31          'gender' => [
32              'required',
33              'regex:/^(male|female)$/i',
34          ],
35          'biography' => 'required'
36      ], [
37          'gender.regex' => "Gender format is invalid: must equal 'male' or 'female'"
38      ]);
39
40      $author = Author::create($request->all());
41      $data = $this->item($author, new AuthorTransformer());
42
43      return response()->json($data, 201);
44  }
```

Listing 10-44. Running the Test Suite After Adding Max Validation

```
# vagrant@homestead:~/Code/bookr$
$ phpunit

OK (42 tests, 200 assertions)
```

You now have a solid endpoint for creating authors with valid data. Now you need to make sure that creating the author adds a Location header (Listing 10-45).

Listing 10-45. Test for the Location Header When an Author Is Created

```
216  /** @test **/
217  public function store_returns_a_valid_location_header()
218  {
219      $postData = [
```

```
220         'name' => 'H. G. Wells',
221         'gender' => 'male',
222         'biography' => 'Prolific Science-Fiction Writer'
223     ];
224
225     $this
226         ->post('/authors', $postData,
227             ['Accept' => 'application/json'])
228         ->seeStatusCode(201);
229
230     $data = $this->response->getData(true);
231     $this->assertArrayHasKey('data', $data);
232     $this->assertArrayHasKey('id', $data['data']);
233
234     // Check the Location header
235     $id = $data['data']['id'];
236     $this->seeHeaderWithRegExp('Location', "#/authors/{$id}$#");
237 }
```

This test doesn't need to check every detail since another test already covers checking the response data. The test focuses on asserting the value of the Location header and checks for a valid id. You use your custom seeHeaderWithRegExp assertion to make sure the location header is correct (Listing 10-46).

Listing 10-46. Running the Test Suite After Adding the Location Header Test

```
$ phpunit

There was 1 failure:

1) Tests\App\Http\Controllers\AuthorsControllerTest::store_returns_a_valid_locat\
ion_header
Response should have the header 'Location' but does not.
Failed asserting that false is true.

/home/vagrant/Code/bookr/tests/TestCase.php:29
/home/vagrant/Code/bookr/tests/TestCase.php:45
/home/vagrant/Code/bookr/tests/app/Http/Controllers/AuthorsControllerTest.php:235

FAILURES!
Tests: 43, Assertions: 204, Failures: 1.
```

The first code update you will make is defining the GET /authors/id route as a named route so you can more easily generate a route URL. Modify the route in app/Http/routes.php (Listing 10-47).

Listing 10-47. Making the Authors Route a Named Route

```
$app->group([
    'prefix' => '/authors',
    'namespace' => 'App\Http\Controllers'
], function (\Laravel\Lumen\Application $app) {
    // …
    $app->get('/{id:[\d]+}', [
```

187

```
        'as' => 'authors.show',
        'uses' => 'AuthorsController@show'
    ]);
    // ...
});
```

Now you can add the Location header in the AuthorsController@store route (Listing 10-48).

Listing 10-48. Adding the Location Header in the AuthorsController

```
27  public function store(Request $request)
28  {
29      $this->validate($request, [
30          'name' => 'required|max:255',
31          'gender' => [
32              'required',
33              'regex:/^(male|female)$/i',
34          ],
35          'biography' => 'required'
36      ], [
37          'gender.regex' => "Gender format is invalid: must equal 'male' or 'female'"
38      ]);
39
40      $author = Author::create($request->all());
41      $data = $this->item($author, new AuthorTransformer());
42
43      return response()->json($data, 201, [
44          'Location' => route('authors.show', ['id' => $author->id])
45      ]);
46  }
```

Let's see if your suite passes now (Listing 10-49).

Listing 10-49. Running the Test Suite

```
# vagrant@homestead:~/Code/bookr$
$ phpunit

OK (43 tests, 205 assertions)
```

All features pass for the POST /authors endpoint!

The PUT /authors/{id} Endpoint

Next up is the ability to update an author. You will add the following features:

- It will have the ability to change author name, gender, and biography.
- It will have the ability to validate name, gender, and biography.
- It should not match an invalid route, such as /authors/foobar.
- It should 404 an invalid author.

You will start out by writing a test to update an author (Listing 10-50).

Listing 10-50. Test to Successfully Update an Author

```
239  /** @test **/
240  public function update_can_update_an_existing_author()
241  {
242      $author = factory(\App\Author::class)->create();
243
244      $requestData = [
245          'name' => 'New Author Name',
246          'gender' => $author->gender === 'male' ? 'female' : 'male',
247          'biography' => 'An updated biography',
248      ];
249
250      $this
251          ->put(
252              "/authors/{$author->id}",
253              $requestData,
254              ['Accept' => 'application/json']
255          )
256          ->seeStatusCode(200)
257          ->seeJson($requestData)
258          ->seeInDatabase('authors', [
259              'name' => 'New Author Name'
260          ])
261          ->notSeeInDatabase('authors', [
262              'name' => $author->name
263          ]);
264
265      $this->assertArrayHasKey('data', $this->response->getData(true));
266  }
```

Your test updates all the author fields and then chains assertions together to ensure the proper status code and that the response has correct author data. Next, the test asserts that the updated record is found in the database and that the old author data is not found. Lastly, you continue to ensure your API contains a data key.

The minimum code needed to get the controller passing is in Listing 10-51.

Listing 10-51. Writing the AuthorsController@update Code

```
48  public function update(Request $request, $id)
49  {
50      $author = Author::findOrFail($id);
51
52      $author->fill($request->all());
53      $author->save();
54
55      $data = $this->item($author, new AuthorTransformer());
56
57      return response()->json($data, 200);
58  }
```

The code in AuthorsController@update should be familiar. Let's see if it passes (Listing 10-52).

Listing 10-52. Running the Test Suite

```
$ phpunit

OK (44 tests, 212 assertions)
```

Next up is validation testing. The validation rules will be the same as the AuthorsController@store method, so let's refactor both methods to use the same rules. With your tests passing, let's refactor the validation out of the @store method. You will write a private method at the end of the AuthorsController to deal with validation (Listing 10-53).

Listing 10-53. Custom Method for Author Validation

```
60  /**
61   * Validate author updates from the request.
62   *
63   * @param Request $request
64   */
65  private function validateAuthor(Request $request)
66  {
67      $this->validate($request, [
68          'name' => 'required|max:255',
69          'gender' => [
70              'required',
71              'regex:/^(male|female)$/i',
72          ],
73          'biography' => 'required'
74      ], [
75          'gender.regex' => "Gender format is invalid: must equal 'male' or 'female'"
76      ]);
77  }
```

Nothing new in this method; you just copied the original AuthorsController@store validation code into a private method. Let's use the validateAuthor() method in the @store controller method (Listing 10-54).

Listing 10-54. Refactoring the AuthorsController@store Method

```
27  public function store(Request $request)
28  {
29      $this->validateAuthor($request);
30
31      $author = Author::create($request->all());
32      $data = $this->item($author, new AuthorTransformer());
33
34      return response()->json($data, 201, [
35          'Location' => route('authors.show', ['id' => $author->id])
36      ]);
37  }
```

Let's see if the code passes the tests (Listing 10-55).

Listing 10-55. See If Tests Pass After the Refactor

```
# vagrant@homestead:~/Code/bookr$
$ phpunit

OK (44 tests, 212 assertions)
```

Your code passes the tests, so you can write the next validation tests for the AuthorsController@update method (Listing 10-56).

Listing 10-56. Writing a Test for AuthorsController@update Validation

```
268   /** @test **/
269   public function update_method_validates_required_fields()
270   {
271       $author = factory(\App\Author::class)->create();
272       $this->put("/authors/{$author->id}", [], ['Accept' => 'application/json']);
273       $this->seeStatusCode(422);
274       $data = $this->response->getData(true);
275
276       $fields = ['name', 'gender', 'biography'];
277
278       foreach ($fields as $field) {
279           $this->assertArrayHasKey($field, $data);
280           $this->assertEquals(["The {$field} field is required."], $data[$field]);
281       }
282   }
```

Now, run the test suite to verify that your new validation test fails (Listing 10-57).

Listing 10-57. Testing the Update Validation Method

```
# vagrant@homestead:~/Code/bookr$
$ phpunit

There was 1 failure:

1) Tests\App\Http\Controllers\AuthorsControllerTest::update_method_validates_req\
uired_fields
Failed asserting that 200 matches expected 422.

/home/vagrant/Code/bookr/vendor/laravel/lumen-framework/src/Testing/CrawlerTrait\
.php:412
/home/vagrant/Code/bookr/tests/app/Http/Controllers/AuthorsControllerTest.php:273

FAILURES!
Tests: 45, Assertions: 213, Failures: 1.
```

You can now use your refactored validation to make the new test pass (Listing 10-58).

Listing 10-58. Using the New validateAuthor() Method

```
39  public function update(Request $request, $id)
40  {
41      $this->validateAuthor($request);
42      $author = Author::findOrFail($id);
43
44      $author->fill($request->all());
45      $author->save();
46
47      $data = $this->item($author, new AuthorTransformer());
48
49      return response()->json($data, 200);
50  }
```

Your test suite should be back to green (Listing 10-59).

Listing 10-59. Running the Test Suite

```
# vagrant@homestead:~/Code/bookr$
$ phpunit

OK (45 tests, 219 assertions)
```

Another thing you can clean up is the duplicated test code for validating an author. Let's refactor your tests to test both the @update and @store methods at the same time. You can start by refactoring the store_method_validates_required_fields test in the AuthorsControllerTest (Listing 10-60).

Listing 10-60. Testing the Create and Update Validation Fields

```
140  /** @test **/
141  public function validation_validates_required_fields()
142  {
143      $author = factory(\App\Author::class)->create();
144      $tests = [
145          ['method' => 'post', 'url' => '/authors'],
146          ['method' => 'put', 'url' => "/authors/{$author->id}"],
147      ];
148
149      foreach ($tests as $test) {
150          $method = $test['method'];
151          $this->{$method}($test['url'], [], ['Accept' => 'application/json']);
152          $this->seeStatusCode(422);
153          $data = $this->response->getData(true);
154
155          $fields = ['name', 'gender', 'biography'];
156
157          foreach ($fields as $field) {
158              $this->assertArrayHasKey($field, $data);
159              $this->assertEquals(["The {$field} field is required."], $data[$field]);
160          }
161      }
162  }
```

Note that the method name has been updated to reflect the scope of the test after refactoring. The $tests array defines the outline for testing both @create and @update validation. The foreach is basically the same as the original test except that now the tests use the dynamic values from the $tests array.

All of your tests should still be passing at this point if you want to run the test suite before you start refactoring the next test. The next test you will refactor is the store_invalidates_incorrect_gender_data test in the same file (Listing 10-61).

Listing 10-61. Refactoring Invalid Gender Test

```
164  /** @test **/
165  public function validation_invalidates_incorrect_gender_data()
166  {
167      $author = factory(\App\Author::class)->create();
168      $tests = [
169          // Create
170          [
171              'method' => 'post',
172              'url' => '/authors',
173              'data' => [
174                  'name' => 'John Doe',
175                  'biography' => 'An anonymous author'
176              ]
177          ],
178
179          // Update
180          [
181              'method' => 'put',
182              'url' => "/authors/{$author->id}",
183              'data' => [
184                  'name' => $author->name,
185                  'biography' => $author->biography
186              ]
187          ]
188      ];
189
190      foreach ($tests as $test) {
191          $method = $test['method'];
192          $test['data']['gender'] = 'unknown';
193          $this->{$method}($test['url'], $test['data'], ['Accept' => 'application/
             json']);
194
195          $this->seeStatusCode(422);
196
197          $data = $this->response->getData(true);
198          $this->assertCount(1, $data);
299          $this->assertArrayHasKey('gender', $data);
200          $this->assertEquals(
201              ["Gender format is invalid: must equal 'male' or 'female'"],
202              $data['gender']
203          );
204      }
205  }
```

Let's run your test suite to see if your code still passes the tests (Listing 10-62).

Listing 10-62. Running the Test Suite

```
# vagrant@homestead:~/Code/bookr$
$ phpunit


OK (45 tests, 231 assertions)
```

Onto refactoring the next test: the *store_invalidates_name_when_name_is_just_too_long* test, which you will rename since it's testing create and update (Listing 10-63).

Listing 10-63. Refactoring Test When the Name is Just Too Long

```
207  /** @test **/
208  public function validation_invalidates_name_when_name_is_just_too_long()
209  {
210      $author = factory(\App\Author::class)->create();
211      $tests = [
212          // Create
213          [
214              'method' => 'post',
215              'url' => '/authors',
216              'data' => [
217                  'name' => 'John Doe',
218                  'gender' => 'male',
219                  'biography' => 'An anonymous author'
220              ]
221          ],
222
223          // Update
224          [
225              'method' => 'put',
226              'url' => "/authors/{$author->id}",
227              'data' => [
228                  'name' => $author->name,
229                  'gender' => $author->gender,
230                  'biography' => $author->biography
231              ]
232          ]
233      ];
234
235      foreach ($tests as $test) {
236          $method = $test['method'];
237          $test['data']['name'] = str_repeat('a', 256);
238
239          $this->{$method}($test['url'], $test['data'], ['Accept' => 'application/
             json']);
240
241          $this->seeStatusCode(422);
242
243          $data = $this->response->getData(true);
```

```
244          $this->assertCount(1, $data);
245          $this->assertArrayHasKey('name', $data);
246          $this->assertEquals(["The name may not be greater than 255 characters."],
                 $data['name']);
247      }
248  }
```

Your tests are still passing at this point and you have one more validation-related test to refactor. Before you finish the final test, it's noticeable how much your refactor data is exactly the same in each validation test. Let's extract a method for the data at the end of the AuthorsControllerTest (Listing 10-64).

Listing 10-64. Extract Boilerplate Validation Data

```
334  /**
335   * Provides boilerplate test instructions for validation.
336   * @return array
337   */
338  private function getValidationTestData()
339  {
340      $author = factory(\App\Author::class)->create();
341      return [
342          // Create
343          [
344              'method' => 'post',
345              'url' => '/authors',
346              'status' => 201,
347              'data' => [
348                  'name' => 'John Doe',
349                  'gender' => 'male',
350                  'biography' => 'An anonymous author'
351              ]
352          ],
353
354          // Update
355          [
356              'method' => 'put',
357              'url' => "/authors/{$author->id}",
358              'status' => 200,
359              'data' => [
360                  'name' => $author->name,
361                  'gender' => $author->gender,
362                  'biography' => $author->biography
363              ]
364          ]
365      ];
366  }
```

The only thing to note in the new method is the status key, which allows a validation test that succeeds to test the status code for each type of operation.

Now that you have the new *getValidationTestData()* method, let's drop it in to your tests (Listing 10-65).

Listing 10-65. Updated Gender Validation Test

```
164  /** @test **/
165  public function validation_invalidates_incorrect_gender_data()
166  {
167      foreach ($this->getValidationTestData() as $test) {
168          $method = $test['method'];
169          $test['data']['gender'] = 'unknown';
170          $this->{$method}($test['url'], $test['data'], ['Accept' => 'application/
             json']);

173          $this->seeStatusCode(422);

175          $data = $this->response->getData(true);
176          $this->assertCount(1, $data);
177          $this->assertArrayHasKey('gender', $data);
178          $this->assertEquals(
179              ["Gender format is invalid: must equal 'male' or 'female'"],
180              $data['gender']
181          );
182      }
183  }
```

Now let's try using your new method in the *store_is_valid_when_name_is_just_long_enough* test and rename it to match its new purpose (Listing 10-66).

Listing 10-66. Refactored Test When the Name is Just Long Enough

```
227  /** @test **/
228  public function validation_is_valid_when_name_is_just_long_enough()
229  {
230      foreach ($this->getValidationTestData() as $test) {
231          $method = $test['method'];
232          $test['data']['name'] = str_repeat('a', 255);

234          $this->{$method}($test['url'], $test['data'], ['Accept' => 'application/
             json']);

236          $this->seeStatusCode($test['status']);
237          $this->seeInDatabase('authors', $test['data']);
238      }
239  }
```

With your refactored test using the new getValidationTestData() your test is straightforward. Now let's update the *validation_invalidates_name_when_name_is_just_too_long* to use your new method (Listing 10-67).

Listing 10-67. Updated Test When Name is Just Too Long

```
184  /** @test **/
185  public function validation_invalidates_name_when_name_is_just_too_long()
186  {
```

```
187    foreach ($this->getValidationTestData() as $test) {
188        $method = $test['method'];
189        $test['data']['name'] = str_repeat('a', 256);
190
191        $this->{$method}($test['url'], $test['data'], ['Accept' => 'application/
           json']);
192
193        $this->seeStatusCode(422);
194
195        $data = $this->response->getData(true);
196        $this->assertCount(1, $data);
197        $this->assertArrayHasKey('name', $data);
198        $this->assertEquals(["The name may not be greater than 255 characters."],
           $data['name']);
299    }
200 }
```

Now that validation covers both creating and updating, you can remove the update_method_
validates_required_fields test you originally started writing and then ensure the code passes the full test
suite (Listing 10-68).

Listing 10-68. Running the Test Suite After Refactoring

```
# vagrant@homestead:~/Code/bookr$
$ phpunit

OK (45 tests, 237 assertions)
```

The refactoring of the AuthorsController and AuthorsControllerTest has the code looking really clean.
Your test coverage allowed you to rip out duplicate code and have confidence that things are still working.

The DELETE /authors/{id} Endpoint

The last author endpoint you will work on in this chapter is the DELETE /authors/{id} route. If you recall
the schema design of the books table, you added a foreign key constraint to the author_id field that will
CASCADE when an author is deleted. This means that when your author is deleted, all the books associated
with that author will be deleted.

You have simple criteria for your first test:

- The author should not exist in the authors table after delete.

- No books with the author's id should exist in the books table.

- A 204 status code should be returned with no content when the delete succeeds.

You will add your remaining tests above the private function getValidationTestdata() method to
keep the test organized (Listing 10-69).

Listing 10-69. Successful Delete Test

```
284 /** @test **/
285 public function delete_can_remove_an_author_and_his_or_her_books()
286 {
```

```
287        $author = factory(\App\Author::class)->create();
288
289        $this
290            ->delete("/authors/{$author->id}")
291            ->seeStatusCode(204)
292            ->notSeeInDatabase('authors', ['id' => $author->id])
293            ->notSeeInDatabase('books', ['author_id' => $author->id]);
294    }
```

And the @destroy implementation above the private validateAuthor() method (Listing 10-70).

Listing 10-70. Implementing the AuthorsController@destroy Method

```
52    public function destroy($id)
53    {
54        Author::findOrFail($id)->delete();
55
56        return response(null, 204);
57    }
```

The final test ensures that a 404 response is returned when an invalid author id is passed (Listing 10-71).

Listing 10-71. Test Trying to Delete an Invalid ID

```
296    /** @test **/
297    public function deleting_an_invalid_author_should_return_a_404()
298    {
299        $this
300            ->delete('/authors/99999', [], ['Accept' => 'application/json'])
301            ->seeStatusCode(404);
302    }
```

This test already passes because you used findOurFail($id) but you will keep it anyway just in case things change in the future. You could replace the findOrFail() with find() to see the failure if you want to experiment before replacing it with findOrFail().

Let's run the test suite before concluding the chapter (Listing 10-72).

Listing 10-72. Running the Test Suite

```
# vagrant@homestead:~/Code/bookr$
$ phpunit

OK (47 tests, 241 assertions)
```

ⓘ Git Commit: Add the Authors Resource API

b06c563 (https://bitbucket.org/paulredmond/apress-bookr/commits/b06c563)

Conclusion

You are done with the basics of the /authors routes and this chapter! The biggest thing introduced in this chapter was how to include associated entity data in responses with Fractal. You also got lots of practice refactoring methods and tests, and making sure things still pass afterwards.

Now that you have two working entities, in the next chapter you will use existing entities to build out a book bundles feature. The chapter will also introduce how to add multiple entity associations in a many-to-many relationship through the API. You will also cover embedded relationships.

CHAPTER 11

Book Bundles

In this chapter, you will be building a simple book bundle implementation. A book bundle is basically a collection of books bundled together under a common theme. For example, a "Database Primer" book bundle might include books about database design, database theory, and database administration.

The outline for the API endpoints you will cover this chapter will be as shown in Listing 11-1.

Listing 11-1. Basic REST /Bundles Endpoints

```
GET     /bundles/{id} Get individual bundle details
PUT     /bundles/{id}/books/{bookId} Add a Book to a Bundle
DELETE  /bundles/{id}/books/{bookId} Remove a Book from a Bundle
```

Your book routes in Listing 11-1 are *nested REST resources*, meaning they represent books in the context of the /bundles functionality. You will use these nested resources to manage adding and removing books from bundles.

You won't code basic CRUD endpoints for /bundles in this chapter—you should be equipped with enough knowledge to complete CRUD endpoints for /bundles on your own. The focus of this chapter will be on new functionality you haven't learned yet.

Defining the Relationship Between Books and Bundles

The Bundle and Book model relationship will be a many-to-many (https://laravel.com/docs/5.2/eloquent-relationships#many-to-many) relationship—you may also know this relationship as "has and belongs to many" (HABTM). It is reasonable that one book could be included in multiple bundles, and that a bundle will have many books (as the name implies).

In this section, you will define the tables, relationships, and data needed for your tests and seed data. Once you have your schema and seed data, you can start coding features.

Let's start defining the data and the relationships needed. First, you need a bundles table that contains data such as the bundle name (Listing 11-2).

Listing 11-2. Creating the bundles Table

```
# vagrant@homestead:~/Code/bookr$
$ php artisan make:migration \
create_bundles_table --create=bundles
```

If you recall, the *--create* flag will generate the migration with Schema::create() in the CreateBundlesTable::up() method and Schema::drop() in the CreateBundlesTable::down() method.

The bundle will simply have title and description fields with the usual timestamps (Listing 11-3).

Listing 11-3. The CreateBundlesTable Migration

```php
1   <?php
2
3   use Illuminate\Database\Schema\Blueprint;
4   use Illuminate\Database\Migrations\Migration;
5
6   class CreateBundlesTable extends Migration
7   {
8       /**
9        * Run the migrations.
10       *
11       * @return void
12       */
13      public function up()
14      {
15          Schema::create('bundles', function (Blueprint $table) {
16              $table->increments('id');
17              $table->string('title');
18              $table->text('description');
19              $table->timestamps();
20          });
21      }
22
23      /**
24       * Reverse the migrations.
25       *
26       * @return void
27       */
28      public function down()
29      {
30          Schema::drop('bundles');
31      }
32  }
```

Next, your *many-to-many* relationship needs a pivot table. The convention for a many-to-many relationship pivot table will be derived from the alphabetical order of the related model names. In your case, the convention for "Books" and "Bundles" will be a "book_bundle" table. You will use the convention, but you can also customize things, as you might now expect, in Eloquent if needed. The next migration will look like Listing 11-4.

Listing 11-4. Creating the Migration for the book_bundle Table

```
# vagrant@homestead:~/Code/bookr$
$ php artisan make:migration \
create_book_bundle_table --create=book_bundle
```

And the migration will look like Listing 11-5.

Listing 11-5. The CreateBookBundleTable Migration Class

```php
1   <?php
2
3   use Illuminate\Database\Schema\Blueprint;
4   use Illuminate\Database\Migrations\Migration;
5
6   class CreateBookBundleTable extends Migration
7   {
8       /**
9        * Run the migrations.
10       *
11       * @return void
12       */
13      public function up()
14      {
15          Schema::create('book_bundle', function (Blueprint $table) {
16              $table->increments('id');
17              $table->integer('book_id')->unsigned();
18              $table->integer('bundle_id')->unsigned();
19              $table->timestamps();
20          });
21      }
22
23      /**
24       * Reverse the migrations.
25       *
26       * @return void
27       */
28      public function down()
29      {
30          Schema::drop('book_bundle');
31      }
32  }
```

The book_id and bundle_id fields correlate with the id column on the books and bundles tables, including being an unsigned integer. Other than that, there's nothing new here.

Now you can run your migrations and make sure they work as expected (Listing 11-6).

Listing 11-6. Running the Database Migrations

```
# vagrant@homestead:~/Code/bookr$
$ php artisan migrate:refresh
Rolled back: 2016_01_20_052512_remove_books_authors_column
Rolled back: 2016_01_20_051118_associate_books_with_authors
Rolled back: 2016_01_20_050526_create_authors_table
Rolled back: 2015_12_29_234835_create_books_table
Migrated: 2015_12_29_234835_create_books_table
Migrated: 2016_01_20_050526_create_authors_table
```

```
Migrated: 2016_01_20_051118_associate_books_with_authors
Migrated: 2016_01_20_052512_remove_books_authors_column
Migrated: 2016_01_24_041900_create_bundles_table
Migrated: 2016_01_30_165357_create_book_bundle_table
```

Now that you have your migrations working, the next step is creating a Bundle model so that you can define the associations (Listing 11-7).

Listing 11-7. Creating the app/Bundle.php File

```
# vagrant@homestead:~/Code/bookr$
$ touch app/Bundle.php
```

Open the *app/Bundle.php* and define the Bundle model with the code in Listing 11-8.

Listing 11-8. The Bundle Eloquent Model

```php
1  <?php
2
3  namespace App;
4
5  use Illuminate\Database\Eloquent\Model;
6
7  class Bundle extends Model
8  {
9      protected $fillable = ['title', 'description'];
10
11     public function books()
12     {
13         return $this->belongsToMany(\App\Book::class);
14     }
15 }
```

The Bundle::books() method defines the Book model as a belongs-to-many relationship. You have seen the belongsTo() and hasMany associations when you associated Book and Author, so this should already look familiar. For more information on Eloquent relationships, see the Eloquent relationships (https://laravel.com/docs/5.2/eloquent-relationships) documentation.

You need to update the Book model in app/Book.php to define the inverse of this relationship, which is identical (Listing 11-9).

Listing 11-9. Defining the Bundle Relationship in the Book Model

```php
21  public function bundles()
22  {
23      return $this->belongsToMany(\App\Bundle::class);
24  }
```

The last thing you will do is define the factory so that you can create model seed data. Add the code in Listing 11-10 to the end of the *database/factories/ModelFactory.php* file.

Listing 11-10. Model Factory for the Bundle Model

```
38  $factory->define(\App\Bundle::class, function ($faker) {
39
40      $title = $faker->sentence(rand(3, 10));
41
42      return [
43          'title' => substr($title, 0, strlen($title) - 1),
44          'description' => $faker->text
45      ];
46  });
```

Next, create a new database seeder file (Listing 11-11) and seed code (Listing 11-12):

Listing 11-11. Creating the BundlesTableSeeder Class

```
# vagrant@homestead:~/Code/bookr$
$ touch database/seeds/BundlesTableSeeder.php
```

Listing 11-12. The BundlesTableSeeder Class

```
1   <?php
2
3   use Illuminate\Database\Seeder;
4
5   class BundlesTableSeeder extends Seeder
6   {
7       /**
8        * Run the database seeds.
9        *
10       * @return void
11       */
12      public function run()
13      {
14          factory(\App\Bundle::class, 5)->create()->each(function ($bundle) {
15              $booksCount = rand(2, 5);
16              $bookIds = [];
17
18              while ($booksCount > 0) {
19                  $book = \App\Book::whereNotIn('id', $bookIds)
20                      ->orderByRaw("RAND()")
21                      ->first();
22
23                  $bundle->books()->attach($book);
24                  $bookIds[] = $book->id;
25                  $booksCount--;
26              }
27          });
28      }
29  }
```

The Bundles seeder class creates five bundles and then loops through each one. In the callback, a random amount of books (between 2 and 5) will be defined with rand(2, 5). The while loop finds a random book in the database that has not been used yet with the whereNotIn('id', $bookIds) call and returns the first result. Next, the book is attached to the current bundle, and added to the ignore array so the book will not be in the same bundle twice.

You need to add the new *BundlesTableSeeder* class to the database/seeds/DatabaseSeeder.php file (Listing 11-13).

Listing 11-13. Adding the BundlesTableSeeder to the DatabaseSeeder

```
7   /**
8    * Run the database seeds.
9    *
10   * @return void
11   */
12  public function run()
13  {
14      // $this->call('UserTableSeeder');
15      $this->call(BooksTableSeeder::class);
16      $this->call(BundlesTableSeeder::class);
17  }
```

You are ready to run the migrations again and seed the new bundle data (Listing 11-14).

Listing 11-14. Migrating and Seeding Application Data

```
# vagrant@homestead:~/Code/bookr$
$ composer dump-autoload
$ php artisan migrate:refresh
...
$ php artisan db:seed
Seeded: BooksTableSeeder
Seeded: BundlesTableSeeder
```

Remember that when you add new seeder classes you need to update the Composer autoloader with the *composer dump-autoload command* so artisan can find the seeder class. If all went well, you should have some seed data in the bundles table and book_bundle table.

You now have the correct data model and associations to move onto your next endpoint, which is returning an individual bundle with related books.

The GET /bundles/{id} Endpoint

With your data and model relationships in place, you are ready to start working on the individual bundle response. Your API endpoint (/bundles/{id}) response resembles the JSON in Listing 11-15.

Listing 11-15. Example Bundle Response

```
{
    "data":{
        "id":1,
```

```
    "title":"Eveniet numquam quos doloribus nemo dolore culpa voluptatem nobis in omnis
    aut",
    "description":"Perferendis minus omnis accusantium reiciendis totam. Quoautem
    ratione amet facere quam. Iure sunt qui odio sint.",
    "created":"2015-12-06T03:14:58+0000",
    "updated":"2015-12-06T03:14:58+0000",
    "books":{
        "data":[
            {
                "id":6,
                "title":"Et ipsam facilis rerum expedita doloribus quasi aliquam numquam
                provident rerum mollitia",
                "description":"Itaque cumque est et vitae voluptatibus ad. Rerum
                repellendus consequatur labore eum nostrum. Ut et ut voluptate maiores.",
                "author":"Angelina Doyle",
                "created":"2015-12-06T03:14:58+0000",
                "updated":"2015-12-06T03:14:58+0000"
            },
            {
                "id":33,
                "title":"Dolorem at cum esse",
                "description":"Commodi et consequuntur quia culpa. Totam earum ad
tempore cumque dolor. In ratione voluptas quisquam et est quaerat rem.",
                "author":"Rylan Lind II",
                "created":"2015-12-06T03:14:58+0000",
                "updated":"2015-12-06T03:14:58+0000"
            }
        ]
    }
  }
}
```

You are ready to create your BundleTransformer file (Listing 11-16).

Listing 11-16. Creating the BundleTransformer Class and Test

```
# vagrant@homestead:~/Code/bookr$
$ touch tests/app/Transformer/BundleTransformerTest.php
$ touch app/Transformer/BundleTransformer.php
```

Next, you are going to cheat a little and write all the bundle transformer tests beforehand (Listing 11-17).

Listing 11-17. Testing the Bundle Transformer

```
1  <?php
2
3  namespace Tests\App\Transformer;
4
5  use TestCase;
```

```php
 6  use App\Transformer\BundleTransformer;
 7  use Laravel\Lumen\Testing\DatabaseMigrations;
 8
 9  class BundleTransformerTest extends TestCase
10  {
11      use DatabaseMigrations;
12
13      /**
14       * @var BundleTransformer
15       */
16      private $subject;
17
18      public function setUp()
19      {
20          parent::setUp();
21
22          $this->subject = new BundleTransformer();
23      }
24
25      /** @test **/
26      public function it_can_be_initialized()
27      {
28          $this->assertInstanceOf(
29              BundleTransformer::class,
30              $this->subject
31          );
32      }
33
34      /** @test **/
35      public function it_can_transform_a_bundle()
36      {
37          $bundle = factory(\App\Bundle::class)->create();
38
39          $actual = $this->subject->transform($bundle);
40
41          $this->assertEquals($bundle->id, $actual['id']);
42          $this->assertEquals($bundle->title, $actual['title']);
43          $this->assertEquals(
44              $bundle->description,
45              $actual['description']
46          );
47          $this->assertEquals(
48              $bundle->created_at->toIso8601String(),
49              $actual['created']
50          );
51          $this->assertEquals(
52              $bundle->updated_at->toIso8601String(),
53              $actual['updated']
54          );
55      }
56
```

```
57      /** @test **/
58      public function it_can_transform_related_books()
59      {
60          $bundle = $this->bundleFactory();
61
62          $data = $this->subject->includeBooks($bundle);
63          $this->assertInstanceOf(
64              \League\Fractal\Resource\Collection::class,
65              $data
66          );
67          $this->assertInstanceOf(
68              \App\Book::class,
69              $data->getData()[0]
70          );
71          $this->assertCount(2, $data->getData());
72      }
73 }
```

I have included all the tests needed to cover the BundleTransformer; this test is just like the other transformer tests you've already covered. You might have noticed the call to $this->bundleFactory() in the *it_can_transform_related_books* test, which you haven't written yet. You might have also noticed the setUp() method used to initialize the subject of your tests as $this->subject, which is a convenient way to set up the test subject before of each test.

You are ready to write the actual transformer class, write the bundleFactory() method, and get tests back to green. Next, you will write the BundleTransformer implementation in app/Transformer/BundleTransformer.php (Listing 11-18).

Listing 11-18. Implementing the BundleTransformer Class

```php
1   <?php
2
3   namespace App\Transformer;
4
5   use App\Bundle;
6   use League\Fractal\TransformerAbstract;
7
8   /**
9    * Class BundleTransformer
10   * @package App\Transformer
11   */
12  class BundleTransformer extends TransformerAbstract
13  {
14      protected $defaultIncludes = ['books'];
15
16      /**
17       * Include a bundle's books
18       * @param Bundle $bundle
19       * @return \League\Fractal\Resource\Collection
20       */
21      public function includeBooks(Bundle $bundle)
22      {
23          return $this->collection($bundle->books, new BookTransformer());
```

```
24        }
25
26        /**
27         * Transform a bundle
28         *
29         * @param Bundle $bundle
30         * @return array
31         */
32        public function transform(Bundle $bundle)
33        {
34            return [
35                'id' => $bundle->id,
36                'title' => $bundle->title,
37                'description' => $bundle->description,
38                'created' => $bundle->created_at->toIso8601String(),
39                'updated' => $bundle->updated_at->toIso8601String(),
40            ];
41        }
42    }
```

The BundleTransformer will always include books; therefore this transformer has books in the
$defaultIncludes array.

Next, let's define the bundleFactory() method in the base tests/TestCase.php file right after the
bookFactory() method in order to easily create bundle records in the database for testing purposes
(Listing 11-19).

Listing 11-19. Defining the bundleFactory() Method in the TestCase Class

```
78    /**
79     * Convenience method for creating a book bundle
80     *
81     * @param int $count
82     * @return mixed
83     */
84    protected function bundleFactory($bookCount = 2)
85    {
86        if ($bookCount <= 1) {
87            throw new \RuntimeException('A bundle must have two or more books!');
88        }
89
90        $bundle = factory(\App\Bundle::class)->create();
91        $books = $this->bookFactory($bookCount);
92
93        $books->each(function ($book) use ($bundle) {
94            $bundle->books()->attach($book);
95        });
96
97        return $bundle;
98    }
```

The bundleFactory() method first makes sure that a $bookCount of at least 2 is passed; otherwise it will throw a \RuntimeException. Next, a bundle is created in the test database. You use the TestCase::bookFactory() method to create multiple books, and then you loop through each book and attach it to your bundle. Finally, you return the bundle.

Before moving on, verify that all tests pass (Listing 11-20).

Listing 11-20. Running the Test Suite

```
# vagrant@homestead:~/Code/bookr$
$ phpunit

OK (50 tests, 250 assertions)
```

With the BundleTransformer class in place you can create test file for the Bundle controller at *tests/app/Http/Controllers/BundlesControllerTest.php* with the first failing test for the BundlesController@show method (Listing 11-21 and Listing 11-22).

Listing 11-21. Creating the BundlesController and Test File

```
# vagrant@homestead:~/Code/bookr$
$ touch app/Http/Controllers/BundlesController.php
$ touch tests/app/Http/Controllers/BundlesControllerTest.php
```

Listing 11-22. Writing the Test for the BundlesController@show Method

```php
1   <?php
2
3   namespace Tests\App\Http\Controllers;
4
5   use TestCase;
6   use Laravel\Lumen\Testing\DatabaseMigrations;
7
8   class BundlesControllerTest extends TestCase
9   {
10      use DatabaseMigrations;
11
12      /** @test **/
13      public function show_should_return_a_valid_bundle()
14      {
15          $bundle = $this->bundleFactory();
16
17          $this->get("/bundles/{$bundle->id}", ['Accept' => 'application/json']);
18          $this->seeStatusCode(200);
19          $body = $this->response->getData(true);
20
21          $this->assertArrayHasKey('data', $body);
22          $data = $body['data'];
23
24          // Check bundle properties exist in the response
25          $this->assertEquals($bundle->id, $data['id']);
26          $this->assertEquals($bundle->title, $data['title']);
```

```
27            $this->assertEquals($bundle->title, $data['title']);
28            $this->assertEquals(
29                $bundle->description,
30                $data['description']
31            );
32            $this->assertEquals(
33                $bundle->created_at->toIso8601String(),
34                $data['created']
35            );
36            $this->assertEquals(
37                $bundle->updated_at->toIso8601String(),
38                $data['updated']
39            );
40
41            // Check that book data is in the response
42            $this->assertArrayHasKey('books', $data);
43            $books = $data['books'];
44
45            // Check that two books exist in the response
46            $this->assertArrayHasKey('data', $books);
47            $this->assertCount(2, $books['data']);
48
49            // Verify keys for one book...
50            $this->assertEquals(
51                $bundle->books[0]->title,
52                $books['data'][0]['title']
53            );
54            $this->assertEquals(
55                $bundle->books[0]->description,
56                $books['data'][0]['description']
57            );
58            $this->assertEquals(
59                $bundle->books[0]->author->name,
60                $books['data'][0]['author']
61            );
62            $this->assertEquals(
63                $bundle->books[0]->created_at->toIso8601String(),
64                $books['data'][0]['created']
65            );
66            $this->assertEquals(
67                $bundle->books[0]->updated_at->toIso8601String(),
68                $books['data'][0]['updated']
69            );
70        }
71 }
```

The test is long but simple. You get the bundle response and go through all the data to make sure your bundle endpoint contains all the response data. The controller isn't complicated but you want to make sure you test all the expected data. In fact, the implementation is only a few lines (Listing 11-23).

Listing 11-23. The Initial Version of the BundlesController

```php
1   <?php
2
3   namespace App\Http\Controllers;
4
5   use App\Bundle;
6   use App\Transformer\BundleTransformer;
7
8   /**
9    * Class BundlesController
10   * @package App\Http\Controllers
11   */
12  class BundlesController extends Controller
13  {
14      public function show($id)
15      {
16          $bundle = Bundle::findOrFail($id);
17          $data = $this->item($bundle, new BundleTransformer());
18
19          return response()->json($data);
20      }
21  }
```

You've seen the @show method a few times. All you need to do at the moment is find the bundle and run the response through Fractal. The BundleTransformer automatically includes the bundle's books in the response. You still need to define a BundlesController@show route in the app/Http/routes.php file before your tests will pass again. You might as well take this opportunity to write all the routes for this chapter at once (Listing 11-24).

Listing 11-24. Adding the /bundles Routes

```php
41  $app->group([
42      'prefix' => '/bundles',
43      'namespace' => 'App\Http\Controllers'
44  ], function (\Laravel\Lumen\Application $app) {
45
46      $app->get('/{id:[\d]+}', [
47          'as' => 'bundles.show',
48          'uses' => 'BundlesController@show'
49      ]);
50
51      $app->put(
52          '/{bundleId:[\d]+}/books/{bookId:[\d]+}',
53          'BundlesController@addBook'
54      );
55
56      $app->delete(
57          '/{bundleId:[\d]+}/books/{bookId:[\d]+}',
58          'BundlesController@removeBook'
59      );
60  });
```

With the routes defined you are ready to see if your test suite is fully passing again (Listing 11-25).

Listing 11-25. Running the Test Suite

```
# vagrant@homestead:~/Code/bookr$
$ phpunit
OK (51 tests, 266 assertions)
```

Adding a Book to a Bundle

Up to this point, you have relied on seed data and factories to associate bundles and books. You need an API endpoint to define the relationship for books contained within a bundle. You will write the API to allow adding and removing a single book per request. Adding a book will use the PUT/bundles/ {bundleId:[\d]+}/books/{bookId:[\d]+} nested route.

Let's start by writing the failing test for adding a book to an existing bundle in the *tests/app/Http/ Controllers/BundlesControllerTest.php* file (Listing 11-26).

Listing 11-26. Testing the Addition of a Book to a Bundle

```
72   /** @test **/
73   public function addBook_should_add_a_book_to_a_bundle()
74   {
75       $bundle = factory(\App\Bundle::class)->create();
76       $book = $this->bookFactory();
77
78       // Bundle should not have any associated books yet
79       $this->notSeeInDatabase('book_bundle', ['bundle_id' => $bundle->id]);
80
81       $this->put("/bundles/{$bundle->id}/books/{$book->id}", [],
82           ['Accept' => 'application/json']);
83
84       $this->seeStatusCode(200);
85
86       $dbBundle = \App\Bundle::with('books')->find($bundle->id);
87       $this->assertCount(1, $dbBundle->books,
88           'The bundle should have 1 associated book');
89
90       $this->assertEquals(
91           $dbBundle->books()->first()->id,
92           $book->id
93       );
94
95       $body = $this->response->getData(true);
96
97       $this->assertArrayHasKey('data', $body);
98       // Ensure the book id is in the response.
99       $this->assertArrayHasKey('books', $body['data']);
100      $this->assertArrayHasKey('data', $body['data']['books']);
101
102      // Make sure the book is in the response
103      $books = $body['data']['books'];
104      $this->assertEquals($book->id, $books['data'][0]['id']);
105  }
```

Your test creates a bundle and a book separately because you don't want them associated, and you assert that the new bundle does not have any books. You associate a book with the bundle with a PUT request and then get the bundle from the database to ensure the book is now associated with the bundle. Lastly, the test ensures the response contains the newly associated book and has the expected response.

Next, you will write the `BundlesController::addBook()` method which adds a book to the bundle (Listing 11-27).

Listing 11-27. The Initial Method for Adding a Book

```
22  /**
23   * @param int $bundleId
24   * @param int $bookId
25   * @return \Illuminate\Http\JsonResponse
26   */
27  public function addBook($bundleId, $bookId)
28  {
29      $bundle = \App\Bundle::findOrFail($bundleId);
30      $book = \App\Book::findOrFail($bookId);
31
32      $bundle->books()->attach($book);
33      $data = $this->item($bundle, new BundleTransformer());
34
35      return response()->json($data);
36  }
```

The implementation is really simple: the controller makes sure that both the bundle and book are valid records and attaches the book to the bundle with the `attach()` method. Let's make sure your new controller method satisfies your tests (Listing 11-28).

Listing 11-28. Running the Test Suite

```
# vagrant@homestead:~/Code/bookr$
$ phpunit

OK (52 tests, 274 assertions)
```

Remove a Book from a Bundle

Now that you have a way to add a book to a bundle, you need a way to remove a book too. Removing a book from a bundle resembles adding a book and will not take much effort to test and implement. First, write the test for removing a book (Listing 11-29).

Listing 11-29. Test for Removing a Book from a Bundle

```
107  /** @test **/
108  public function removeBook_should_remove_a_book_from_a_bundle()
109  {
110      $bundle = $this->bundleFactory(3);
111      $book = $bundle->books()->first();
112
```

```
113     $this->seeInDatabase('book_bundle', [
114         'book_id' => $book->id,
115         'bundle_id' => $bundle->id
116     ]);
117
118     $this->assertCount(3, $bundle->books);
119
120     $this
121         ->delete("/bundles/{$bundle->id}/books/{$book->id}")
122         ->seeStatusCode(204)
123         ->notSeeInDatabase('book_bundle', [
124             'book_id' => $book->id,
125             'bundle_id' => $bundle->id
126         ]);
127
128     $dbBundle = \App\Bundle::find($bundle->id);
129     $this->assertCount(2, $dbBundle->books);
130 }
```

Let's break down the code in this test:

- Create a bundle with three associated books.

- Get the first associated book and ensures the database association.

- Assert that the bundle has three associated books.

- Make a DELETE request and check for a 204 response.

- Verify that the removed book is not associated with the bundle anymore.

- Verify that the bundle only has two associated books in the database after deleting the association.

The controller method is just like the addBook() method, except that you call detach() instead of attach() to remove the book from the bundle.

Up next is the controller method for removing a book from a book bundle (Listing 11-30).

Listing 11-30. Removing a Book in the BundlesController

```
38  public function removeBook($bundleId, $bookId)
39  {
40      $bundle = \App\Bundle::findOrFail($bundleId);
41      $book = \App\Book::findOrFail($bookId);
42
43      $bundle->books()->detach($book);
44
45      return response(null, 204);
46  }
```

The removeBook method finds the bundle and book records, and then detaches the association between the bundle and book. The response sends back a null response body with a 204 No Content on success.

Next, finalize your bundle features by running the full test suite (Listing 11-31).

Listing 11-31. Running the Test Suite

```
# vagrant@homestead:~/Code/bookr$
$ phpunit

OK (53 tests, 279 assertions)
```

---

❶ Git Commit: Add the Bundles API Resource

e720e5c (https://bitbucket.org/paulredmond/apress-bookr/commits/492e78b)

Conclusion

You learned how to deal with adding and removing many-to-many associations through API requests, in addition to basic GET responses for all bundles and individual bundles. You now have enough experience in this book to write tests for the remaining /bundle CRUD operations and then implement each one. I demonstrated one way to represent many-to-many associations through an AP; you can now expand upon it with things like bulk adding and removing of books from a bundle.

In the next and final chapter of this book, you will explore polymorphic relationships, as well as some performance optimizations to your queries for associated records.

Ratings

The final chapter will focus on adding the ability to rate things. When you think of ratings, you might think of book ratings, but actually you can apply ratings to multiple things. Specifically, you will add ratings to *authors*. Using Eloquent makes it easy to apply data like ratings to multiple models (as you will see shortly) using polymorphic relationships (https://laravel.com/docs/5.2/eloquent-relationships#polymorphic-relations). Polymorphic relationships allow a model (ratings) to belong to more than one model. In the context of your API, ratings make sense for authors, books, and bundles.

Your ratings will be a five star rating system based on an integer value between 1 and 5. You will be laying all the groundwork in this chapter so that adding ratings to multiple models in your API will be almost effortless.

Database Design

Eloquent provides polymorphic associations out of the box and it's really easy to get something working quickly. Your database design will start by defining a migration for the ratings table. Based on the polymorphic documentation, you should come up with something like Listing 12-1.

Listing 12-1. Creating the Ratings Table Migration

```
# vagrant@homestead:~/Code/bookr$
$ php artisan make:migration \
create_ratings_table --create=ratings
Created Migration: 2015_12_12_061605_create_ratings_table
```

The migration for the ratings table will define the value, the associated model id, and the model type (Listing 12-2).

Listing 12-2. Ratings Table Database Migration Code

```
1   <?php
2
3   use Illuminate\Database\Schema\Blueprint;
4   use Illuminate\Database\Migrations\Migration;
5
6   class CreateRatingsTable extends Migration
7   {
8       /**
9        * Run the migrations.
10       *
11       * @return void
```

© Paul Redmond 2016
P. Redmond, *Lumen Programming Guide*, DOI 10.1007/978-1-4842-2187-7_12

```
12        */
13        public function up()
14        {
15            Schema::create('ratings', function (Blueprint $table) {
16                $table->increments('id');
17                $table->integer('value')->unsigned();
18                $table->integer('rateable_id')->unsigned();
19                $table->string('rateable_type');
20                $table->timestamps();
21            });
22        }
23
24        /**
25         * Reverse the migrations.
26         *
27         * @return void
28         */
29        public function down()
30        {
31            Schema::drop('ratings');
32        }
33    }
```

Your migration defines an unsigned integer field of value to hold the rating. The polymorphic association needs two other fields: rateable_id and rateable_type. The former is the id of the "owning" model (Author) and the latter is the class name of the "owning" model (App\Author). The rest of the migration should be familiar at this point.

With the ratings table defined, your next step is to create a new Rating model and update your Author model to support ratings. Create the *app/Rating.php* model with the code in Listing 12-3.

Listing 12-3. The Rating Model

```
1   <?php
2
3   namespace App;
4
5   use Illuminate\Database\Eloquent\Model;
6
7   class Rating extends Model
8   {
9       /**
10       * @inheritdoc
11       */
12      protected $fillable = ['value'];
13
14      public function rateable()
15      {
16          return $this->morphTo();
17      }
18  }
```

Notice the correlation between the method name of rateable() and the database field name prefix of rateable_. The *return $this->morphTo()* call is defining the polymorphic inverse relationship. You also define the value field as the only fillable field since the other fields will be managed by Eloquent automatically.

Next, you are going to create a PHP Trait (http://php.net/manual/en/language.oop5.traits.php) that models can use to add the other end of the polymorphic relationship easily. Create a file at *app/Rateable.php* with the code in Listing 12-4.

Listing 12-4. The Rateable Trait

```php
1   <?php
2
3   namespace App;
4
5   /**
6    * Trait to enable polymorphic ratings on a model.
7    *
8    * @package App
9    */
10  trait Rateable
11  {
12      public function ratings()
13      {
14          return $this->morphMany(Rating::class, 'rateable');
15      }
16  }
```

When a model uses the Rateable trait, the ratings() method will define a one-to-many polymorphic relationship, meaning that the Author model will have many ratings and a single Rating will *belongTo* an Author. Other models can add this trait to implement ratings, and this makes it easy at a glance to see that a model is "rateable."

Next, add the new trait to the Author and Book models (Listing 12-5).

Listing 12-5. Adding the Rateable Trait

```php
class Book extends Model
{
    use Rateable;

    // ...
}
```

```php
class Author extends Model
{
    use Rateable;

    // ...
}
```

I've provided one code sample for both models since adding the trait is such a small amount of code. Now your models can store ratings in the database! You are ready to create a factory and seed data now for ratings.

First, append the factory in Listing 12-6 to the database/factories/ModelFactory.php file.

Listing 12-6. The Rating Factory

```
48  $factory->define(\App\Rating::class, function ($faker) {
49      return [
50          'value' => rand(1, 5)
51      ];
52  });
```

The factory randomly assigns 1-5 stars for a rating. Note that you will not use factory()->create() on the ratings factory. You will mostly use factory()->make() and then save the ratings through other models.

To use your new factory, you will refactor the *database/seeds/BooksTableSeeder.php* file to insert ratings into author and book seed data (Listing 12-7).

Listing 12-7. Adding Ratings to the Books Database Seeder

```
 9  /**
10   * Run the database seeds.
11   *
12   * @return void
13   */
14  public function run()
15  {
16      $authors = factory(App\Author::class, 10)->create();
17      $authors->each(function ($author) {
18          $author->ratings()->saveMany(
19              factory(App\Rating::class, rand(20, 50))->make()
20          );
21
22          $booksCount = rand(1, 5);
23
24          while ($booksCount > 0) {
25              $book = factory(App\Book::class)->make();
26              $author->books()->save($book);
27              $book->ratings()->saveMany(
28                  factory(App\Rating::class, rand(20, 50))->make()
29              );
30              $booksCount--;
31          }
32      });
33  }
```

Now your database seeder is creating ratings for each author, and then ratings for each book. You use *rand(20, 50)* to add between 20 and 50 ratings with ratings()->saveMany(). As noted earlier, you call *factory(App\Rating::class, rand(20, 50))->make()* and use the associated models to persist ratings to the database. You should be able to seed the database now with the artisan command (Listing 12-8).

Listing 12-8. Migrating and Seeding the Database

```
# vagrant@homestead:~/Code/bookr$
$ php artisan migrate:refresh
...
$ php artisan db:seed
```

```
Seeded: BooksTableSeeder
Seeded: BundlesTableSeeder
```

If you inspect the database you should see ratings in the `ratings` table for both authors and books. Eloquent and Laravel make it easy to model data quickly and get stuff done!

Rating an Author

The design of the author ratings API will be a nested resource specific to author ratings. The following are examples of the author rating endpoints you will be writing:

- `POST /authors/1/ratings` for adding a new rating
- `DELETE /authors/1/ratings/1` for deleting an existing author rating

Define the new author rating routes in *app/Http/routes.php* to get started (Listing 12-9).

Listing 12-9. Author Ratings Routes in app/Http/routes.php

```
27  $app->group([
28      'prefix' => '/authors',
29      'namespace' => 'App\Http\Controllers'
30  ], function (\Laravel\Lumen\Application $app) {
31      $app->get('/', 'AuthorsController@index');
32      $app->post('/', 'AuthorsController@store');
33      $app->get('/{id:[\d]+}', [
34          'as' => 'authors.show',
35          'uses' => 'AuthorsController@show'
36      ]);
37      $app->put('/{id:[\d]+}', 'AuthorsController@update');
38      $app->delete('/{id:[\d]+}', 'AuthorsController@destroy');
39
40      // Author ratings
41      $app->post('/{id:[\d]+}/ratings', 'AuthorsRatingsController@store');
42      $app->delete(
43          '/{authorId:[\d]+}/ratings/{ratingId:[\d]+}',
44          'AuthorsRatingsController@destroy'
45      );
46  });
```

Note the `{authorId:[\d]+}` route param, which is needed to differentiate with the `ratingId`—route params must be unique. You will organize author rating management in a new controller but nest the routes within the `/authors` resource routes.

Adding an Author Rating

The first route you will test is adding a new rating to an author. When the Controller endpoint is complete you will expect a response similar to Listing 12-10.

Listing 12-10. Example Response from AuthorsRatingsController@store

```
{
    "data":{
        "id":1409,
        "value":"5",
        "type":"App\\Author",
        "links":[
            {
                "rel":"author",
                "href":"http:\/\/localhost:8000\/authors\/1"
            }
        ],
        "created":"2015-12-12T16:42:24+0000",
        "updated":"2015-12-12T16:42:24+0000"
    }
}
```

Let's get to work on writing tests and a controller for your work. First, let's create the Author's ratings controller and test (Listing 12-11).

Listing 12-11. Creating the AuthorRatingsController and Test File

```
# vagrant@homestead:~/Code/bookr$
$ touch tests/app/Http/Controllers/AuthorsRatingsControllerTest.php
$ touch app/Http/Controllers/AuthorsRatingsController.php
```

Your first test in the *tests/app/Http/Controllers/AuthorsRatingsControllerTest.php* file will test adding a new rating to an author (Listing 12-12).

Listing 12-12. Test for Adding Author Ratings

```
1   <?php
2
3   namespace Tests\App\Http\Controllers;
4
5   use TestCase;
6   use Laravel\Lumen\Testing\DatabaseMigrations;
7
8   class AuthorsRatingsControllerTest extends TestCase
9   {
10      use DatabaseMigrations;
11
12      /** @test **/
13      public function store_can_add_a_rating_to_an_author()
14      {
15          $author = factory(\App\Author::class)->create();
16
17          $this->post(
18              "/authors/{$author->id}/ratings",
19              ['value' => 5],
20              ['Accept' => 'application/json']
```

```
21          );
22
23          $this
24              ->seeStatusCode(201)
25              ->seeJson([
26                  'value' => 5
27              ])
28              ->seeJson([
29                  'rel' => 'author',
30                  'href' => route('authors.show', ['id' => $author->id])
31              ]);
32
33          $body = $this->response->getData(true);
34          $this->assertArrayHasKey('data', $body);
35
36          $data = $body['data'];
37          $this->assertArrayHasKey('links', $data);
38      }
39  }
```

This test submits a rating of "5" and makes sure that the value is returned. The test also checks for a links key which will contain an *href* to the created rating resource and an href to the author associated with this rating.

HATEOAS

For those keeping track, this book hasn't talked about or addressed HATEOAS (`https://en.wikipedia.org/wiki/HATEOAS`) (Hypermedia as the Engine of Application State) much at all, but I have provided a few examples how you can use the `route()` helper function to make generating links between data simple.

You can leverage Fractal transformers to take care of HATEOAS data and I encourage you to learn more of the theory and good practices around writing RESTful services, including HATEOAS, if you are not familiar.

Before you start working on the controller, you will need another Fractal transformer for ratings. The transformer will need to be a little smarter than your previous transformers since it will transform multiple types, and you want to provide additional data about a rating and how it relates to other models.

Create the new rating transformer file and accompanying test (Listing 12-13).

Listing 12-13. Creating the RatingTransformer and Test Files

```
$ touch tests/app/Transformer/RatingTransformerTest.php
$ touch app/Transformer/RatingTransformer.php
```

The initial *RatingTransformerTest* class will include the basic initialization test you add for each transformer and a test to transform an author rating (Listing 12-14).

225

Listing 12-14. Initial RatingTransformerTest Class

```php
1   <?php
2
3   namespace Tests\App\Transformer;
4
5   use TestCase;
6   use App\Transformer\RatingTransformer;
7   use Laravel\Lumen\Testing\DatabaseMigrations;
8
9   class RatingTransformerTest extends TestCase
10  {
11      use DatabaseMigrations;
12
13      /**
14       * @var RatingTransformer
15       */
16      private $subject;
17
18      public function setUp()
19      {
20          parent::setUp();
21
22          $this->subject = new RatingTransformer();
23      }
24
25      /** @test **/
26      public function it_can_be_initialized()
27      {
28          $this->assertInstanceOf(RatingTransformer::class, $this->subject);
29      }
30
31      /** @test **/
32      public function it_can_transform_a_rating_for_an_author()
33      {
34          $author = factory(\App\Author::class)->create();
35          $rating = $author->ratings()->save(
36              factory(\App\Rating::class)->make()
37          );
38
39
40          $actual = $this->subject->transform($rating);
41
42          $this->assertEquals($rating->id, $actual['id']);
43          $this->assertEquals($rating->value, $actual['value']);
44          $this->assertEquals($rating->rateable_type, $actual['type']);
45          $this->assertEquals(
46              $rating->created_at->toIso8601String(),
47              $actual['created']
48          );
49          $this->assertEquals(
50              $rating->updated_at->toIso8601String(),
```

```
51                    $actual['created']
52            );
53
54            $this->assertArrayHasKey('links', $actual);
55            $links = $actual['links'];
56            $this->assertCount(1, $links);
57            $authorLink = $links[0];
58
59            $this->assertArrayHasKey('rel', $authorLink);
60            $this->assertEquals('author', $authorLink['rel']);
61            $this->assertArrayHasKey('href', $authorLink);
62            $this->assertEquals(
63                route('authors.show', ['id' => $author->id]),
64                $authorLink['href']
65            );
66        }
67    }
```

Like all the other transformer tests you've covered, you test that the transformer can be initialized. The *it_can_transform_a_rating_for_an_author* test checks for keys and values to make sure the transformer formats data as you expect. The test also verifies the links property, which should contain an author resource with an href to the author API entity.

Listing 12-15 shows what your first RatingTransformer implementation looks like.

Listing 12-15. First Version of the RatingTransformer Implementation

```
1    <?php
2
3    namespace App\Transformer;
4
5    use App\Rating;
6    use League\Fractal\TransformerAbstract;
7
8    /**
9     * Class RatingTransformer
10    * @package App\Transformer
11    */
12   class RatingTransformer extends TransformerAbstract
13   {
14       /**
15        * Transform a Rating
16        *
17        * @param Rating $rating
18        * @return array
19        */
20       public function transform(Rating $rating)
21       {
22           return [
23               'id' => $rating->id,
24               'value' => $rating->value,
25               'type' => $rating->rateable_type,
26               'links' => [
```

```
27                       [
28                            'rel' => 'author',
29                            'href' => route('authors.show', ['id' => $rating->rateable_id])
30                       ]
31                  ],
32                  'created' => $rating->created_at->toIso8601String(),
33                  'updated' => $rating->updated_at->toIso8601String(),
34             ];
35         }
36  }
```

You've side-stepped the failing test for RatingsAuthorsController that you originally wrote in this section to work on the RatingTransformer. You cannot run the full test suite, but the initial passing version of the RatingTransfomer hard-codes the author link data and your RatingTransformer tests should pass now (Listing 12-16).

Listing 12-16. Running Tests for the RatingTransformer

```
# vagrant@homestead:~/Code/bookr$
$ phpunit --filter=RatingTransformerTest

OK (2 tests, 12 assertions)
```

Before you write the passing implementation for the AuthorsRatingsController, let's refactor the transformer to be more dynamic and capable of transforming a rating for other entities (Listing 12-17).

Listing 12-17. Refactoring the RatingTransformer to Support Multiple Models

```
1   <?php
2
3   namespace App\Transformer;
4
5   use App\Rating;
6   use League\Fractal\TransformerAbstract;
7
8   /**
9    * Class RatingTransformer
10   * @package App\Transformer
11   */
12  class RatingTransformer extends TransformerAbstract
13  {
14      /**
15       * Transform a Rating
16       *
17       * @param Rating $rating
18       * @return array
19       */
20      public function transform(Rating $rating)
21      {
22          return [
23              'id' => $rating->id,
24              'value' => $rating->value,
```

```php
25                'type' => $rating->rateable_type,
26                'links' => [
27                    [
28                            'rel' => $this->getModelName($rating->rateable_type),
29                            'href' => $this->getModelUrl($rating)
30                    ]
31                ],
32                'created' => $rating->created_at->toIso8601String(),
33                'updated' => $rating->updated_at->toIso8601String(),
34            ];
35        }
36
37    /**
38     * Get a human-friendly model name
39     *
40     * @param $rateable_type
41     * @return string
42     */
43    private function getModelName($rateable_type)
44    {
45        return strtolower(preg_replace("/^App\\\/", '', $rateable_type));
46    }
47
48    /**
49     * Generate a URL to the rated model resyource
50     *
51     * @param Rating $rating
52     * @return string
53     */
54    private function getModelUrl(Rating $rating)
55    {
56        $author = \App\Author::class;
57        $book = \App\Author::class;
58
59        switch ($rating->rateable_type) {
60            case $author:
61                $named = 'authors.show';
62                break;
63            case $book:
64                $named = 'books.show';
65                break;
66            default:
67                throw new \RuntimeException(sprintf(
68                    'Rateable model type for %s is not defined',
69                    $rating->rateable_type
70                ));
71        }
72
73        return route($named, ['id' => $rating->rateable_id]);
74    }
75 }
```

You've added two private methods for dealing with dynamic model data, getModelName() and getModelUrl(). These methods are not *perfect* but they get the job done by providing a more human-readable rel type. You will have to keep adding more models to the switch statement in getModelUrl() method when you want to make something "rateable," but for now it works.

Your tests should still pass after the refactor. In real life, you might have to deal with failures along the way, but through the power of books, you get the passing code immediately (Listing 12-18).

Listing 12-18. Running the RatingTransformer Tests After Refactoring

```
# vagrant@homestead:~/Code/bookr$
$ phpunit --filter=RatingTransformerTest

OK (2 tests, 12 assertions)
```

The getModelUrl() will throw an exception if it doesn't recognize the $rating->rateable_type so you need to write a test for that (Listing 12-19).

Listing 12-19. Test for a Thrown Exception in RatingTranformerTest

```
68  /**
69   * @test
70   * @expectedException \RuntimeException
71   * @expectedExceptionMessage Rateable model type for Foo\Bar is not defined
72   */
73  public function it_throws_an_exception_when_a_model_is_not_defined()
74  {
75      $rating = factory(\App\Rating::class)->create([
76          'value' => 5,
77          'rateable_type' => 'Foo\Bar',
78          'rateable_id' => 1
79      ]);
80
81      $this->subject->transform($rating);
82  }
```

You directly create a rating with a fake rateable_type to trigger the exception. This test also uses PHPUnit test annotations (https://phpunit.de/manual/current/en/appendixes.annotations.html#appendixes.annotations.expectedException) to ensure that \RuntimeException is thrown with the correct message.

Your transformer passes fully and is ready to use. You can now starting writing the first version of your controller at app/Http/Controllers/AuthorsRatingsController.php and get your tests to pass (Listing 12-20).

Listing 12-20. The AuthorsRatings Controller

```
1  <?php
2
3  namespace App\Http\Controllers;
4
5  use App\Author;
6  use Illuminate\Http\Request;
7  use App\Transformer\RatingTransformer;
8
9  /**
```

```
10    * Manage an Author's Ratings
11    */
12  class AuthorsRatingsController extends Controller
13  {
14      public function store(Request $request, $authorId)
15      {
16          $author = Author::findOrFail($authorId);
17
18          $rating = $author->ratings()->create(['value' => $request->get('value')]);
19          $data = $this->item($rating, new RatingTransformer());
20
21          return response()->json($data, 201);
22      }
23  }
```

The controller simply checks for a valid author and creates a new rating associated with the author. The controller returns the new rating data with a 201 created response. The full test suite should pass now that you've implemented the controller (Listing 12-21).

Listing 12-21. Running the Full Test Suite

```
# vagrant@homestead:~/Code/bookr$
$ phpunit

OK (57 tests, 299 assertions)
```

For your own satisfaction, you can post a rating via the command line on 'nix systems, as shown in Listing 12-22.

Listing 12-22. Adding an Author Rating with Curl

```
# vagrant@homestead:~/Code/bookr$
$ php artisan migrate:refresh
$ php artisan db:seed
$ curl --data "value=5" -X POST http://bookr.app/authors/1/ratings
{
    "data":{
        "id":1188,
        "value":"5",
        "type":"App\\Author",
        "links":[
            {
                "rel":"author",
                "href":"http:\/\/bookr.app\/authors\/1"
            }
        ],
        "created":"2016-02-02T05:55:42+0000",
        "updated":"2016-02-02T05:55:42+0000"
    }
}
```

Now that the code has passed the tests, you will write a test to ensure you get a 404 response back when the author id is invalid in AuthorsRatingsControllerTest (Listing 12-23).

Listing 12-23. Test for Trying to Add a Rating to an Invalid Author

```
40  /** @test **/
41  public function store_fails_when_the_author_is_invalid()
42  {
43      $this->post('/authors/1/ratings', [], ['Accept' => 'application/json']);
44      $this->seeStatusCode(404);
45  }
```

Since you already wrote Author::findOrFail($authorId); this test will pass. Be careful of tests that pass without writing additional code. To verify that your test is indeed valid, temporarily update the controller to Listing 12-24.

Listing 12-24. Revert AuthorsRatingsController to Make Test Fail

```
14  public function store(Request $request, $authorId)
15  {
16      $author = Author::find($authorId);
17
18      $rating = $author->ratings()->create(['value' => $request->get('value')]);
19      $data = $this->item($rating, new RatingTransformer());
20
21      return response()->json($data, 201);
22  }
```

After changing the AuthorsRatingsController::store() method, you should get the test failure shown in Listing 12-25.

Listing 12-25. Test Failure After Reverting the AuthorsRatingsController

```
# vagrant@homestead:~/Code/bookr$
$ phpunit

There was 1 failure:

1) Tests\App\Http\Controllers\AuthorsRatingsControllerTest::store_fails_when_the\
_author_is_invalid
Failed asserting that 400 matches expected 404.

/home/vagrant/Code/bookr/vendor/laravel/lumen-framework/src/Testing/CrawlerTrait\
.php:412
/home/vagrant/Code/bookr/tests/app/Http/Controllers/AuthorsRatingsControllerTest.php:44

FAILURES!
Tests: 58, Assertions: 300, Failures: 1.
```

Your test will guard against to responding with a 404 when the database lookup fails. Revert the AuthorsRatingsController.php file to Listing 12-26 to get back to green.

Listing 12-26. Restoring the Correct Store Method

```
14  public function store(Request $request, $authorId)
15  {
16      $author = Author::findOrFail($authorId);
17
18      $rating = $author->ratings()->create(['value' => $request->get('value')]);
19      $data = $this->item($rating, new RatingTransformer());
20
21      return response()->json($data, 201);
22  }
```

Check the tests to make sure everything is working as expected (Listing 12-27).

Listing 12-27. Running the Full Test Suite

```
# vagrant@homestead:~/Code/bookr$
$ phpunit

OK (58 tests, 300 assertions)
```

Deleting an Author Rating

Your next feature will be the ability to *delete* an existing author rating. You already defined the application delete route earlier in this chapter (Listing 12-28).

Listing 12-28. The Delete Route for Author Ratings

```
$app->delete(
    '/{authorId}:[\d]+}/ratings/{ratingId:[\d]+}',
    'AuthorsRatingsController@destroy'
);
```

The outline for your acceptance criteria:

- Delete should remove an existing rating from an author.

- The ratings table should no longer associate the rating to the author.

- The rating should no longer exist in the database.

Let's write the first failing test for deleting a rating from an author in the AuthorsRatingsControllerTest (Listing 12-29).

Listing 12-29. Test to Delete a Rating from an Author

```
47  /** @test **/
48  public function destroy_can_delete_an_author_rating()
49  {
50      $author = factory(\App\Author::class)->create();
51      $ratings = $author->ratings()->saveMany(
52          factory(\App\Rating::class, 2)->make()
53      );
54
```

```
55      $this->assertCount(2, $ratings);
56
57      $ratings->each(function (\App\Rating $rating) use ($author) {
58          $this->seeInDatabase('ratings', [
59              'rateable_id' => $author->id,
60              'id' => $rating->id
61          ]);
62      });
63
64      $ratingToDelete = $ratings->first();
65      $this
66          ->delete(
67              "/authors/{$author->id}/ratings/{$ratingToDelete->id}"
68          )
69          ->seeStatusCode(204);
70
71      $dbAuthor = \App\Author::find($author->id);
72      $this->assertCount(1, $dbAuthor->ratings);
73      $this->notSeeInDatabase(
74          'ratings',
75          ['id' => $ratingToDelete->id]
76      );
77  }
```

First, you seed data for the test; data factory code should look familiar because it is basically the same as the database seeding you saw earlier in this chapter. You then check to make sure that you save two ratings in the database with ratings()->saveMany() so you can verify that the rating count decreases by one after deleting one rating. Next, you loop through each rating and just double check that each rating is properly associated with the author.

With the data seeded and verifying associations, your test gets the rating to be deleted and makes the DELETE request and you expect a 204 status code in return. Last, you verify that the rating was removed by getting the author from the database and asserting that the author only has one rating, and the rating you deleted is no longer in the ratings table.

Technically, the framework takes care of the database associations checked in this test, but extra checking does not hurt and makes me feel safer that my test is accurate.

Moving on, you make sure your new test causes a failure (Listing 12-30).

Listing 12-30. Running the Failing Test

```
# vagrant@homestead:~/Code/bookr$
$ phpunit

There was 1 failure:

1) Tests\App\Http\Controllers\AuthorsRatingsControllerTest::destroy_can_delete_an_author_
rating
Failed asserting that 404 matches expected 204.

/home/vagrant/Code/bookr/vendor/laravel/lumen-framework/src/Testing/CrawlerTrait.php:412
/home/vagrant/Code/bookr/tests/app/Http/Controllers/AuthorsRatingsControllerTest.php:69

FAILURES!
```

```
Tests: 59, Assertions: 304, Failures: 1.
```

With the failing test in place, let's write the first implementation of the AuthorsRatingsController@ destroy method (Listing 12-31).

Listing 12-31. Implementation for Deleting an Author Rating

```
24   /**
25    * @param $authorId
26    * @param $ratingId
27    * @return \Laravel\Lumen\Http\ResponseFactory
28    */
29   public function destroy($authorId, $ratingId)
30   {
31       /** @var \App\Author $author */
32       $author = Author::findOrFail($authorId);
33       $author
34           ->ratings()
35           ->findOrFail($ratingId)
36           ->delete();
37
38       return response(null, 204);
39   }
```

Your controller ensures the author exists and then uses the author to find the $ratingId. The request can fail if the $authorId is invalid *or* the $ratingId is invalid. You should write some additional tests in the AuthorsRatingsControllerTest class just to ensure that this method fails in the way you expect (Listing 12-32).

Listing 12-32. Test API Cannot Delete Another Author's Rating

```
79   /** @test **/
80   public function destroy_should_not_delete_ratings_from_another_author()
81   {
82       $authors = factory(\App\Author::class, 2)->create();
83       $authors->each(function (\App\Author $author) {
84           $author->ratings()->saveMany(
85               factory(\App\Rating::class, 2)->make()
86           );
87       });
88
89       $firstAuthor = $authors->first();
90       $rating = $authors
91           ->last()
92           ->ratings()
93           ->first();
94
95       $this->delete(
96           "/authors/{$firstAuthor->id}/ratings/{$rating->id}",
97           [],
98           ['Accept' => 'application/json']
99       )->seeStatusCode(404);
100  }
```

The test creates factory data for two authors. You then grab the first author and a rating from the second author. Your delete request expects a 404 response because the rating id is invalid in the context of the author from which you try to delete a rating. This test will pass because you've already added $author->ratings()->findOrFail($ratingId) to the controller's destroy method. You can swap out the code to get the test failing.

You should also expect a 404 if the author id is not valid in the AuthorsRatingsControllerTest. You have already seen variations of this test multiple times in this book.

Listing 12-33. Test Expecting a 404 When the Author Is Invalid

```
102   /** @test **/
103   public function destroy_fails_when_the_author_is_invalid()
104   {
105       $this->delete(
106           '/authors/1/ratings/1',
107           [],
108           ['Accept' => 'application/json']
109       )->seeStatusCode(404);
110   }
```

You code should fully pass, but you'll run the test suite once more before moving on to the next topic (Listing 12-34).

Listing 12-34. Running the Full Test Suite

```
$ phpunit

OK (61 tests, 308 assertions)
```

You are done with managing author ratings, although I did not cover all the API endpoints you might make to manage ratings an application. You could also provide an endpoint to do bulk operations, like removing multiple ratings with one request when it makes sense. You should be equipped with enough knowledge now to develop and test these concepts.

Ratings in the Author API

Now that you have the database schema and basic rating management, you are going to add rating data to the /author API. Your feature will be to provide an API that includes an author's rating average and rating count. When building this feature you need to keep in mind *how* the ratings might be used. In the simplest form, perhaps an author page will show a five star graphical scale.

The API needs to provide enough information to allow the UI to display the ratings. The consumer might need to know things like the maximum rating possible, how many people rated the author, the average rating, and the average rating as a percentage.

With that data in mind, your first attempt might look like Listing 12-35.

Listing 12-35. Example Author Response With Ratings

```
{
    "data":{
        "id":1,
        "name":"Roslyn Medhurst",
        "gender":"female",
```

```
        "biography":"Nemo accusantium et blanditiis.",
        "rating":{
            "average":3.32,
            "max":5,
            "percent":66.4,
            "count":56
        },
        "created":"2015-12-12T14:36:50+0000",
        "updated":"2015-12-12T14:36:50+0000"
    }
}
```

Now that you have an idea of what your API might respond with, your test plan will include:

- Testing typical rating values when an author has been rated

- Testing the rating data when an author has not been rated yet

You'll start by writing new tests in the *tests/app/Transformer/AuthorTransformerTest.php* class. The first test you will cover is to modify the existing it_can_transform_an_author test to add rating data (Listing 12-36).

Listing 12-36. Testing the AuthorTransformer Rating Data

```
25  /** @test **/
26  public function it_can_transform_an_author()
27  {
28      $author = factory(\App\Author::class)->create();
29
30      $author->ratings()->save(
31          factory(\App\Rating::class)->make(['value' => 5])
32      );
33
34      $author->ratings()->save(
35          factory(\App\Rating::class)->make(['value' => 3])
36      );
37
38      $actual = $this->subject->transform($author);
39
40      $this->assertEquals($author->id, $actual['id']);
41      $this->assertEquals($author->name, $actual['name']);
42      $this->assertEquals($author->gender, $actual['gender']);
43      $this->assertEquals($author->biography, $actual['biography']);
44      $this->assertEquals($author->created_at->toIso8601String(), $actual['created']);
45      $this->assertEquals($author->updated_at->toIso8601String(), $actual['created']);
46
47      // Rating
48      $this->assertArrayHasKey('rating', $actual);
49      $this->assertInternalType('array', $actual['rating']);
50      $this->assertEquals(4, $actual['rating']['average']);
51      $this->assertEquals(5, $actual['rating']['max']);
52      $this->assertEquals(80, $actual['rating']['percent']);
53      $this->assertEquals(2, $actual['rating']['count']);
54  }
```

You start by adding ratings to the author data under test. To make it easy to calculate averages, you add two ratings individually, and factory()->make() allows you to override the rating value. Next, you add assertions that the rating key exists and is an array. Last, you verify the value of each individual rating key you expect.

Your test will fail with the error shown in Listing 12-37.

Listing 12-37. Running the Modified Test

```
# vagrant@homestead:~/Code/bookr$
$ phpunit --filter=it_can_transform_an_author

There was 1 failure:

1) Tests\App\Transformer\AuthorTransformerTest::it_can_transform_an_author
Failed asserting that an array has the key 'rating'.

/home/vagrant/Code/bookr/tests/app/Transformer/AuthorTransformerTest.php:48

FAILURES!
Tests: 1, Assertions: 7, Failures: 1.
```

Your implementation of this feature will update the *app/Transformer/AuthorTransformer.php* file to include the "ratings" key and do all the ratings calculations (Listing 12-38).

Listing 12-38. Implementing Ratings in the AuthorTransformer

```
19  /**
20   * Transform an author model
21   *
22   * @param Author $author
23   * @return array
24   */
25  public function transform(Author $author)
26  {
27      return [
28          'id'        => $author->id,
29          'name'      => $author->name,
30          'gender'    => $author->gender,
31          'biography' => $author->biography,
32          'rating' => [
33              'average' => (float) sprintf(
34                  "%.2f",
35                  $author->ratings->avg('value')
36              ),
37              'max' => (float) sprintf("%.2f", 5),
38              'percent' => (float) sprintf(
39                  "%.2f",
40                  ($author->ratings->avg('value') / 5) * 100
41              ),
42              'count' => $author->ratings->count(),
43          ],
44          'created'   => $author->created_at->toIso8601String(),
```

```
45              'updated'   => $author->created_at->toIso8601String(),
46          ];
47  }
```

If you run the test suite, things should pass again (Listing 12-39).

Listing 12-39. Running the Test Suite

```
# vagrant@homestead:~/Code/bookr$
$ phpunit

OK (61 tests, 314 assertions)
```

Your change will affect all of your responses containing an author. Unfortunately, the rating data is lazy-loaded right now, meaning that each Author record in the /authors request will result in a new query. If you are returning 100 authors in your response, that will result in 100 queries to the ratings table. Listing 12-40 is an example from the *app/storage/logs/lumen.log* file where I am outputting queries from the ORM.

Listing 12-40. Example of a Lazy-Loaded Query

```
[2015-12-17 21:20:56] lumen.INFO: select * from `ratings` where `ratings`.`ratea\
ble_id` = ? and `ratings`.`rateable_id` is not null and `ratings`.`rateable_type\
` = ? [1,"App\\Author"]
```

To get this type of logging working in your app, you are going to use the *app/Providers/AppServiceProvider.php* class to add some database logging so you can visualize the actual queries generated by Eloquent (Listing 12-41).

Listing 12-41. Adding Database Logging to the AppServiceProvider

```
 1  <?php
 2
 3  namespace App\Providers;
 4
 5  use DB;
 6  use Log;
 7  use Illuminate\Support\ServiceProvider;
 8
 9  class AppServiceProvider extends ServiceProvider
10  {
11      /**
12       * Register any application services.
13       *
14       * @return void
15       */
16      public function register()
17      {
18          //
19      }
20
21      public function boot()
22      {
```

```
23          if (env('DB_LOGGING', false) === true) {
24              DB::listen(function($query) {
25                  Log::info($query->sql, $query->bindings, $query->time);
26              });
27          }
28      }
29  }
```

You've added a listener that will log out the SQL query and bindings when the environment variable DB_LOGGING=true is set. To start using this listener, you need to enable the AppServiceProvider and configure the environment variable.

To enable the AppServiceProvider, open up *bootstrap/app.php* and look for the "Register Service Providers" section and uncomment the *AppServiceProvider* class (Listing 12-42).

Listing 12-42. Enabling the AppServiceProvider in bootstrap/app.php

```
81  $app->register(App\Providers\AppServiceProvider::class);
```

Add the following to your *.env* file in the root of the project (I would also recommend adding it to the .env example file for other developers to grab). Setting the variable to true (Listing 12-43) enables logging.

Listing 12-43. Enabling DB Logging in .env

```
DB_LOGGING=true
```

Setting it to false or not defining the variable will disable logging (Listing 12-44).

Listing 12-44. Disabling DB Logging in .env.example

```
DB_LOGGING=false
```

⚠ **Chatty Logs**   It's probably not a good idea to use DB::listen() to log database queries in production; use the DB logging feature as a development convenience to see SQL queries. You can just as easily enable MySQL's logging capabilities to get the same effect. I prefer to toggle it on/off in development because I don't always need (or want) to see database logs while I develop.

Now that you have database logging in place, make a request to the */authors* endpoint to visualize the queries. In the next section, you will work on preventing excess queries to get author rating data.

Eager Loading Ratings

After taking an aside and understanding that your transformer can create additional unnecessary (and unintentional) queries, what can you do about it? Enter eager loading (https://laravel.com/docs/5.2/eloquent-relationships#eager-loading).

The official documentation for eager loading does a great job of explaining the (potential) problem and how to avoid it. Let's update your AuthorsController@index method to use eager loading and check how your database logging changes compared to doing a query for each individual author. Open the *app/Http/Controllers/AuthorsController.php* file and update the index route (Listing 12-45).

Listing 12-45. Using Eager Loading on the Authors Index Route

```
11  public function index()
12  {
13      $authors = Author::with('ratings')->get();
14
15      return $this->collection($authors, new AuthorTransformer());
16  }
```

If you make a request to /authors with database logging turned on, the request should only generate two queries (Listing 12-46).

Listing 12-46. Queries Logged with Eager Loading

```
[2015-12-18 05:33:07] lumen.INFO: select * from `authors`
[2015-12-18 05:33:07] lumen.INFO: select * from `ratings` where `ratings`.`ratea\
ble_id` in (?, ?, ?, ?, ?, ?, ?, ?, ?, ?) and `ratings`.`rateable_type` = ? [1,2\
,3,4,5,6,7,8,9,10,"App\\Author"]
```

Much better! Now your transformer is not creating unnecessary queries.

 You Can Still Generate Extra Queries!

In the AuthorTransformer you can still create extra queries by calling the $author->ratings() method. For example, $author->ratings()->avg('value') makes an additional query even if you use eager loading to get the author and ratings. You should use $author->ratings->avg('value') as seen in your transformer to avoid extra queries.

At this point, you should run the test suite again since you changed your code to use eager loading (Listing 12-47).

Listing 12-47. Running the Test Suite

```
# vagrant@homestead:~/Code/bookr$
$ phpunit

OK (61 tests, 314 assertions)
```

The remaining author routes in the AuthorsController don't really need to use eager loading because only one record is being requested and you will not generate additional queries. Eager loading is most important when you are getting a collection of records and looping over them.

 Git Commit: Add Author Ratings

c5989e9 (https://bitbucket.org/paulredmond/apress-bookr/commits/c5989e9)

Conclusion

In this chapter, you learned how to use polymorphic relationships in your API and then expose the data from your Fractal transformer. You are well-equipped to add ratings to books and then use the API to create your own front end too! Along the way you learned about eager loading (`https://laravel.com/docs/5.2/eloquent-relationships#eager-loading`) and just touched on the subject of query optimization.

Where to Go From Here

Congratulations! Thanks for reading and working through the whole book. The main objective of this book is two-fold: to show that any PHP developer can pick up this book and write Lumen APIs with no previous Laravel Experience, and to let you practice test-driven development in an API context.

A wonderful artifact of writing this book in a test-driven manner is that I have high confidence that the code samples in this book do work. I am not claiming that the book is *100% free from bugs* or full test coverage, but the *code feels solid*.

There are many things not covered in the scope of this book that may one day become a follow-up or a more advanced book. For instance, I did not cover writing APIs with multi-tenancy in mind and I did not cover authentication. This book was about building a foundation.

If you want to share this book with others in your company, meetups, newsletters, and conferences, please get in touch with me on Twitter @paulredmond (https://twitter.com/paulredmond).

Laravel

If you have a solid understanding of Laravel (https://laravel.com/), you pretty much know Lumen (apart from a few API differences). If you have not worked with Laravel, I hope you read through the documentation at https://laravel.com/docs/. Chances are that most readers have already at least experimented with Laravel.

Laravel is the other half of my current development toolkit. Together, Laravel and Lumen provide all the core developer tools I need to write web applications and APIs. I have the same basic workflow between writing Laravel and Lumen apps. Having the same workflow makes me feel very productive, and the APIs are familiar.

Lumen has other features you can read about in the Laravel documentation, such as a queue system and scheduled jobs. Knowing that you don't have to bring in third-party libraries to get a queue going in Lumen or Laravel is a huge win. Lumen also benefits from some more advanced Eloquent features that I did not cover in this book, but you can learn about them in the documentation.

Laracasts

Laracasts (https://laracasts.com/) are the best resource for learning Laravel (and thus Lumen), period. At the time of writing, they have a free series called Laravel from Scratch at https://laracasts.com/series/laravel-5-from-scratch. The paid subscription is valuable and will give you hours of videos on Laravel, general programming, development tools, and even JavaScript.

© Paul Redmond 2016

P. Redmond, *Lumen Programming Guide*, DOI 10.1007/978-1-4842-2187-7

Mockery

We used Mockery (`http://docs.mockery.io/en/latest/`) to unit test certain things in this book and I can't encourage you enough to become very familiar with this library. Mockery is a must in my own unit testing toolbelt.

Guzzle

Guzzle (`http://docs.guzzlephp.org/`) is my favorite PHP HTTP client library. When you write APIs, you need a way for other applications to communicate with your API. If you haven't used Guzzle, I recommend writing an HTTP client for the application you wrote in this book. It would be a good exercise. Sometimes your own APIs will need to communicate with other internal APIs.

Index

A

$app->group, 9, 165, 187, 213, 223
Artisan console
   commands
      db:seed, 29–30, 34, 51–53, 56–57, 143–145, 206, 222, 231
      make:migration, 27, 137–138, 143, 201–202, 219
      migrate:refresh, 30, 34, 51–53, 56–57, 138, 140, 143–145, 203, 206, 222, 231
Author Model Factory, 142
/authors, 165–199, 223–224, 230–241
AuthorsController, 165–166, 168–171, 178–192, 195, 197–198, 223, 228, 241
AuthorsRatings Controller, 230
Authors Transformer, 166–168, 177–178

B

Book API
   create a new project, 7–9, 17, 21
Book bundle, 199, 201–217
/books API, 33, 125
BooksController, 23–25, 31–32, 35–38, 43–44, 48–50, 52, 54–60, 63, 97, 105, 111, 114–116, 182
BooksController@index, 25, 31, 35, 43, 48, 50, 55, 63, 66, 90–92, 116, 118, 155, 160
BooksControllerTest, 23–24, 33, 35–36, 38–39, 41, 43, 44, 47, 49–50, 52–54, 56–57, 59, 66–67, 91–92, 94, 96, 117–118, 120, 132, 145–146, 148, 150–153, 155
/books/ route, 33, 39, 52–54, 170
BooksTableSeeder.php, 29, 142, 222
BookTransformer, 98–99, 101, 106–107, 115–117, 120, 151
Bundle model factory, 204–205
/bundles, 201, 204–214, 216–217
BundlesController, 211, 213–216
BundleTransformer, 207–211, 213, 215

C

Carbon, 29, 101, 120–121, 123, 142, 148, 152
Composer, 1, 7, 17, 22, 30, 74, 90, 97, 206
   commands
      dump-autoload, 30, 206
   create-project, 7, 17
Custom validation messages, 132–134, 185

D

Database migration
   authors, 27–28, 137–139, 143–144, 202–203
   books table, 27–28, 30, 137–139, 143–144, 203
DatabaseMigrations trait, 65–67, 126
Database seeder, 28–29, 142, 144, 205, 222
Date Mutators, 101
dd(), 44, 147, 150–151
Debugging
   dd(), 44, 147, 151

E

Eloquent
   author model, 140–142, 152, 159–162, 167, 220–221, 238
   book model, 31, 45, 67, 97, 141, 201, 204
   database logging, 239–241
   eager loading, 177, 240–242
   many to many, 138, 201–202, 217
   mass assignment, 43, 45
   MassAssignmentException, 45
   methods
      all(), 31, 37, 43–44, 46, 48, 53, 57, 94–95, 116, 119, 122, 127, 129, 150, 170, 182–183, 185, 188–190, 192
      attach(), 215–216
      create(), 43–44, 67–69, 91–92, 99, 117, 128, 133, 145, 161, 169, 191–198, 205, 208, 224, 235

delete(), 55, 57, 59, 198, 235
detach(), 216
fill(), 51
findOrFail(), 37, 79–80, 198
ModelNotFoundException, 35–39, 44, 53,
    56–59, 69, 80–85, 115, 122, 129
morphMany(), 221
one to many, 138, 141–142, 221
polymorphic relationships, 138, 217, 219,
    221, 242
properties
    $fillable, 45, 51, 141, 147, 150, 220
relationships, 141, 201, 204, 240, 242
Environment setup
    database connection, 1, 20, 147
    The .env file, 19–21
Exception Handling
    Handler contract, 71
    Handler.php, 71–72, 78, 80, 84
    HandlerTest.php, 74, 78, 85
    HttpException, 72–73, 78–80, 84

■ F, G

Facades, 12, 20–21, 111
Faker, 65–66, 69, 142, 145, 205, 222
Fractal
    FractalServiceProvider.php, 112, 175
    including other models, 171–181
    installing fractal, 97
    manager, 101–106, 108–109, 113,
        172–174, 177
    parseIncludes(), 176–177, 180
    serializer, 102–111, 113, 172–177
Fractal Response Class
    FractalResponse::collection(), 107–109
    FractalResponse::item(), 105–106, 109

■ H

Homestead
    book API setup, 7, 26, 65
    Homestead.yaml, 2, 8, 18–19, 65
    project setup, 65
    vagrant, 1, 2, 7, 19–21, 23–28, 30, 34, 36, 38–39,
        41–42, 44–45, 47, 50–55, 57, 73
    vagrant provision, 8, 18, 65

■ I

Installation
    Linux–Debian/Ubuntu, 5–6
    Linux–Red Hat, 4
    Mac OSX, 2–3
    Windows, 6

■ J, K

JSON Exceptions, 72–74
JsonResponse, 43, 55–56, 59, 75–79, 83, 85–87,
    127, 215

■ L

Log facade, 12
Lumen
    app.php config, 9, 12, 14, 20, 71, 111, 114, 240
    enable eloquent, 20
    enable facades, 12, 20–21
    project setup, 65
    requirements, 1, 74

■ M

Max Length, 131–132
Middleware
    global middleware, 11–13
    route middleware, 11, 13–14
Mockery, 74–77, 79, 85, 88, 103–104, 177, 244
MockeryPHPUnitIntegration, 76, 104
Mocking Carbon, 120
Model factory
    book model factory, 66, 68
    factory(), 67, 69, 153–155, 222, 238
    factory()->create(), 67, 69, 222
    in tests, 66–69, 145–146
MySQL, 1–6, 19–21, 28, 65, 240

■ N, O

Nested REST resources, 201

■ P, Q

Phpdotenv, 18, 65
PHPUnit, 21–22, 36, 47, 65, 67, 76–77, 79, 91–92, 98,
    101, 146, 160–161, 230
    --filter, 36, 38–39, 44–45, 47, 51–52, 54–56, 67,
        76, 79, 99, 101, 103, 126, 128, 147–154,
        160–161, 230, 238
    Pending tests, 33–34

■ R

Rateable trait, 221
Rating model factory, 220
Ratings, 219–244
Rating transfomer, 225
Request Object
    $request->all(), 43–44, 46, 48, 51, 53, 58, 94, 119,
        122, 127, 152, 182–183, 186, 188–190

$request->wantsJson(), 16, 72–73, 78, 84

Required, 5–6, 10, 23, 125, 128–129, 131–134, 149, 153, 156, 183–184, 186, 188, 190–192

response()
    response()->json(), 43, 55
    response()->make(), 16

Response object, 11, 14–16

Route groups, 9–11, 13–15, 25, 165

Routes
    Hello World Route, 10–11
    named routes, 48, 63
    route(), 34, 38, 40, 48–49, 52, 54, 56, 60, 62, 225
    route parameters, 10–11

routes.php
    BooksController@destroy, 54–55, 63, 153–154
    BooksController@index, 25, 31, 35, 43, 48, 50, 55, 63, 66, 90–92, 118, 155, 160
    BooksController@show, 35, 38–40, 43, 48, 50, 53, 55, 60, 63, 79–81, 92–93, 118
    BooksController@store, 43, 48, 50, 55, 63, 93, 94, 119, 121, 125, 128, 146–147, 149, 153
    BooksController@update, 50, 55, 63, 95–96, 121–122, 125, 128–129, 131, 134, 151–153

S

Service container, 12, 15, 43, 111–112, 114–115, 124, 175

Service provider
    FractalServiceProvider.php, 112, 175
    resolve a service, 71, 111, 113–115, 134

T

Test database, 49, 51, 65–66, 69, 83, 88, 146, 211

Testing
    CrawlerTrait, 24, 35, 51, 54, 91, 94, 156, 184, 232, 234
    methods
        get(), 10, 14–15, 82, 241
        isEmpty(), 54, 62, 69, 153
        notSeeInDatabase, 49, 51, 54, 61–62, 69, 95, 122, 130, 152, 153, 157, 158, 189, 198, 214, 216, 234
        post(), 42
        seeHeaderWithRegExp(), 46–47, 61, 161, 187
        seeInDatabase(), 42, 50, 61, 69, 93, 96, 121, 123, 131, 148, 152, 186, 189, 196, 234
        seeJson(), 25, 81, 94, 95, 152
        seeJsonEquals(), 52, 56, 62, 91–92, 117
        seeStatusCode(), 24, 34, 36, 39–40, 46, 49, 52, 54, 56, 59–62, 68–69, 82, 92, 96, 118, 123, 130–132, 157–158, 161, 168, 181, 184–187, 189, 191–194, 196, 198, 211, 216, 232, 234–236

U

Unit Tests, 21–22, 74, 76, 98, 103, 244

V, W, X, Y, Z

Validation, 125–135, 149, 153–157, 183–186, 190–192, 195–196

Get the eBook for only $5!

Why limit yourself?

Now you can take the weightless companion with you wherever you go and access your content on your PC, phone, tablet, or reader.

Since you've purchased this print book, we're happy to offer you the eBook in all 3 formats for just $5.

Convenient and fully searchable, the PDF version enables you to easily find and copy code—or perform examples by quickly toggling between instructions and applications. The MOBI format is ideal for your Kindle, while the ePUB can be utilized on a variety of mobile devices.

To learn more, go to www.apress.com/companion or contact support@apress.com.